THE RETARDED ADULT
IN THE COMMUNITY

Third Printing

THE RETARDED ADULT IN THE COMMUNITY

By

ELIAS KATZ, Ph.D.

Psychologist, University of California Medical Center
Consultant, San Francisco Aid Retarded Children, Incorporated
Former Director, Work-Training Center and
Independent Living Rehabilitation Program
San Francisco, California

With a Foreword by

Mary E. Switzer

Administrator of the Social and Rehabilitation Service
United States Department of Health, Education and Welfare
Washington, D. C.

CHARLES C THOMAS • PUBLISHER
Springfield • Illinois • U.S.A.

Published and Distributed Throughout the World by

CHARLES C THOMAS • PUBLISHER

BANNERSTONE HOUSE

301-327 East Lawrence Avenue, Springfield, Illinois, U.S.A.

©*1968, by* CHARLES C THOMAS • PUBLISHER

ISBN 0-398-00981-3

Library of Congress Catalog Card Number: 68-11694

First Printing, 1968
Second Printing, 1972
Third Printing, 1977

With THOMAS BOOKS *careful attention is given to all details of manufacturing and design. It is the Publisher's desire to present books that are satisfactory as to their physical qualities and artistic possibilities and appropriate for their particular use.* THOMAS BOOKS *will be true to those laws of quality that assure a good name and good will.*

This book may be reproduced royalty free for United States Governmental purposes.

Printed in the United States of America
N-1

To Florence

FOREWORD

THROUGHOUT THIS BOOK is woven the basic premise that the mentally retarded adult *can* become a valuable and productive member of society. The author has accurately described the potential of the retardate while establishing realistic limits for the expectations of employers and the public in general. His writing covers every conceivable facet of a complex subject and represents a virtual encyclopedia of pertinent information. The result is a highly comprehensive volume which will serve for many years as an effective textbook for rehabilitation students and a useful reference work for professionals in the field.

Dr. Elias Katz has here provided us with new insights into the definitions of mental retardation in each of its many forms. He has concisely described the various methods used in the rehabilitation of retarded persons. He has drawn in bold, new strokes the functions of the mentally retarded adult in the community, and he has shown the extent of the public's vested interest in utilizing the abilities of retarded workers.

There has been a growing awareness that mentally retarded adults have job capabilities far more significant than many observers had assumed after examining test scores. Emerging is yet another example of the human personality's unique refusal to be classified in absolute terms. Now Dr. Katz has crystallized this line of thought and, moreover, carried it to its logical conclusion. He has further dispelled the myth of the "typical retardate," taken these individuals from an institutionalized milieu and placed them against a background of the world as we all know it in our daily lives. He has indicated the natural position which the retarded worker occupies in this environment.

We welcome this book as an outstanding addition to our literature on a subject of increasing concern. Its influence will ultimately touch the lives of millions of Americans. It has been said that a good writer has the capacity to make the familiar new and the new familiar. Dr. Elias Katz is a good writer.

Mary E. Switzer

Administrator of the
Social and Rehabilitation Service

PREFACE

Who are the mentally retarded adults in the community? Can they live in the community or must they be cared for in state institutions? Can they have an independent life? Can they hold jobs, marry, raise families? What lies ahead for the retarded child and his family when he becomes an adult? How should the community be organized to make a brighter future for the retarded adult?

This book has developed from a deep conviction based on personal experience that most retarded adults have untapped potentials for making a good adjustment in the community. However, only when there is clear understanding of their needs and a "total push" to meet these needs can their promise be fulfilled. Emphasis therefore is placed on comprehensive, co-ordinated community programming.

This book is intended as a text for educators, rehabilitation counselors, physicians, social workers, psychologists, nurses, and others working with the mentally retarded and their families, with stress on interdisciplinary service.

The retarded adult in the community is a human being. This, in itself, justifies all efforts to help him realize to the fullest his personal, social, and vocational potentials.

ELIAS KATZ, PH.D.

ACKNOWLEDGMENTS

I AM DEEPLY indebted to the public agencies, organizations, journals, publishers, and individuals who contributed to this book.

Acknowledgment is due to the Vocational Rehabilitation Administration, U. S. Department of Health, Education, and Welfare, which awarded San Francisco Aid Retarded Children, Inc., a grant to help prepare this manuscript for publication. I am grateful to Mrs. Margarete M. Connolly, Executive Director of San Francisco Aid Retarded Children, Inc., for her counsel and encouragement.

The following kindly granted permission to use case material from their files:

Abilities, Inc., Albertson, Long Island, New York;
Adult Psychiatry Clinic, University of California Medical Center, San Francisco, California;
Parents and Friends of the Mentally Retarded of Bridgeport, Connecticut;
California Department of Rehabilitation, Sacramento;
Peter Cohen, M.D., Associate Professor of Pediatrics, University of California Medical Center, San Francisco, California;
Mrs. Frances Costa, Director, EBARC Work Training Center, Hayward, California;
Hot Springs Rehabilitation Center, Arkansas;
Langley Porter Neuropsychiatric Institute, San Francisco, California;
Mental Retardation Services Board of Los Angeles County, California;
Exceptional Children's Foundation, Los Angeles, California;
Rita Mattei, Santa Cruz, California;
Structured Community Services for the Mentally Retarded, Milwaukee, Wisconsin;

New York City Association for the Help of Retarded Children, Inc.;

San Francisco Aid Retarded Children, Inc.;

San Francisco Information and Referral Service for the Mentally Retarded;

Mrs. Marie Rexroth, R.N., Department of Public Health, San Francisco, California;

Mrs. Myra Schapps, M.S.W., Los Angeles, California;

Arthur Segal, M.S.W., University of California, Berkeley, California;

Beatrice Vennert, R.N., Bridgeport, Connecticut;

Douglas Clark, M.A., El Cerrito, California.

My wife, Florence, has been my inspiration and has assisted me in every way to bring this book to completion.

E. K.

ABBREVIATIONS

AAMD—American Association on Mental Deficiency
AFDC—Aid to Families with Dependent Children
AHRC—Association for the Help of Retarded Children
AJMD—American Journal on Mental Deficiency
AMA—American Medical Association
APA—American Psychiatric Association
APA—American Psychological Association
ARC—Association for Retarded Children
ATD—Aid to the Permanently and Totally Disabled (also known as Aid to the Needy Disabled)
BVR—Bureau of Vocational Rehabilitation
CAP—Community Action Program (Office of Economic Opportunity)
CEC—Council for Exceptional Children, National Education Association (NEA)
CP—Cerebral Palsy
DPH—Department of Public Health
DVR—Division of Vocational Rehabilitation
DR—Department of Rehabilitation
EBARC—East Bay Association for Retarded Children
ECF—Exceptional Children's Foundation
EdD—Doctor of Education
EMR—Educable mentally retarded
FSA—Family Service Association
FSIQ—Full Scale IQ (Wechsler-Bellevue Intelligence Scale)
GAP—Group for the Advancement of Psychiatry
GATB—General Aptitude Test Battery
ILRP—Independent Living Rehabilitation Program
IQ—Intelligence Quotient
IRS(MR)—Information and Referral Service for the Mentally Retarded
ITPA—Illinois Test of Psycholinguistic Abilities

LARC—Ladies Auxiliary, Association for Retarded Children
MA—Mental Age
MDTA—Manpower Development and Training Act
MR—Mental Retardation (journal)
MSW—Master of Social Work
NARC—National Association for Retarded Children
NASW—National Association of Social Workers
NASWHP—National Association of Sheltered Workshops and Homebound Programs
NIH—National Institutes of Health
NIMH—National Institute of Mental Health
NRA—National Recreation Association
NRA—National Rehabilitation Association
NRCA—National Rehabilitation Counseling Association
OEO—Office of Economic Opportunity (Antipoverty Program)
OJT—On-the-Job Training
OMAT—Office of Manpower and Training
OVR—Office of Vocational Rehabilitation (now Vocational Rehabilitation Administration, U. S. Department of Health, Education, and Welfare)
PhD—Doctor of Philosophy
PL—Public Law (federal)
PSIQ—Performance Scale IQ (Wechsler-Bellevue Intelligence Scale)
RN—Registered Nurse
S-B—Stanford-Binet Intelligence Scale (Form L, M, or L-M)
SES—State Employment Service
SFCCMR—San Francisco Coordinating Council on Mental Retardation
SFCRW—San Francisco Community Rehabilitation Workshop
SMR—Severely mentally retarded
SQ—Social Quotient (from Vineland Social Maturity Scale)
SRS—Social and Rehabilitation Service
TAT—Thematic Apperception Test
TMR—Trainable mentally retarded
UCPA—United Cerebral Palsy Association
USDHEW—U. S. Department of Health, Education, and Welfare

USES—U. S. Employment Service
VA—Veterans Administration
VAC—Vocational Adjustment Center
VISTA—Volunteers in Service to America
VNA—Visiting Nurses Association
VRA—Vocational Rehabilitation Administration (formerly Office of Vocational Rehabilitation)
VSIQ—Verbal Scale IQ (Wechsler-Bellevue Intelligence Scale)
WAIS—Wechsler Adult Intelligence Scale
W-B—Wechsler-Bellevue Intelligence Scale
WICHE—Western Interstate Commission on Higher Education
W-TC—Work-Training Center

CONTENTS

Page

Foreword vii

Preface ix

Acknowledgments xi

Abbreviations xiii

Chapter
I. WHAT IS MEANT BY THE RETARDED ADULT IN THE

    COMMUNITY? 3

    Definitions of Mental Retardation 6

        Subaverage General Intellectual Functioning 6

        Impairment in Adaptive Behavior 7

        Differences Among Mentally Retarded Adults 9

        Variations of Abilities and Performances Within

           the Individual Retarded Adult 11

    Potentials of the Mentally Retarded Adult 12

        Profit from Vocational Rehabilitation 12

        Good Community Adjustment of Former Patients of

           State Institutions for the Retarded 13

        Successful Marriage 14

        The Beginning of Adulthood for the Mentally Retarded .. 16

        Relationship to the Community 20

        Distinction Between the Mentally Retarded and the

           Mentally Ill Adult 23

        Questions for Discussion 25

        References 26

II. WHY BE CONCERNED ABOUT THE RETARDED ADULT IN

    THE COMMUNITY? 28

    Size of the Problem 28

    Effect Upon the Family 30

    Connection Between Poverty and the Retarded 31

    Health Problems 32

Chapter   *Page*

  Manifestations of Antisocial Behavior 32
  The Effectiveness of Special Education in the
    Public Schools 34
  Community Adjustment of Former Institutional Patients.. 36
  Protection of Legal Rights and Privileges 38
  Help for Achieving Higher Levels of Functioning 39
  Questions for Discussion 40
  References 41

  III. HOW IS THE RETARDED ADULT EVALUATED IN THE
        COMMUNITY? 43
  Psychological Evaluation 43
  Social Evaluation 47
  Medical Evaluation 51
  Psychiatric Evaluation 55
  Work Evaluation by Vocational Rehabilitation Counselor.. 59
  Work Evaluation in Workshops for the Handicapped 62
  Diagnostic Team Approach to Comprehensive
    Evaluation 65
  Questions for Discussion 71
  References 71

  IV. WHAT ARE THE NEEDS OF THE RETARDED ADULT IN
        THE COMMUNITY? 73
  Physiological Needs 73
  Psychosocial Needs 74
  The Expressed Needs of the Mentally Retarded Adult 75
  Translating Expressed Needs into Community Services .. 79
  Questions for Discussion 81
  References 81

  V. HOW ARE SOME NEEDS OF THE RETARDED ADULT MET
        IN THE COMMUNITY? 82
  Residential Needs 82
    Living Independently 82
    Living at Home 83
    Family Care and Foster Care 83

Chapter *Page*

Halfway House 84

Vocational Needs 86

The More Able Retarded Adult 86

The Less Able Retarded Adult 86

The Least Able Retarded Adult 88

Marriage Adjustment 88

Health and Medical Needs 91

Counseling and Therapy Needs 93

Group Therapy 97

Work as Therapy 100

Educational Needs 104

Recreational Needs 105

Camping 107

Creative Activities 109

Spectator Sports 109

Religious Activity 110

Questions for Discussion 113

References 113

VI. HOW ARE THE VOCATIONAL NEEDS OF THE MORE ABLE
RETARDED ADULT MET IN THE COMMUNITY? 116

Federal-State Vocational Rehabilitation Programs and
the More Able Retarded Adults 117

Available Vocational Rehabilitation Services for the
More Able Retarded Adults 120

Comprehensive Vocational Evaluation 120

Medical Examination 120

Psychological Evaluation 120

Social Evaluation 121

Work Evaluation 121

Case Review 121

Vocational Training 122

Job Placement 122

Vocational Counseling 125

Follow-up of Rehabilitated Retarded Clients 126

Chapter   *Page*

Records and Reports 126

The Role of Workshops for the Handicapped in
Rehabilitating More Able Retarded Adults 127

Questions for Discussion 132

References 133

VII. HOW ARE THE NEEDS OF THE LESS ABLE RETARDED
ADULT MET IN LONG-TERM WORKSHOPS? 135

Evaluation of Social and Vocational Potentials 133

The Role of Workshops in Relation to Less Able
Retarded Adults 143

Rehabilitation for Independent Living 149

Few Long-term Workshops 151

Questions for Discussion 152

References 153

VIII. HOW ARE THE NEEDS OF THE LEAST ABLE RETARDED
ADULT MET IN THE COMMUNITY? 154

Characteristics of the Least Able Retarded Adult 154

Living Arrangements 155

Parent Counseling 157

Meeting Their Needs in the Home 159

Public Health Nursing Services 159

Homemaker Services 163

Baby-sitting 163

Meeting Their Needs Outside the Home 164

Activity Centers (day facilities) 164

Respite Care 166

Questions for Discussion 166

References 167

IX. WHAT COUNSELING IS AVAILABLE TO PARENTS OF THE
RETARDED ADULT IN THE COMMUNITY? 168

Problems Facing the Parents 168

Institutional Placement: Case of Stanley J. 172

Siblings of Retarded Adults: Case of Martin F. 174

Vocational Preparation: Case of Howard Z. 177

Chapter *Page*

Marriage of Retarded Adults: Case of Randy W.
and Loretta S. 179
The Emotionally Disturbed Retarded Adult:
Case of Thomas R. 181
Questions for Discussion 185
References 185

X. WHAT IS THE MOST EFFECTIVE PROGRAM FOR THE
RETARDED ADULT IN THE COMMUNITY? 186
Ten Basic Principles Underlying a Program for the
Retarded Adult in the Community 186
Direct Services 190
Information and Referral Service for the
Mentally Retarded 190
Comprehensive Evaluation of Needs and Potentials 190
Financial Assistance 191
Residential Arrangements 191
Clinical Services 191
Medical Care 191
Dental Care 191
Psychiatric Care 192
Physical Rehabilitation Services 192
Public Health Nursing 192
Personal Counseling 193
Family Counseling 193
Vocational Services 194
Vocational Rehabilitation Services 194
Selective Placement in Competitive Employment 195
Special Placement in Civil Service 195
Workshops for the Handicapped 195
Independent Living Rehabilitation Services 197
Activity Centers 198
Respite Care 198
Homemaker Services and Baby-sitter Services 198
Socio-recreative Programming 199

Chapter   *Page*

Religious Activity 199

Adult Education 200

Guardianship 200

Transportation 201

Supportive Aspects 202

Financial Support for the Program 202

Education and Participation of the Public 202

Trained Staff 204

Coordination Among Community Agencies and

  Individuals Serving the Retarded Adult 205

  Central Registry of the Retarded 206

  Case Finding 207

Research on Retarded Adults 208

Questions for Discussion 210

References 210

XI.   WHAT ARE SOME APPROACHES TO PROGRAM PLANNING

      FOR THE RETARDED ADULT IN COMMUNITY? 213

The San Francisco Coordinating Council on

  Mental Retardation 217

The Bridgeport Story 221

Structured Community Approach: Milwaukee 223

Greater Cleveland Mental Retardation Planning Project..226

The Joint Agencies Agreement: Los Angeles County 228

The Area Center for the Mentally Retarded 231

Questions for Discussion 233

References 234

XII. CURRENT TRENDS AND IDEAS 236

National Action 236

Research and Development Center 237

National Survey 237

Neighborhood Centers in Poverty Areas 238

Comprehensive Coordinated Programming 238

Comprehensive Evaluation 239

Participation in Program Planning 239

Chapter *Page*

Extended Follow-up 240

Long-term Workshops for the Less Able 240

Supervised Teams 241

Junior College and Adult Education 242

The Generalist 243

The Large State Institution for the Retarded—

An Anachronism 243

Conclusion 245

Question for Discussion 247

References 247

Appendix

A. Array of Direct Services for the Retarded 250

B. Institute of Industrial Launderers National

MDTA-on-the-Job Training Project 251

Index 257

THE RETARDED ADULT
IN THE COMMUNITY

Chapter I

WHAT IS MEANT BY THE RETARDED ADULT IN THE COMMUNITY?

To clarify what is meant by the retarded adult in the community, two hypothetical cases, Joseph L. and Albert S., are presented.

Joseph L., a tall, well-built, slow-moving man of twenty-five has been employed regularly as a helper in a service station since he left school. He lives with his parents and two younger sisters in a neatly furnished three-bedroom home in the middle-class suburbs of a large city. His family seems pleased with his general adjustment. He has some good friends he has known since school days and is friendly with his fellow employees at the service station.

When Joseph L. started school, it was noted that he was learning very slowly and he was referred to the school psychologist. He was found to have an IQ of 62 on the Stanford-Binet Intelligence Scale, Form L.[1] He was placed in a special class for the educable mentally retarded. Subsequent intelligence test scores were in the IQ range between 60 and 70. He remained in special classes throughout his schooling. In high school he did poorly in academic subjects, but he did well in the shops. He was "graduated" at the age of eighteen, receiving a "Special" diploma. Shortly after graduation he was employed in the service station where he still works. He enjoys his job and he will be getting his second raise next month.

Albert S., a tall, well-built, slow-moving man of twenty-five, lives with his parents and two younger sisters in a neatly furnished three-bedroom home in the middle-class suburbs of a large city.

When he started school it was noted that he was learning very slowly and he was referred to the school psychologist. He was found to have an IQ of 62 on the Stanford-Binet Intelligence Scale, Form L. He was placed in a special class for educable mentally retarded. Subsequent intelligence test scores were in the IQ range between 60 and 70. He remained in special classes throughout his schooling. In

3

high school he did poorly in academic subjects, but he did well in the shops. He made no friends during his school years and spent much time wandering around the city alone. His parents were concerned about this, but did not know how to help him. He was "graduated" at the age of eighteen receiving a "Special" diploma. After leaving school he did not seem able to hold a job for more than a few days at a time. Because he was having trouble finding a permanent job, he was referred by an understanding neighbor to the vocational rehabilitation office. There he was interviewed by a vocational rehabilitation counselor.

He was assigned to a nearby workshop for vocational evaluation. Although he had poor work habits and inadequate skills, the workshop staff concluded that he could be trained as a janitor's helper. The counselor arranged for a six-months' period of on-the-job training in a building maintenance company. During the first few months of training he had difficulties with his immediate supervisor. His counselor held regular meetings with him and helped him work through his problems. At the end of the training period, he was ready for a job and his counselor placed him as a janitor's helper in a small office building. He occasionally gets into trouble with his employer and still has no friends. However, he does manage to earn a minimum wage and to keep himself occupied in his spare time. The counselor is keeping the case open because he is not sure that Albert's serious problems with his employer are over, and he believes he will need further help to stay on the job.

Are both these men mentally retarded? Is neither mentally retarded? Is one mentally retarded and not the other? Both Joseph L. and Albert S. have the same intelligence test scores, socioeconomic background, and education, but they differ widely in social and vocational adjustment. Albert S. has had such serious problems of adjustment in addition to a low IQ, that he has needed, and still may need, the assistance of a professional counselor to help him. In this book Albert S. is considered a mentally retarded adult. On the other hand, Joseph L. is making a good adjustment in the community. Even though he has a low IQ, was classified as a mentally retarded child, and educated as such, he would *not* be considered a mentally retarded adult. The reason for making this distinction between Joseph L. and Albert S. lies in their differences in adaptive behavior. The definition of mental retardation of the American Association on

Mental Deficiency (AAMD) is as follows: "Mental retardation refers to subaverage general intellectual functioning which originates during the developmental period and is associated with impairment in adaptive behavior."[2]

The AAMD definition marks a milestone in thinking about the mentally retarded, since it incorporates the concept of impairment in adaptive behavior. This is an important amplification of most previous definitions which defined the mentally retarded primarily in terms of their intelligence. Two important elements in the definition are *subaverage general intellectual functioning,* succinctly stated as low IQ or low measured intelligence, and *impairment in adaptive behavior,* often referred to as lack of social competency or poor social adjustment.* Thus the mentally retarded adult is one who demonstrates not only comparatively low intelligence but also poor social adjustment or lack of social maturity. In terms of the AAMD definition, although both men have equally low general intellectual functioning, Albert S. *is* mentally retarded and Joseph L. is *not* at present identified as mentally retarded. The difference between them is ascribable to Albert's *impairment in adaptive behavior.*

While in agreement with the AAMD definition, for practical purposes, this book narrows the definition of mental retardation to include *only those adults with subaverage general intellectual functioning whose adaptive behavior is so impaired that it comes to the attention of their families or social agencies, making it necessary to provide special services for them.* Thus, Albert S. is mentally retarded because, in addition to subaverage general intellectual functioning, his impairment in adaptive behavior is of such a nature that he cannot get along in the community without the help of his family and social agencies. On the other hand, Joseph L. is *not* at present identified as a mentally retarded adult, because, despite his low IQ, he has no disabling impairment in adaptive behavior that limits his ability to function without outside help.

————

* This book is not concerned with that part of the AAMD definition, ". . . which originates during the developmental period . . ."[3] since emphasis is on adult behavior rather than on causes and early treatment of mental retardation.

DEFINITIONS OF MENTAL RETARDATION

Subaverage General Intellectual Functioning

General intellectual functioning may be assessed by objective intelligence tests such as the Stanford-Binet Intelligence Scales[4] or the Wechsler-Bellevue Intelligence Scales,[5] which were developed and standardized for this purpose. The AAMD has defined an individual's subaverage general intellectual functioning as performance which is more than one standard deviation* below the population mean of his own age group. To characterize the relative degree of severity of impairment in general intellectual functioning, an individual may be classified in one of five levels of subaverage general intellectual functioning: borderline, mild, moderate, severe, and profound—depending on his intelligence test score expressed as an IQ score. The purposes of establishing these levels are to define more clearly an individual's abilities and to use this knowledge to help him achieve his highest potentials. Table I presents the levels of measured intelligence for intelligence test scores characterizing subaverage general intellectual functioning.

TABLE I

LEVELS OF MEASURED INTELLIGENCE*

Levels	Description	Range in Standard Deviation Units†	IQ Range Wechsler-Bellevue‡	Stanford-Binet§
	No retardation	above −1.00	above 84	above 83
I	Borderline	−1.01 to −2.00	70-84	68-83
II	Mild	−2.01 to −3.00	55-69	52-67
III	Moderate	−3.01 to −4.00	40-54	36-51
IV	Severe	−4.01 to −5.00	−	20-35
V	Profound	below −5.00	−	below 20

* Adapted from Heber.[2, 3]
† Standard deviation is a statistical unit expressing the variability or dispersion from the mean of a range of measurements in a sample.
‡ Wechsler-Bellevue refers to Wechsler Adult Intelligence Scale (WAIS); Wechsler-Bellevue (W-B) Intelligence Scales, Form I and Form II; Wechsler Intelligence Scale for Children (WISC).
§ Stanford-Binet refers to Stanford-Binet Intelligence Scale, Form L, Form M, and Form L-M.

Any discussion of subaverage general intellectual functioning opens up large areas of ambiguity in current thinking and practice

---

* A statistical unit which expresses the variability or dispersion from the mean of a range of measurements in a sample. One standard deviation below the mean includes 34.13 per cent of the population.

in relation to the retarded adult in the community. It has been often stated that 3 per cent of the population is mentally retarded. The 3 per cent figure, when extrapolated to the approximately 200,000,000 population of the United States, suggests that there are about 6,000,000 retarded persons.

Whom does the 3 per cent actually refer to? Table I indicates that about 3 per cent of the total population falls into the AAMD levels II, III, IV, and V. What about level I (borderline retardation) which includes about 13 per cent of the total population? Are all persons in level I mentally retarded? The answer is No. According to the AAMD definition, persons in levels I, II, III, IV, and V would be classified as mentally retarded if their adaptive behavior is impaired.* The large number of adults with IQ scores in level I—borderline retardation and many in level II—mild retardation whose adaptive behavior is not impaired are not identified as mentally retarded. It is only when such persons need and seek help from their families or social agencies that they are identified as mentally retarded.

Impairment in Adaptive Behavior

Adaptive behavior is a complex process involving learning ability and social adjustment.

> Learning ability refers to the facility with which knowledge is acquired as a function of experience. . . . Social adjustment . . . at the adult level . . . is assessed in terms of the degree to which the individual is able to maintain himself independently in the community and in gainful employment as well as by his ability to meet and conform to other personal and social responsibilities and standards set by the community.[6]

At present it is not possible to define adaptive behavior with the same precision as general intellectual functioning because objective and standardized tests have not as yet been developed for this purpose. The closest approach to obtaining an objective measure of adaptive behavior is the Vineland Social Maturity Scale. According to Doll,[7] the Vineland Social Maturity Scale "provides a definite outline of detailed performances in respect

---

* Persons in levels III, IV, and V of measured intelligence usually are impaired in adaptive behavior.

to which children show a progressive capacity for looking after themselves and for participating in those activities which lead toward ultimate independence as adults. The items of the Scale are now arranged in order of increasing average difficulty and represent progressive maturation in self-help, self-direction, locomotion, occupation, communication and social relations. This maturation in social independence may be taken as a measure of progressive development in social competence."

The AAMD has defined an individual's impairment in adaptive behavior as performance which is more than one standard deviation below the population mean of his own age group. To

TABLE II

LEVELS OF ADAPTIVE BEHAVIOR*

Levels	Description	Range in Standard Deviation Units†	SQ‡ Range Vineland Social Maturity Scale
	No retardation of adaptive behavior	above −1.00	above 83
I	Mild but apparent and significant negative deviation from norms and standards of adaptive behavior. (Capable of social and vocational adequacy with proper education and training. Frequently needs supervision and guidance under serious social or economic stress.)§	−1.01 to −2.25	64-83
II	Moderate but definite negative deviation from norms and standards of adaptive behavior. (Capable of self-maintenance in unskilled or semi-skilled occupations; needs supervision and guidance when under mild social or economic stress.)	−2.26 to −3.50	38.63
III	Severe negative deviation from norms and standards of adaptive behavior. (Can contribute partially to self-support under complete supervision; can develop self-protection skills to a minimal useful level in controlled environment.)	−3.51 to −4.75	25-37
IV	Profound negative deviation from norms and standards of adaptive behavior. (Some motor and speech development; totally incapable of self-maintenance; needs complete care and supervision.)	below −4.75	below 25

* Adapted from Heber.[2, 3]
† See Table I.
‡ SQ refers to Social Quotient derived from Vineland Social Maturity Scale. See Doll.[7]
§ See Sloan and Birch.[8]

characterize the relative degree of severity of impairment in adaptive behavior, an individual may be classified in one of four levels: mild, moderate, severe, and profound, depending on his score on the Vineland Social Maturity Scale. A suggested behavioral description appropriate to each level has been formulated.[8]

Table II presents the levels of impairment in adaptive behavior together with the associated behavioral descriptions appropriate for each level.

Since the development of the Vineland Social Maturity Scale, it has been recognized that there are limitations to its use as an instrument for measuring adaptive behavior. There are wide variations in adaptive behavior in different socioeconomic settings. For example, if Albert S. were living in a slum area where there is considerable unemployment and a low standard of living, his adaptive behavior might not be considered impaired by his family, neighbors, or local social agencies, since he would be functioning much like those around him even though his intelligence level is lower than theirs. Similarly, if Joseph L. lived in a high socioeconomic setting and his family were well-to-do professionals, it is likely that he would be considered by those around him as greatly impaired in adaptive behavior, and help would be sought from many public and private agencies to evaluate his needs and to prepare him for the future. Several investigators have been working on the problem of measuring social competency.[9, 10, 11] As yet no replacement for the Vineland Social Maturity Scale has emerged from these studies. Despite its limitations it is the best means of measuring impairment in adaptive behavior.

Differences Among Mentally Retarded Adults

It is not fully appreciated that mentally retarded adults are not a homogeneous group but are individuals who differ widely from one another. Even within the same IQ level there is wide variation in their physical capacities, interests, and abilities.

Ralph J. and Arthur T. are both thirty-three years of age, each with an IQ of 61. Ralph is myopic and wears thick-lensed glasses,

ARTHUR ----------

RALPH   ——————

SURVEY OF DEGREE OF PHYSICAL HANDICAP*

Cerebral Palsy Program, Department of Pediatrics
University of California School of Medicine, San Francisco

Name_____ Sex_____ No. _____ Date _____

Diagnosis_____ B.D. _____

_____ Rated by:_____ Age_____

	NON—HANDICAPPING		HANDICAPPING		Comments
	Minimal	Mild	Moderate	Severe	
VISION	(A) No trouble with vision; no glasses needed	( ) Some correction needed; may wear glasses; not handicapped in seeing	(R) Quite handicapped in seeing; vision not correctible by glasses	( ) Almost blind totally blind	Left eye totally Rt. eye
HEARING	(R) No trouble with hearing	( ) Some difficulty in hearing; may wear hearing aid satisfactorily	(A) Quite handicapped in hearing; has difficulty when wearing hearing aid	( ) Almost deaf; totally deaf	Left ear Rt. ear
SPEECH (verbal)	( ) Speech can be understood without difficulty by a stranger	(R) Some difficulty in being understood by a stranger; able to get ideas across in speech	( ) Speech hard for a stranger or immediate family to understand; hard to get ideas across in speech	(A) Almost totally unable to communicate by speech; totally without speech	
SITTING BALANCE	(A) (R) No difficulty in sitting in a chair or at table	( ) Somewhat unsteady in sitting in a chair or at a table, but not handicapped in doing so	( ) Quite handicapped in sitting in a chair or at a table; needs a relaxation chair and tray	( ) Unable to maintain sitting balance unless fully supported	
ARM-HAND USE	(A) No difficulty in using arms and hands for self-help activity	( ) Some difficulty in using arms and hands for self-help, but not handicapped in doing so	(R) Quite handicapped in using arms and hands for many self-help activities	( ) Unable to use arms and hands for any self-help activity	Left arm Rt. arm
WALKING	(A) No difficulty in walking	(R) Braces needed; unsteady gait; but able to get around	( ) Quite handicapped in walking; cannot walk independently	( ) Unable to walk	Left arm Rt. leg

* Prepared by Elias Katz, Ph. D., Psychologist, Cerebral Palsy Program, with the cooperation of Dr. Peter Cohen, Associate Professor of Pediatrics, and Supervisor, Cerebral Palsy Program, and Staff Members.
    For method of rating, and additional descriptions of behavior for each category, see Manual, which can be obtained on request.

Figure 1.   Differences in degree of physical handicap in two retarded adults.

while Arthur has excellent vision. Arthur has a moderate hearing loss in both ears and wears a hearing aid which compensates only a little. His speech is very hard to understand. Ralph has good speech. He has a mild left hemiplegia which affects both his arm and his leg. This has resulted in his using his left arm only as a helping hand. He limps noticeably and has never been active in sports or athletics. Arthur, on the other hand, played baseball with other young people. Even though he has trouble hearing the announcements, he goes to the ball park on weekends to cheer his favorite team.

Some of the differences between Ralph J. and Arthur T. are graphically illustrated in Figure 1.

Variations of Abilities and Performances Within the Individual Mentally Retarded Adult

Even more important than differences among retarded adults is the wide variation of abilities within each individual.

Sam L. is twenty-one years of age, has good speech, and relates well to others, yet his judgment and ability are very faulty. He consistently obtains IQ scores in the 50's and 60's, with low scores on Vocabulary, as well as on Performance subtests of the Wechsler-Bellevue Intelligence Scales. His good verbal skills and his personable appearance make his mental retardation less apparent. This outward appearance of normalcy has worked against him at times. He has been given jobs by prospective employers who find that he is unable to perform them. He is usually fired after one or two days on the job. His family is concerned that he is unemployed and keeps urging him to seek help from the Vocational Rehabilitation Agency.

Daniel M., a strong, well-developed man, has an IQ of 75. While in school he attended special classes for the mentally retarded. In the secondary school he showed remarkable aptitude in playing football, especially as a lineman. After graduating with a "Special" diploma, he was recruited to play with a minor league football team. Unfortunately, he was belligerent and was constantly in trouble with his teammates, the coach, and opposing teams. He could not be kept on the team because of his personality problems. He was able to find work as a laborer and could do the required work, but he continued to lose jobs because of his difficulties with co-workers and employers. He was finally referred to the Vocational Rehabilitation Agency. A vocational rehabilitation counselor is now working with him to help him learn to get along with other people.

The Retarded Adult in the Community

POTENTIALS OF THE MENTALLY RETARDED ADULT

Most mentally retarded persons have untapped potentials for achieving higher levels of personal, social, and vocational functioning than they are presently achieving. The whole system of special education of mentally retarded children in the public schools is based on public understanding of, and support for, the idea that most retarded children have the potentials of becoming independent citizens and can be helped to accomplish these goals through specialized training. There does not appear to be the same widespread understanding of, and support for, the idea that most retarded adults also have the potentials for becoming good citizens if provided with needed services.

Some areas in which mentally retarded adults have achieved their possibilities are job placement in gainful employment, community adjustment after leaving state institutions for the mentally retarded, and personal adjustment in marriage. It must be emphasized that most retarded adults who achieved success along these lines received special help to make this possible.

Profit from Vocational Rehabilitation

A dramatic report of improvement in mentally retarded adults' vocational functioning as a result of vocational rehabilitation services provided to them has been published by the U. S. Vocational Rehabilitation Administration.[12]

> Over seven thousand mentally retarded persons were rehabilitated in fiscal year 1963 [out of a total of 125,000 persons rehabilitated].
> Persons with mental retardation constituted 5.4 per cent of all rehabilitants. In 1958 this proportion was only 2.1 per cent. Correspondingly in 1963 there were 3.1 mentally retarded persons rehabilitated per unit of 100,000 population in the nation, as compared to 0.9 per unit of 100,000 population in 1958.
> Over two-thirds of the mentally retarded rehabilitated were under the age of twenty.
> For those states reporting race, over 85 per cent of the rehabilitants were white; 68 per cent were males. Only 5 per cent of the retarded had dependents.
> Nearly all of the retarded were capable of activity outside the home without help.
> The largest single source of referral for the retarded clients was

educational institutions.

Before receiving rehabilitation services, three-quarters of the retardates were primarily dependent on family and friends for support. Seventeen per cent were being supported by public funds.

Approximately 90 per cent were not earning wages before receiving rehabilitation services. After receiving service, fewer than 10 per cent of the retarded were not wage earners.

Approximately 40 per cent of the mentally retarded entered service-type occupations, 20 per cent were closed as unskilled workers, and 17 per cent became semiskilled workers.

Edward C. is a thirty-three-year-old man, tall and slender, with marked difficulty in expressing himself verbally. He has been diagnosed as cerebral palsy, mixed athetoid and spastic, with mental retardation. His IQ scores have averaged in the 50's with no subtests higher than 60. He cannot answer questions except by grunts and pointing. He gets around the community quite well on public transportation. He lives with his mother, who works in a canning factory.

When he left school, he could find no work. A friend of the family referred him to the local association for retarded children, which in turn referred him to the State Vocational Rehabilitation Agency. He was evaluated and accepted for vocational rehabilitation services. The counselor's efforts were directed to finding him a job to meet his needs within his limitations. The counselor met with him regularly, and finally was able to place him in a job as a warehouseman's helper. In this job he pulls a truck carrying loads of items and deposits them at various points in the warehouse. He works well under supervision but cannot be left alone to work independently. The case was closed six months after he proved his ability to stay with the job. The counselor checked the placement after a two-year period, and found that his employer and co-workers enjoy his friendly ways, and that he continues to put forth much effort to do a good job.

Good Community Adjustment of Former Patients of State Institutions for the Retarded

Another area in which retarded adults have demonstrated their potentials is in their transition from being patients in state institutions for the retarded to making satisfactory adjustments in the community. Goldstein[13] made an extensive review of follow-up studies of mentally retarded adults who had been paroled from state institutions for the mentally retarded. He concluded that the majority of higher-grade retarded former patients would probably make a relatively successful adjustment in their communities "when training, selection, placement, and supervision are all at an optimum."

Mary C. is a forty-year-old woman now living in a small town in a rural area. As a child she had attended special classes for educable mentally retarded children in her community. When she was eleven years old, her parents and her sister were killed in an automobile accident, in which she was slightly hurt. She was then placed in the home of her maiden aunt, one of the survivors of the accident. There was constant friction and many management problems. She ran away three times, each time demonstrating little capacity for protecting herself from sexual advances by men with whom she found herself.

When she was fourteen years old, she was placed in juvenile hall where psychological tests indicated that she had an IQ of 52, could read and write at the third-grade level, and was an immature personality. About six months later she was committed to a state institution for the retarded. There she became a model patient, working for several years as a helper on the wards. She was given an assignment in the laundry and worked well on the job of folding and stacking linens. When the staff felt she was ready for community placement, arrangements were initiated to work with her more intensively. A staff social worker held regular meetings with her to discuss community adjustment problems. The institutional school staff assigned her to their homemaking training program. Later she was interviewed by a vocational rehabilitation counselor working in the community to which it was planned to send her. All efforts were coordinated at regular staff conferences. A boarding home was located in a nearby community and she moved in.

The vocational rehabilitation counselor continued to see her and soon located a job in a self-service laundry where she helped the proprietor fold the finished laundry. She has been living in the boarding home where she has her own room. She shares the social life of the family with which she boards and sometimes helps out by being a baby-sitter for the younger children. On several occasions when she felt "blue" she contacted her former social worker in the institution, arranged an appointment to see her, and was given help.

Successful Marriage

Successful marriage is another area in which some mentally retarded adults have demonstrated higher potentials than anticipated. Studies by Bass,[14] and Lee, Hegge, and Voelker[15] found only a small number of mentally retarded adults* who had successful marriages. The general impression from their reports is that marriage in which one or both partners are mentally retarded would be fraught with grave difficulties. On the other hand, Jastak[16] found that, judging by frequency of separation or divorce, the mentally retarded in his sample in Delaware were not significantly different from the nonretarded population. While further information on this subject is essential before generalizations can be made, there is ample evidence from studies that there are many mentally retarded adults who do marry and make a good adjustment in their marriage.[17]

Alice R. and Bill M. are happily married and have lived in their one-bedroom apartment in a lower middle-class neighborhood for the past three years. Bill is twenty-eight years old and works full time in a Goodwill Industries facility helping the warehouse truck dispatcher in the loading and unloading of salvage delivery trucks. Occasionally he has the responsibility of handling the dispatcher's job for a half hour or so, but he does not want to do the job continuously. Alice is a part-time client in a long-term workshop not far from home.

Bill attended classes for the educable mentally retarded in school, remaining until he was eighteen years old. In high school he made C's and D's in most subjects, but did well in physical education, carpentry, and machine shop. He is an only child and before his marriage lived with his widowed mother who earned her income as a teacher of kindergarten children. After he was graduated, he tried different jobs, but because his work was too slow, he was fired each time. One day he was passing the local Goodwill Industries and decided to apply for a job. He was accepted as a sorter of salvage items. A few weeks later he was assigned to the dispatcher, where he is now employed at $1.50 per hour, earning a little above the minimum wage.

About nine months after joining Goodwill Industries, he met Alice at a party. She was a slender, neatly dressed young woman of twenty-one years, at that time being evaluated by vocational rehabilitation. She had attended classes for the educable mentally retarded, and had been "graduated" at the age of eighteen. Her IQ

---

* By their definitions, which did not necessarily coincide with the definition used in this book.

scores had been consistently between 65 and 75. Her speech was not easy to understand especially when she became excited in new situations. Her parents (father worked as a building superintendent in a small office building; mother was a housewife, who had completed high school and one year of college) had always been interested in Alice's welfare and had tried to help her in school work and in developing a richer social life. She has an older sister, who is married, and a younger brother who is being drafted into the Army sometime during the next three months. After she left school, Alice did very little with her time beyond taking care of her room, cleaning the house, and spending time with her former school friends.

When she was twenty-one years old, she suddenly decided that she would like to get a job and become more independent. Her parents arranged appointments with the Vocational Rehabilitation Agency. After some joint interviews which the rehabilitation counselor conducted with Alice and her parents, it was decided that she should go to a workshop for evaluation. Although she did not meet the mental requirements for vocational rehabilitation services, meet the basic requirements for vocational rehabilitation services, workshop as a long-term client, working at slightly less than half the norm of a nonhandicapped worker. It was at this time that she met Bill. Their friendship developed rapidly and after a few months of keeping company they decided to get married. Their parents at first were opposed to the idea, expressing concern about Bill's earning enough to maintain an independent home, and over the prospect of the couple having children. After a number of family discussions it was finally agreed that the couple could manage financially with a combination of Bill's salary, Alice's workshop earnings, and additional financial help from their parents as needed. Both Alice and Bill agreed that it would be best for them not to have children. To prevent pregnancy Alice was fitted with an intrauterine contraceptive device, and the couple agreed to continue using it. They have followed through on this matter, and there have been no pregnancies.

THE BEGINNING OF ADULTHOOD FOR THE MENTALLY RETARDED

Is there a sharp line of demarcation between adolescence and adulthood? Is it a matter of chronological age, mental age, social maturity, legal status, custom? From the following definitions of the start of adulthood it is obvious that there is wide variability in determining when childhood ends and adulthood begins. In common law a man or woman attains adulthood (full age, majority) on the last day of the twenty-first year of age. In some states a woman is an adult on becoming eighteen years of age. "In civil law a male is an adult after the age of fourteen years, and females after twelve years."[18] For many purposes, such as determining eligibility for the draft, and, in many states, marrying without parental consent or drinking alcoholic beverages without legal restriction, being eighteen signifies the start of adulthood. For other purposes, the age of twenty-one years is considered the start of adulthood, e.g., being able to vote, thereby assuming one of the most important privileges and responsibilities of citizenship.

While there are differences in the age which designates the start of adulthood, it is noteworthy that this is always expressed in a chronological age. In this book, however, a different concept is used to designate the start of adulthood among mentally retarded persons. The start of adulthood for the mentally retarded person is considered the period following the completion of the *compulsory phase* of his education. In this era of compulsory education for all, the education of the mentally retarded is usually carried on up to the age of eighteen, although this is by no means universally the case.

While the mentally retarded adolescent is still in school his major needs are met. He is supervised, receives training and counseling, and his day is filled with activities. After he is "graduated," the picture changes completely. The school is no longer there to meet his needs, and he is on his own. He must find gainful employment, recreation, and social activities which the school no longer provides. Now he has new privileges and responsibilities which he may not be able to meet without help. It is well known that the period after normal high school students graduate is a very difficult one for them. How much more difficult it is for those with subaverage general intellectual functioning and impairment of adaptive behavior! For these reasons the start of adulthood in the mentally retarded will be considered the period immediately after they leave school, regardless of whether their chronological age is sixteen, eighteen, or twenty-one. Since there is no compulsory education beyond twenty-one years of age, to all intents and purposes the mentally retarded person is always considered an adult after he is twenty-one years old. However, he may be considered an adult at any age below twenty-one if he is no longer a student in a compulsory school situation.

When they leave the public school program, whether at sixteen, eighteen, or twenty-one years of age, the mentally retarded may not have achieved the social maturity nor have obtained the training necessary to cope with the social and vocational demands made on adults. For the retarded person the process of growing up may be going on and may extend beyond the age of eighteen or twenty-one. Some normal persons with this delay in development are characterized as "late bloomers" and are accepted as such. A similar delay in maturation is noted in many retarded adults. This has implications for giving the mentally retarded the benefits of more extended periods of schooling and more opportunities to develop their potentials. For these retarded persons the designation of adulthood might best be postponed for a later time than law and custom now dictate.

> Edward E. is a seventeen-year-old adolescent, living in a run-down section of a large city. He attends a class for educable mentally retarded students in the nearby senior high school. He is short, somewhat obese, clumsy in gait, and has poor speech. Physically he looks younger than his age. He is very shy, and his only friends are those he knows in school. His IQ is 55 and his achievement test scores place him in the third grade in reading and arithmetic. The school psychologist has characterized him as being a moderately mentally retarded, immature adolescent. His school program includes homemaking, carpentry, athletics, and academic work. Although his best subject has been the homemaking activity, he has been making slow but steady progress in academic subjects. He is becoming less shy. For the past few months he has been spending two hours a week helping the school janitor. The school janitor reported to his teacher that Edward was showing some interest in this type of work. Edward's teacher, after a conference with the school psychologist, believes that Edward would need more training in homemaking and in academic subjects, and would have to get over his extreme shyness before he is ready to leave school. If Edward could remain

in school after he becomes eighteen, he might develop greater social maturity. He might also continue training which could help him get a job and make a generally more adequate community adjustment. This would make it more possible for him to meet the demands which will be made upon him as an adult.

At what age the retarded are considered adult is of considerable importance. At eighteen, for example, the mentally retarded is considered adult and eligible for special benefits under the Aid to the Permanently and Totally Disabled Program.* Eligibility for these benefits is determined by the county welfare department. The following is quoted from a circular[19] describing this program in one state:

Aid to Needy Disabled Program

For Needy Persons Who are Permanently and Totally Disabled

What is a Permanent and Total Disability?
    a. A major physical, emotional, or mental handicap
    b. That will probably continue throughout lifetime, and
    c. Prevents regular employment or homemaking.

To be Eligible
    Age: at least 18 years of age
    Residence:
        a. three of the past nine years in this state. One of these three years must be the year immediately before applying for aid; or
        b. become disabled while a resident of this state.
    Property: does not own real or personal property beyond a certain amount.
    Income: insufficient income to meet needs.

What Kind of Help Is Available?
    Financial assistance
    Medical care
    Supplying of special devices, such as wheelchairs, braces, and other equipment and devices
    Work training
    Assistance with special problems
    Assistance with living arrangements
    Attendant care
    Other services.

---

* Aid to the Permanently and Totally Disabled, also known as Aid to the Needy Disabled, is abbreviated ATD.

Where to Apply
You may apply at your local County Welfare Department. This booklet was prepared by the State Department of Social Welfare to provide information about the Aid to Needy Disabled Program.

It should be noted that funds for the ATD program come largely from Federal sources. The administration of the funds is a state-county responsibility, with actual disbursement of funds being done at the county level. Since there are wide variations in the organization, operation, and attitudes of staff in different parts of the United States, there are differences in the amounts of funds and the types of services provided for retarded adult clients under this program.*

Joan D. is an adolescent with Down's syndrome (mongolism)†, now seventeen years of age. She lives with her mother and four younger children, her father having deserted the family a few years before. Her mother receives a total grant under AFDC‡ of $212 per month, which is sufficient to cover the basic needs of the family, with nothing extra. Joan, with an IQ of 46, attends classes for the trainable mentally retarded (TMR) in her neighborhood.

She has frequent colds and misses school occasionally. Her family's AFDC caseworker is a recent college graduate with little experience in social work and with a case load of 120 families. There is little time to be of help to Mrs. D. with her many problems.

When Joan becomes eighteen years of age, she will be eligible for ATD. Her case will be transferred to a trained social worker with a case load of forty-five to sixty clients. Her social worker will be able not only to spend time counseling Joan but also will be able to make funds available for medical and rehabilitation services and for vocational training if necessary. Joan's mother is looking forward to the time when Joan can "go on ATD."

RELATIONSHIP TO THE COMMUNITY

Since this book is concerned with the mentally retarded adult

---

* In June 1964, 501,429 persons were receiving grants under the Aid to the Permanently and Totally Disabled Program (ATD). Average payment was $78.50 per month.[20]

† Down's syndrome and mongolism are used interchangeably.

‡ Aid to Families with Dependent Children.

in the community, it is necessary to explain the use of the term *community.* By community is meant an area where people live or work under normal conditions.

Traditionally, large state institutions for the mentally retarded (variously known as state school, state hospital, state colony, state home) were built remote from population centers and isolated from the mainstream of community living. The schools having been conceived primarily as custodial institutions, the retarded patient was taken out of the community, placed in the institution, and expected to live there indefinitely.

In recent years there has been general agreement that these traditional large state institutions are not the best way to serve the retarded person who needs to be institutionalized. As a result, construction of new large state institutions for the retarded remote from population centers has been virtually discontinued in most states. Instead the emphasis is on construction of smaller state institutions closer to population centers. Within the state institutions for the retarded, there has been a shift from custodial to rehabilitative services, with a strong effort to return the institutionalized retardate back to the community.

There seems little doubt that a step forward has been taken in the change in concept from large state institutions remote from population centers to smaller state institutions closer to population centers. However, before vast expenditures of funds are made to implement this concept the question is raised as to whether this is the best way to deal with the mentally retarded. If these funds were used to develop adequate facilities, programs, and services in the community to meet the needs of retarded children and adults, there would be no reason to place the retarded in even the most advanced state institutions. As community services and programs for retarded adults (including foster homes, halfway houses (see Chapter V), workshops, group home facilities,* recreation programs, vocational rehabilitation services) are increased, it would be possible to more closely

---

* "A facility which provides housing services, personal counseling services, and group activity services for individuals capable of personal self-care and requiring only moderate or minimal supervision."[21]

approach the goal of achieving a more nearly normal and productive life for the retarded. For these reasons, emphasis on community programming for retarded adults is timely and necessary.

As an infant, Robert Q. had been diagnosed as having Down's syndrome. The obstetrician recommended that Robert be placed in a state institution for the retarded, but his parents refused to do so. Robert was the third of a family of four children. His siblings were normal. His father deserted his mother when Robert was three, shortly after his youngest brother was born. The family had received public welfare assistance prior to this time, owing to the father's inability to hold a job. After he left, Mrs. Q. found the situation too difficult, and the children were made wards of the court. The other children were placed in a foster home, but Robert remained with his mother. When he was four, his mother remarried, but this marriage was even more disastrous, with her new husband beating both her and Robert. Shortly thereafter, Robert was placed in a foster home, where he received much love and excellent care.

When he was five years old and ready to enroll in kindergarten, his foster parents were told by the school psychologist that Robert was too slow to be enrolled in regular classes. Tests had indicated that he had an IQ of 38. At a conference among the school psychologist, the county social worker, and the foster parents, it was decided that since there were public school classes for the trainable mentally retarded, and he was not a management problem, he would be better off remaining in the community than being placed in a state institution.

He attended public school classes for the trainable mentally retarded, making slow progress. When he left school at eighteen, the question of institutionalization again arose. His foster parents did not wish to place him in an institution and tried to find some way to keep him in the community. They located a workshop for the handicapped, which agreed to accept him in a few months. During these months at home, Robert showed much interest in housework, especially helping in the kitchen. After admission to the workshop, he did poorly on industrial subcontract work, but did well when given household and kitchen assignments. He was then given special training in housekeeping duties. The staff and his co-workers enjoyed him, as he was friendly and cooperative.

His foster parents learned that there was a small commercial bakery in a nearby city which might be interested in employing

Robert, providing he could get to and from the bakery by himself. The owner of the bakery had a brother with Down's syndrome, and as a consequence, became interested in Robert. Through the county welfare department, another foster home was located about a half mile from the bakery so that Robert could walk to work. These foster parents had provided foster home care for two other young men from state institutions for the mentally retarded. They were aware of some of the problems which mentally retarded adults had in making an adjustment to community life.

From the start, Robert got along well with the other employees: two bakers, two truck drivers, a bookkeeper, and a retail clerk who sold some of the baked goods in a small store in front of the bakery. His work was to sweep the floors, help bring necessary supplies to the bakers, move the racks of baked breads to the slicing and packaging machines, and load the packaged bread into large cartons. In time he was doing his assignment well. He earned the minimum wage of $1.20 per hour. On one occasion, the bakery owner told his social worker that Robert was a slow but steady worker, with a pleasing personality.

The bakery owner invited Robert to his home for dinner on several occasions. He also helped Robert become friendly with a group of young adults who were interested in providing physically handicapped persons with recreation. When they took the handicapped to the circus or to the beach, Robert would help the more handicapped on and off their wheel chairs and would get them soft drinks. One of the handicapped women who volunteered a few hours a week in a public library urged him to visit the local library. There he found many picture books and magazines which he enjoyed looking through. On holidays, Robert travelled to his former foster home to visit with his family.

DISTINCTION BETWEEN THE MENTALLY RETARDED AND THE MENTALLY ILL ADULT

Many people confuse mental retardation and mental illness. The mentally ill adult manifests psychopathological distortions of reality, usually associated with a history of emotional disturbance or of acute personality maladjustments. He may be unable to cope with the pressures of his environment and have to undergo psychotherapy or be placed in a protected setting such as an institution. In his case it is hoped that the emotional disturbance will subside or respond to treatment and that he will return to normal functioning. On the other hand, the most serious problems of the mentally retarded adult arise from impairment in general intellectual functioning, a condition which is not subject to significant improvement with the passage of time or by any known treatment. However, with appropriate training, counseling, and rehabilitative services, the retarded person can be helped to achieve the maximum of his potentialities. To be sure, some mentally retarded adults may be unable to cope with the pressures of their environment. They also may need psychotherapy or even require hospitalization to treat their mental illness. In such cases it is hoped that with treatment the emotional disturbance in the retarded adult will be ameliorated and he will be able to function at his previous level.

Pamela D. is a thirty-three-year-old retarded woman with an IQ of 70, who has always been frail and somewhat nervous. She lives in the lower middle-class section of a small city. She attended special classes for the mentally retarded. She left school at the age of sixteen when her father died and it was necessary for her to work to help support the family. She was employed by a large laundry and dry cleaning plant to do hand ironing of small items. She worked with two other women who had about the same intelligence as she. Pamela did her job quite well for about nine years. Her work was her only interest. She spent evenings and weekends at home with her mother. The personnel manager decided that because she was doing such a good job she should be promoted to a more responsible job with a raise in pay. The new job involved operating a machine iron on another floor of the building. It was also necessary for her to work more rapidly.

She tried very hard to learn the new operation but it was too difficult for her. After a few days her nervousness increased and she seemed less able to work. She also developed splitting headaches and stomach pains. She was advised to see a physician. Her doctor examined her and found no physical illness. He referred her to a psychiatrist. After one interview the psychiatrist decided that what was involved was excessive pressure on the job and that she needed a richer social life. He agreed to treat her in group therapy sessions which he was then conducting. He recommended that she be returned to her previous work assignment.

Once she was returned to her old job she was much happier,

but her physical symptoms did not immediately disappear. With continued therapy her headaches and stomach aches slowly came less often and eventually stopped. During the group therapy sessions, she discussed some of her feelings of loneliness and with encouragement gradually began to attend some groups in a nearby community center.

QUESTIONS FOR DISCUSSION

1.   What are some definitions of *mental retardation* other than the one proposed by the American Association on Mental Deficiency? Evaluate their good points and shortcomings.

2.   You are a state employment service counselor trying to place retarded adults. In a conference with the personnel manager of a large factory where electronic equipment is assembled, he says he has heard about "those crazy dumbbells," and he will not consider hiring such persons. How do you go about trying to change his attitude?

3.   John F. attended adjustment classes for the mentally retarded while in school. Now at thirty-five years of age he is employed as a busboy in a large cafeteria earning $2.10 per hour. He does not like to be reminded that he attended special classes for the mentally retarded in school. Why do you think he feels that way?

4.   The following case is presented for discussion:

Jim B. is a twenty-five-year-old man, who lives with his mother in a two-bedroom apartment in the suburbs of a large city. He is the second of three siblings. His older sister and younger brother are out of the home, his sister married, his brother in the Army. His father died when he was four years old.

He was born prematurely, weighing 3½ pounds, and was in an incubator for five weeks. He developed slowly. His speech has always been hard to understand. When he was first brought to school he was so unhappy that his mother agreed with the school principal that he should be kept home for another year. When he was admitted to school at the age of eight, tests indicated that his IQ was 62—mild mental retardation. During his early school years he made little academic progress, made few friends at school or in his local neighborhood. He was easily upset and frustrated. His mother took him to several physicians and to a chiropractor, but no treatments seemed to help.

Rock Valley College - ERC

He was excluded from school at fourteen after engaging in a series of fights with younger children; during one of these fights he broke a child's nose. For a two-year period he was treated by a psychiatrist in a child guidance clinic with only minimal evidence of improvement in behavior.

When he reached eighteen, his mother arranged for him to become a client of the Aid to the Disabled Program of the welfare department. Subsequently he was interviewed by the Department of Vocational Rehabilitation counselor, but it was determined that rehabilitation services were not feasible for him since there was no prospect of his being employed. He was tried in the local Goodwill Industries workshop but was unable to do any of the assignments, continually was late, and was belligerent with his supervisor. He was soon discharged.

Recently he became involved with a group of young men in his neighborhood who stand on a street corner and get him to throw rocks at passing cars and shout vile language at passersby. The police officer has spoken to his mother and told her that his behavior is likely to lead to his being brought to court and to being sent to jail.

Jim needs help if he is to function adequately in his community. What help does he need? How does he go about getting such help? Efforts have been made to help him in the past. How successful have these efforts been? Do you think he could have been helped at an earlier age?

REFERENCES

1. Terman, Lewis, and Merrill, Maud: *The Measurement of Intelligence.* Boston, Houghton Mifflin Co., 1937.
2. Heber, Rick: Modifications in the manual on terminology and classification in mental retardation. *Amer J Ment Defic, 65*:499, 1961.
3. Heber, Rick (Ed.): A manual on terminology and classification in mental retardation. Monogr. Suppl., *Amer J Ment Defic, 64*(2):3, 1958.
4. Terman, and Merrill: *op. cit.*
5. Wechsler, David: *The Measurement of Adult Intelligence.* Baltimore, Williams and Wilkins, 1944.
6. Heber: *A manual on terminology. . . .* pp. 3-4.
7. Doll, Edgar A.: *The Vineland Social Maturity Scale: Manual of*

Instructions. Minneapolis, Minn., Educational Test Bureau, 1947, p. 1.

8. Sloan, William, and Birch, Jack: A rationale for degrees of retardation. *Amer J Ment Defic, 60:*262, 1955.
9. Cain, Leo F., and Levine, Samuel: *Effects of Community and Institutional Programs on Trainable Mentally Retarded Children.* Washington, D. C., Publications Sales Section, NEA, 1961.
10. Katz, Elias: Changes in social competency ratings of seriously handicapped mentally retarded young adults in a community rehabilitation programme. *J Ment Subnormality (England), 10:*76-82, 1964.
11. Leland, Henry; Nihira, Kazuo; Foster, Ray; Shellhaas, Max, and Kagin, Edwin: *Conference on Measurement of Adaptive Behavior.* Parsons, Kans., Parsons State Hospital and Training Center, 1966. (NIMH Grant No. S-R11 MHO1862-02.)
12. U.S. Dept. of HEW: *Selected Characteristics of the Mentally Retarded Clients Rehabilitated by State Vocational Rehabilitation Agencies in Fiscal Years 1958 and 1963.* Washington, U.S. Gov. Printing Office, April 1964, p. 2.
13. Goldstein, Herbert: Social and occupational adjustment. In Stevens, Harvey A., and Heber, Rick (Eds.): *Mental Retardation: A Review of Research.* Chicago, U. of Chicago, 1964, p. 229.
14. Bass, Medora S.: Marriage, parenthood, and prevention of pregnancy. *Amer J Ment Defic, 68:*318-333, 1963.
15. Lee, John J.; Hegge, Thorlief G., and Voelker, Paul H.: *A Study of Social Adequacy and of Social Failure of Mentally Retarded Youth in Wayne County, Michigan.* Report to U.S. Office of Education, Project No. 178 (Jan. 1957 to June 1959). Detroit, Wayne State University, 1959.
16. Jastak, Joseph F.; MacPhee, Halsey M., and Whiteman, Martin: *Mental Retardation, Its Nature and Incidence. A Population Survey of the State of Delaware.* Newark, Del., U. of Delaware, 1963, p. 138.
17. Goldstein: *op. cit.,* p. 253.
18. *Webster's Unabridged New International Dictionary of the English Language,* 2nd ed. Springfield, Mass., G. and C. Merriam, 1958, p. 37.
19. State of California, Dept. of Social Welfare: *Aid to Needy Disabled Program* (circular). Sacramento, Office of State Printing, Oct. 1965.
20. Moss, John: Social welfare. *Britannica Book of the Year 1965,* p. 738b.
21. U. S. Dept. of HEW: *Planning of Facilities for the Mentally Retarded.* Washington, U. S. Gov. Printing Office, Nov. 1964, p. 9.

Chapter II

WHY BE CONCERNED ABOUT THE RETARDED ADULT IN THE COMMUNITY?

There are urgent reasons for being deeply concerned about mentally retarded adults in the community. The large number of persons involved and the high cost to society make this a matter of considerable importance.

Mental retardation is generally accepted as a serious community and educational problem in childhood. The prevention of mental retardation in the *newborn* is one of the primary goals of biological and health research of the present day. The public supports the idea that mentally retarded *children* and *adolescents* need and can profit from special education and counseling while in school. It is readily apparent, however, both from direct observation as well as from published reports of community services for the mentally retarded that programs for retarded *adults* are either nonexistent or woefully inadequate.

With the exception of vocational rehabilitation services, Aid to the Permanently and Totally Disabled, and a few other programs, there is a tendency to regard mental retardation as largely a problem of childhood. If it is important to accept the problem and to support programs for retarded children, is it logical to ignore the same mentally retarded after they become adults? It seems strange that the community as a whole has *not* been deeply concerned about the welfare of so large a group of handicapped persons in its midst!

SIZE OF THE PROBLEM

Although the precise number of mentally retarded adults is not known, the best estimates would indicate that they comprise no less than one to two per cent of the total population of the United States. The total number of mentally retarded adults would thus be in excess of *2,000,000 persons.** Suppose that each of these mentally retarded adults involves at least one, two, or more persons directly or indirectly affected by the problems he generates, then the staggering impact on literally millions of citizens can be imagined. Can the total cost of services needed by all these retarded persons and by those affected by them be calculated? Can the loss of productivity to society be estimated?

There is one dimension of this problem which has baffled many workers in the field of mental retardation: where are all the mentally retarded adults? They must be in the community because there were fewer than 100,000 adults in state institutions for the retarded in 1965.[1] All surveys of the mentally retarded in the community have located only a very small percentage of the adult retarded, far fewer than anticipated.

In seeking an answer to the question of why so few retarded adults in the community are identified, it should be pointed out that some 85 per cent of the mentally retarded (almost two million retarded adults) are in the mildly and borderline retarded intelligence ranges, while 15 per cent of the retarded (less than one-quarter million retarded adults) are in the moderately, severely, and profoundly retarded levels. The more severely retarded are likely to be noticeable in terms of behavior, appearance, speech, and physical defects. They are more easily identified than the mildly retarded, and, because of the severity of their problems, are often better served. On the other hand, many of the mildly and borderline retarded adults are found in socially, economically, and culturally deprived communities. They tend to look like normal people, may fit into some normal activities, and therefore are not easily identified as mentally retarded. This does not mean that they do not need help. In fact, unless they are given such help as training, counseling, and job placement, they "present a serious problem to society and may comprise a

---

* Based on the assumption that 3 per cent of the total population is mentally retarded, and that of these about one half are adults.

significant number of school dropouts, chronic unemployables, and social outcasts."[2] In many cases, if they get into trouble with the law, they are considered vagrants, delinquents, prostitutes, hoodlums, and are not listed as retarded. Because they are not considered retarded does not alter the fact that they *are* retarded adults and should be identified and treated as such.

EFFECT UPON THE FAMILY

What takes place within each family is not so obvious to the general public—the concern that each parent feels for his retarded child and the impact of the retardate on siblings. The profound grief of parents over their retarded child has been characterized by Olshansky[3] as the "chronic sorrow syndrome." Pearl Buck,[4] Karin Stensland Junkers,[5] and other parents of retarded children have eloquently expressed their own grief, their disappointment, and their search for answers.

The Group for the Advancement of Psychiatry[6] lists many problems which parents of retarded children and adults face:

They may not have fully accepted the diagnosis of mental retardation.

They have varying degrees of guilt feelings about their possible role in the causation of the child's condition.

They resent the fact that this has happened to them and tend to try to find some outside influence on which they can blame the problem.

They hope for a magical solution.

There have been few studies reported as to the effects of the mentally retarded adult who lives at home, upon siblings who are still in the home. To be sure there have been reports of meetings and panel discussions where siblings of retarded children have met and discussed their attitudes and feelings about their retarded family member.[7] Farber and his associates[8] have been studying the effects of severely retarded children on their siblings. Some of these studies of the retarded child help clarify the early development of relationships between young retardates and their siblings. They tell little about relationships between adult retardates and their adult siblings who remain in the home. When the retardate is young, adjustments must be worked through by the family if he is to continue as a family member. These adjustments may be painful and disturbing. After adulthood has been reached and early problems in family relationships are resolved, new and different problems arise.

The impact of the retarded on their families has had far-reaching effects. Since the early 1950's, parents of the retarded have joined hands, and with many others have devoted their efforts to improving conditions for their own children and for all other handicapped persons. Out of their deep conviction that the retarded can be helped, grew the National Association for Retarded Children and its more than one thousand state and local affiliates. The association's basic goal expresses the concern of the parents of retarded persons: ". . . to promote the general welfare of the mentally retarded of all ages everywhere."[9] The work of the National Association for Retarded Children has had deep and abiding influence on research, legislation, and services on the Federal, state, and community levels.

CONNECTION BETWEEN POVERTY AND
THE RETARDED

If poverty is defined as the condition of a wage earner who has an income of less than $3000 per year,[10] then there are large numbers of mentally retarded adults who fall into the poverty class. Indeed, it is likely that only the mentally retarded with borderline intelligence could have the productive capacity to earn $3000 per year or higher. Those persons unable to earn this amount per year must rely on public or private help to survive. In recent years public-assistance grants from Aid to the Needy Disabled have been made available in some states to retarded adults over 18 years of age under certain conditions.[11] The grant, however, allows only a minimal subsistence level of support. Furthermore, many retarded adults cannot qualify for such grants and receive no financial assistance from this source.

Poverty is not alone a matter of dollars and cents or bread and butter. Those who live in slums and socioeconomic ghettos suffer from lack of motivation to advance themselves, from limited experiences, from broken homes and emotionally crippling family life, and from lack of opportunities for gainful work. Despite the strenuous efforts of the War on Poverty, many of the socially and economically deprived will continue to live in communities with low living-standards for years to come. In these poverty-stricken communities, mentally retarded persons will suffer even more than the normal. One of the cardinal recommendations in the Report of the President's Panel on Mental Retardation[12] was

> . . . the root causes of a great part of the problem of mental retardation are to be found in bad social and economic conditions as they affect individuals and families, and . . . correction of these fundamental conditions is necessary to prevent mental retardation successfully on a truly significant scale.

HEALTH PROBLEMS

It has been pointed out by various authorities that the mentally retarded exhibit a higher incidence of health problems than is found in the general population.[13] While the impressions on this score appear to be derived from experience with mentally retarded children, it is likely that the same holds for the retarded adult. Many mentally retarded adults live in low socioeconomic circumstances, in communities where there is evidence of a higher incidence of health problems and higher risk of birth defects. It must be stated that there are few hard facts as to the health of retarded adults. No national health survey has as yet been undertaken to verify many popular beliefs about their health problems.

MANIFESTATIONS OF ANTISOCIAL BEHAVIOR

In recent years few investigators have focussed their attention on the person with low IQ who has exhibited such extreme antisocial behavior as to require confinement in jail. This is in marked contrast to the period in the latter part of the nineteenth century and the early part of the twentieth century when, in the popular mind and among knowledgeable professional workers in all fields, mental deficiency and criminal activities were believed closely linked. Davies[14] opens his book on the mentally retarded in society with a vivid word picture of this earlier thinking:

> What pictures from the literature of the past the very mention of the feebleminded conjures up! Menace to the progress of the race, root of social evils, burden of civilization—this was the way mental retardation used to be widely characterized. To no other form of human inadequacy have so many social blights been attributed: crime, delinquency, degeneracy, poverty, vagrancy, immorality and their train.

Davies' words relative to earlier thinking on the subject of the relationship between mental retardation and the ills of society may appear to be gross exaggerations to modern ears. However, there are some statistics which give reason for concern; for example, the California Study Commission on Mental Retardation,[15] in reviewing services provided by the California Department of Youth Authority, which supervises seriously delinquent males and females below the age of twenty-one, noted the following:

> The percentage of funds or staff time devoted to the mentally retarded is not known, but the 2933 youths who were identified as mentally retarded represent 16.5 per cent of the entire caseload of 17,776. Applying this percentage to the total agency budget and staffing, we may infer an expenditure of close to $4,000,000 for the retarded part of the case load, and the equivalent of more than one hundred full-time professional staff.
>
> Identification of the mentally retarded is regarded by the department with some reservation inasmuch as the instrument used for determining the retardation was the nonlanguage form of a group-type test, the California Test of Mental Maturity. Individual intelligence tests usually show a smaller percentage of those in the retarded area than do group tests.
>
> It is safe to say that 2933 persons with problems indicating mental retardation or slow learning rate are recognized and service is provided by the Youth Authority.

Whether one accepts a 16 per cent figure or a smaller one, it should be of grave concern that this figure is several times more than the expected incidence of mental retardation in a comparable nondelinquent population. If this particular statistic is generalized to the far larger number of adults who come into conflict with the law and may be in confinement, but who may not have been identified as mentally retarded, then the implications for the field of delinquency and correction are disturbing. In what way is society failing to prevent the retarded from becoming delinquent? Does it mean that there is a larger number of retarded adults among the delinquents than is generally believed?

THE EFFECTIVENESS OF SPECIAL EDUCATION
IN THE PUBLIC SCHOOLS

It is generally accepted that mentally retarded children can profit from special education, as evidenced by support of special education by local communities, state legislatures, and the federal government. In recent years the number of children enrolled in special classes for the educable mentally retarded and the trainable mentally retarded* has increased dramatically, especially since many states have declared as mandatory special education of all mentally retarded children. It is estimated that it will be many years before all eligible retarded children are placed in special education classes because of the shortage of trained teachers and of classrooms.

One feature of special education of the mentally retarded is that class size must be small, since retarded children cannot be provided individualized instruction in a regular class of thirty-five to forty children. In many states classes for educable mentally retarded children are limited to eighteen children, and classes for trainable mentally retarded children are limited to twelve children. To make these smaller classes possible, supplementation

---

* Educable mentally retarded children (EMR) are those who are "incapable of coping with a normal-class program . . . most school districts use an IQ range of 50 to 75 as a major criterion, whether this practice is sound or not. The IQ range is ordinarily stretched upward or downward a few points, depending upon many administrative factors."[16] Trainable mentally retarded children (TMR), also known as severely mentally retarded children (SMR), are those "with an approximate IQ range of 25 to 50 with some potential for *acquiring social maturity skills.*"[17]

in the form of excess cost-reimbursement from the state treasury to the local school district which operates such special education classes is needed to cover the extra cost involved. In some communities additional taxes must be levied to cover the higher cost of these classes. Where necessary, retarded children are transported to and from schools. This cost must be added to the expense of their education. The cost of educating a mentally retarded child may thus be as much as two or three times that of an average or above-average child.

The high cost of special education of the mentally retarded in the public schools has raised questions in the minds of the general public and of legislators. Legislators who vote the funds for special education of the mentally retarded have an obligation to their constituents to insure that the most effective use is made of public education funds. Taxpayers who pay local taxes to support general and special education are rightfully interested in knowing what their taxes are being used to accomplish.

Parents of retarded children worry whether the special education being provided for their children will indeed prepare them for a life of security and happiness after leaving school, as they hope it will for their normal children. Teachers of the retarded are concerned whether their methods and content are effective in training their students to cope with the immediate and long-range demands of society.

Special education of the mentally retarded should be a major concern of the public schools. The high cost of special education is justified since special training enables many mentally retarded adults to take their place as useful citizens. Follow-up studies of adults who attended classes for the mentally retarded in the public schools have offered evidence that for many the effort was well justified. Even the Wayne State University study[18] which found much evidence of social inadequacy among adults who had attended public school classes for the mentally retarded in Detroit, came to the following general conclusion:

> If the study says anything, it is that what has been done is not wrong, but rather that it has not been adequate. . . . To revise and improve educational programs which will enhance the social adequacy

of retarded youth in a manner that will reduce their rate of social failure, as indicated in this study, is a major challenge to special education, to general education, and to every social agency.

COMMUNITY ADJUSTMENT OF FORMER INSTITUTIONAL PATIENTS

Since this is a period when mentally retarded adults are being moved from the institution into the community, many questions deserve consideration. How can those adult patients who are most likely to become successful be selected prior to being placed on leave? How well do ex-patients adjust to community life? How can the former patient best be served in the community in order to substantially increase his chances for remaining in the community?

Much interest has developed on how to select those patients in the institution who are most likely to make a successful adjustment when placed in the community. The usual criterion for success is the ability to remain in the community without having to return to the institution. Windle[19] reviewed previous studies on the prognosis for successful community adjustment of mentally retarded adults in state institutions. He came to the disappointing conclusion that little could be generalized from the extensive literature on the subject. He did conclude that "the areas which appear to this reviewer most in need of additional study for prognosis relevance are etiological diagnosis, various abilities and ability patterns, personality, and type of treatment."[20]

Many follow-up studies have been made on the community adjustment of adults who formerly were patients in institutions for the retarded. These studies have reported that some patients were successful and remained in the community, while others were unsuccessful and had to return to the institution.

In one study, Miller[21] reported on a representative sample of patients on leave in the community from California state hospitals for the retarded from 1956 to 1961. She found that thirty-six out of forty-three patients (84%) were returned to the institution one or more times during the five-year period following 1956, although some were not resident patients at the end of the five-year period. This finding suggests that many former patients of these state institutions had a difficult time making a community adjustment.

On the other hand, after reviewing many follow-up studies of the social and occupational adjustment of mentally retarded persons who had been patients in state institutions, Goldstein[22] concluded that a large majority of the retarded patients released had made a generally successful community adjustment.

In a follow-up study by Windle, Stewart, and Brown,[23] the reasons for return to the institution (failure) of 147 patients placed on leave from Pacific State Hospital, California, in 1952 and 1953 were obtained from patients' clinical records. These reasons are reported in Table III. Their study strongly suggests that former patients return to the institution because of antisocial behavior and poor social adjustment. The question may be raised as to whether the major reasons for failure lie not only in the behavior of the patient, but also in the absence of appropriate community services to meet his needs.

TABLE III

PERCENTAGE OF FAILURE* FOR VARIOUS REASONS AMONG 147 PATIENTS RELEASED FROM PACIFIC STATE HOSPITAL 1952-1953†

REASON FOR FAILURE	PERCENTAGE OF FAILURE
Patient's Actions	
Antisocial Behavior: crimes, sexual misbehavior, pregnancy, minor antisocial actions	27
Intolerable Behavior: unhygienic, untidy, temperamental, hyperactive, destructive, insomniac	7
Inadequate Interpersonal Relations: jealous, disrespectful, quarrelsome, domineering	11
Inadequate Work Performance: cannot take orders, has anxiety or poor self-evaluation	12
Voluntary Return and Escape	9
Mental Illness: commitment to mental hospital, psychotic, depressed	7
Health: medical problems, seizures, or too much care required	9
Environmental Lack of Support: parental disinterest, home closed, parental interference, community objection	18

* *Failure* means the patient could not make a community adjustment, and had to be returned to the institution.

† Adapted from Windle, Charles D.; Stewart, E., and Brown, S.: Reasons for community failure of released patients. *Amer J Ment Defic*, 66:213-217, 1961.

The author conducted a follow-up study[24] of 119 mentally retarded adult clients of the Work-Training Center Project (1957 to 1961).[25] These clients (all of whom had been considered not feasible by the State DVR) were provided specialized vocational rehabilitation services including evaluation, social services, work training, job placement, and job follow-up. Table IV indicates that five years after the end of the project, only four former clients (about 3%) were resident patients in state institutions.

TABLE IV

STATUS* OF 119 FORMER CLIENTS OF THE WORK-TRAINING CENTER (W-TC†) FOR THE MENTALLY RETARDED

HISTORY OF INSTITUTIONALIZATION‡	PRESENT STATUS			
	LIVING IN COMMUNITY	IN INSTITUTION FOR RETARDED	IN INSTITUTION FOR MENTALLY ILL	TOTAL
Institutionalization before admission to W-TC	25	1	1	27
No institutionalization before admission to W-TC, but committed since leaving W-TC	7	2	0	9
No institutionalization before or after attending W-TC	83	0	0	83
Total	115	3	1	119

* From unpublished data collected by the author in July 1966.

† Katz. Elias (Ed.): *Final Report, Work-Training Center for the Mentally Retarded,* for Vocational Rehabilitation Administration, Project No. 205 (San Francisco, Calif.: Aid Retarded Children, 1961).

‡ Committed to an institution for the mentally retarded or the mentally ill for periods ranging from a few months to a few years.

In another study,[26] the author reported on fifty-six clients of the Independent Living Rehabilitation Program (1961 to 1965), a therapeutically oriented workshop program for seriously handicapped mentally retarded adults, many of whom were former patients of institutions for the retarded or were eligible to be committed to such institutions. Over the four-year period during which these fifty-six clients were terminated from the program, *not one* was committed to a state institution for the retarded, although four were placed in institutions for the mentally ill, owing to severe emotional problems.

It is difficult to generalize from these studies. However, available information indicates that the existence of community programs designed to meet the needs of retarded ex-patients of state institutions results in significant reduction in the number of those returned to institutions.

PROTECTION OF LEGAL RIGHTS AND PRIVILEGES

There are certain legal rights and privileges of citizenship, e.g., the right to vote, the right to move about freely, and the right of protection by the government of one's person and of one's property. Generally speaking these rights are not questioned, although they may be restricted in times of war, during confinement in an institution, or when the exercise of these rights does harm to others.

It is sometimes forgotten that mentally retarded adults are citizens with the rights and privileges of all other adults. The Report[27] of the President's Panel on Mental Retardation summarized contemporary thinking on this score as follows: ". . . It must be recognized that many of the retarded are at a disadvantage in recognizing and asserting their rights."

A great deal of thought has been given to the need of the more severely handicapped retarded adult for some form of protection of his person and his property, especially when his parents are unable to care for him. In some states plans are being developed for guardianship of the retarded adult to be assumed by a governmental agency when the parents are incompetent to assume this responsibility. In other states guardianship of the retarded adult remains in the hands of non-governmental agencies or individuals. As yet there is no general agreement on the best way to handle the general problem of protection of the severely handicapped retarded adult living in the community.[28]

HELP FOR ACHIEVING HIGHER LEVELS OF FUNCTIONING

A final reason for being concerned about mentally retarded adults in the community is the mounting evidence that they *do* profit from training, rehabilitation, recreation, and creative expression. Those who have visited and observed well-organized and well-operated recreation programs, workshops for the handicapped, or halfway houses have commented on the happiness and the enthusiasm which emanate from the retarded adults participating in the programs. These impressions are reinforced by discussions with the staffs, who often are doing hard jobs under difficult conditions, yet seem to enjoy their work with the retarded adult. There are many reports which demonstrate that contributions of retarded adults are substantially greater when community programs are available to meet their needs.

During the past few years public agencies at the federal, state, and local levels, and private nonprofit community agencies have been increasing the amount of funding, staff, and facilities to serve the mentally retarded. While it is true that much of the focus has been and continues to be on prevention, early treatment, and education of the mentally retarded child, funds are being more liberally allocated to help the retarded adult. There is every indication that the amount of funds for this purpose may be increasing in years to come as the scope and seriousness of the problem becomes clearer.

In spite of encouraging developments, the nagging questions still remain: Are sufficient funds being allocated? Is enough being accomplished with the allotted funds? Are mentally retarded adults being helped to achieve the maximum of their possibilities? There is little doubt that significant progress in vocational rehabilitation, recreation, and employment has been made. A far greater effort in terms of staff, funds, and facilities must be put forth in the next few years if retarded adults are to realize their full potentials as members of society.

QUESTIONS FOR DISCUSSION

1. What are some of the basic legal rights which may have been withheld from mentally retarded adults? How could you account for this?

2. Why do most mentally retarded adults earn less than $3000 per year?

3. Why do you think mentally retarded adults could have more health problems than the nonretarded adult?

4. In what ways does special education for the mentally retarded student in school prepare him for his role as an adult?

5. What evidence is there that mentally retarded adults can become contributing members of the community, instead of being a drain on our economic and social resources?

REFERENCES

1. Scheerenberger, Richard C.: A census of public and private residential facilities for the mentally retarded in the United States and Canada. In *Directory of Residential Facilities for the Mentally Retarded.* Columbus, Ohio, American Association on Mental Deficiency, 1965. (Abstract in *Ment Retard Abstr,* 2:620, 1965.)
2. Philips, Irving (Ed.): *Prevention and Treatment of Mental Retardation.* New York, Basic Books, 1966, p. VIII.
3. Olshansky, Simon: Chronic sorrow: a response to having a mentally defective child. *Soc Casework,* 43:190-193, 1962.
4. Buck, Pearl: *The Child Who Never Grew.* New York, Day, 1952.
5. Junkers, Karin Stensland: *The Child in the Glass Ball,* transl. by Gustaf Lannestock. New York, Abingdon, 1964.
6. Group for the Advancement of Psychiatry: *Mental Retardation: A Family Crisis—the Therapeutic Role of the Physician.* New York, Group for the Advancement of Psychiatry, 1963, p. 129.
7. Schreiber, Meyer, and Feeley, Mary: Siblings of the retarded—A guided group experience. *Children,* 12:221-225, 1965.
8. Farber, Bernard, and Jenne, W. C.: *Family Organization and Parent-child Communication: Parents and Siblings of a Retarded Child.* Monogr., *Society for Research in Child Development,* 28:3-78, 1963.
9. National Association for Retarded Children: *Basic Aims of the National Association for Retarded Children,* Jan. 1966, p. 1.
10. *Public Law 88-452, The Economic Opportunity Act of 1964.* Washington, U.S. Gov. Printing Office, 1964.
11. State of California, Dept. of Social Welfare: *Aid to Needy Disabled Program* (circular). Sacramento, Office of State Printing, 1965.
12. President's Panel on Mental Retardation: *A Proposed Program for National Action to Combat Mental Retardation.* Washington, U. S. Gov. Printing Office, 1962, pp. 8-9.
13. American Medical Association: *Mental Retardation: A Handbook for the Primary Physician.* Chicago, AMA, 1965, p. 55. (Reprinted from the *J Amer Med Ass, 191:*183-232, 1965.)
14. Davies, Stanley P.: *The Mentally Retarded in Society.* New York, Columbia, 1959, p. 4.
15. State of California, Study Commission on Mental Retardation: *The Undeveloped Resource: A Plan for the Mentally Retarded of California.* Sacramento, Study Commission on Mental Retardation, Jan. 1965, p. 32.
16. Rothstein, Jerome: *Mental Retardation: Readings and Resources.* New York, Holt, Rinehart, and Winston, 1961, p. 163.
17. *Ibid.,* p. 332.

42   *The Retarded Adult in the Community*

18. Lee, John J.; Hegge, Thorlief G., and Voelker, Paul H.: *A Study of Social Adequacy and Social Failure of Mentally Retarded Youth in Wayne County, Michigan.* Report to U. S. Office of Education, Project No. 178 (Jan. 1957 to June 1959). Detroit, Wayne State University, 1959.
19. Windle, Charles D.: *Prognosis of Mental Subnormals.* Monogr. Suppl., *Amer J. Ment Defic, 66*(5): 1962.
20. *Ibid,* p. 137.
21. Miller, Dorothy: *Worlds that Fail: Part I. Retrospective Analysis of Mental Patients' Careers.* California Mental Health Research Monogr. No. 6. Sacramento, State Dept. of Mental Hygiene, 1965, p. 88.
22. Goldstein, Herbert: Social and occupational adjustment. In Stevens, Harvey A., and Heber, Rick (Eds.): *Mental Retardation: A Review of Research.* Chicago, U. of Chicago, 1964, p. 253.
23. Windle, Charles D.; Stewart, E., and Brown, S.: Reasons for community failure of released patients. *Amer J Ment Defic, 66*:213-217, 1961.
24. Katz, Elias: Personal communication, 1966.
25. Katz, Elias (Ed.): *Final Report, Work-Training Center for the Mentally Retarded.* (For Vocational Rehabilitation Administration, Project No. 205.) San Francisco, Aid Retarded Children, 1961.
26. Katz, Elias: *Independent Living Rehabilitation Program for Seriously Handicapped Mentally Retarded Adults.* (Final report for Vocational Rehabilitation Administration, Project No. RD-905.) San Francisco, Aid Retarded Children, 1965, p. 112.
27. President's Panel: *op. cit.,* p. 150.
28. Boggs, Elizabeth M.: Legal aspects of mental retardation. In Philips, Irving (Ed.): *Prevention and Treatment of Mental Retardation.* New York, Basic Books, 1966, p. 426.

Chapter III

HOW IS THE RETARDED ADULT EVALUATED IN THE COMMUNITY?

W HEN A MENTALLY retarded adult and his family seek help, the professional worker or social agency to whom they turn must be prepared to provide the best possible service. This can be done only after a careful evaluation. If the problem is relatively simple it can be evaluated by a skilled professional, whether this be a physician, a psychologist, a social worker, or a vocational rehabilitation counselor. If it is a complex problem, it may require thorough and extensive study by a comprehensive evaluation team.

PSYCHOLOGICAL EVALUATION

Psychological evaluation addresses itself to answering a series of questions based on tests and interviews: What is the retarded adult's intellectual functioning level? What variations exist in the different aspects of his intelligence, e.g., do his scores on the Wechsler-Bellevue Intelligence Scale[1] subtests show a wide range of performance in different functions? How should this spread of scores be interpreted? What are his social competencies in relation to other persons of his chronological age in his socio-economic setting? What are his dominant personality characteristics? What are his major mechanisms of adjustment to frustration and conflict? What is his grade level of achievement in the basic academic subjects of reading, arithmetic, and spelling? What are his aptitudes in mechanical, clerical, and home-making areas? What are his personal, social, and vocational interests? What are his recreational and leisure-time activities?

Following is a summary report of a psychological evaluation

of a mentally retarded man who was referred by a vocational rehabilitation counselor seeking to determine whether the applicant should be accepted for vocational rehabilitation services.

Report of Psychological Evaluation

Name: R.........., James   Age: 32 years, 9 months
                                  Sex: Male
Referred by Vocational Rehabilitation Counselor

Reason for Referral

Personality evaluation to assist in determining feasibility for vocational rehabilitation services.

Tests Administered

Wechsler-Bellevue Intelligence Scale[2]
Columbia Mental Maturity Scale[3]
Raven's Progressive Matrices[4]
Rorschach Ink-Blot Test[5]
Thematic Apperception Test[6]
Vineland Social Maturity Scale[7] (mother, informant)

Behavior during Examination

Mr. R. was a brown-haired, brown-eyed, neatly dressed and groomed, rather short man, looking considerably younger than his chronological age. He could see and hear adequately, and evidenced no overt symptoms of neuromuscular involvement of extremities. His speech was relevant but rather hesitant. Frequently he seemed to be searching for the correct word to express an idea but would then give up without success.

He was very shy at all times, never volunteering information, but giving appropriate answers to direct questions. He said he did not see much connection between the psychological evaluation and getting a job.

Psychological Examination Findings

He obtained a Full Scale IQ of 65, with a Verbal Scale IQ of 63 and a Performance Scale IQ of 75. These scores were in the mild to borderline level of subaverage general intellectual functioning.* While most of the subtest scores were in the mentally retarded level, on the Picture Completion subtest (identifying missing parts of pictures) he was able to do as well as a person of average intelligence. This suggests that he may have intellectual capacities along nonverbal lines which are superior to his achievement on verbal tasks. To some degree this is consistent with poor academic skills, a reflection of meager schooling.

---

* See Chapter I, Table I.

The scores on two nonlanguage intelligence tests were in the seven to eight-year mental age range. These tests were performed with a minimum of effort and probably tended to underestimate his intellectual capacity.

On projective tests, he tended to be inhibited, especially in elaborating responses. The Rorschach protocol, both in content and in formal qualities, was characteristic of a mildly mentally retarded person. He perceived mostly animal shapes in the blots, which represents emotionally immature responses. Parts of animals and birds were seen, sometimes presented in a rather perseverative manner. Delays in response suggested an undertone of depression.

While he did not elaborate the Thematic Apperception Test stories, there was present considerable concern about the future. In one story, a young man was seen as "crying—crying about his own future." In another, he said, "The man's sad, thinking of when he grows up." One picture, showing an older and a younger man, elicited the following: "He looks scared to me; somebody's behind him; maybe he's scared he might do something to him, might try to give him poison; he's young-looking—old man hates him." However, in another story, a father is represented as helping his son who has been injured. From these sketchy clues, it would be difficult to develop the personality picture, but a great deal of light was cast when his mother was interviewed.

Mrs. R. was a forceful, talkative, anxious middle-aged woman, with exaggerated costume jewelry and an elaborate hairdo. The contrast between her son and herself was striking. Her overwhelming ways could well have a devastating effect on her son's independence. She tended to minimize her son's obvious mental limitations, repeatedly pleading with the examiner to get a job for him. As reflected in the TAT stories, Mr. R. appears to manifest resentment and fear in relation to his mother's superiority in virtually every sphere. At the same time there was appreciation for his mother's effort to help him make a vocational and personal adjustment.

From information furnished by his mother, he was reported to be functioning at the level of social competence of a seventeen-year-old. This was consistent with his appearance and behavior. He started school at seven years, had reached the fifth-grade level at sixteen years when he dropped out of school. Except for the periods when he was employed, most of his time was spent at home. His reported occupational history included serving as a messenger boy at a very low salary ($100 to $150 per month). He held this job for three years. His mother characterized him as dependable, honest, industrious. She stated that she believed her son could be trained to operate a mimeograph machine, to do simple mail sorting, and simple filing.

Diagnostic Impression

Borderline level of measured intelligence° (AAMD nomenclature); mild depressive trends.

Recommendations

1. Continue in present home situation, providing he has more freedom from his mother's domination. It is questionable whether he can live alone, except in a sheltered setting such as a dormitory-type living arrangement with adult supervision.

2. He would profit from training to carry on a simple routine task within his mental abilities. Such training could be in the realm of simple factory work or elementary filing and sorting tasks.

3. A strong effort should be made to help him develop a more active social life, whether in clubs, church groups, or by attending dances. This would help him to become more independent and more sociable.

4. He should be considered for further evaluation of vocational interests and aptitudes, and training in a workshop, where he might learn better work skills, and ultimately be placed in elementary clerical or simple assembly work.

(CLINICAL PSYCHOLOGIST)

There are basic limitations to psychological evaluation of mentally retarded adults. These limitations stem from two major sources: First, there are few tests of intelligence, personality, aptitude, and interest which have been developed and standardized for use with mentally retarded adults. As an example, the content of some of the Wechsler-Bellevue Intelligence Scale subtests is sometimes beyond the reading comprehension and experience range of a mentally retarded adult who is from a very deprived environment, or who has lived in a remote rural area, or who has lived for many years in a state institution. Under these circumstances the test findings cannot be used to accurately determine intelligence level. In such cases it may be necessary to rely on clinical skill or to admit that this facet of functioning is not clear. Another example is the General Aptitude Test Battery (GATB)[8] of the U. S. Employ-

---

° See Chapter I, Table I.

ment Service, which is widely used in state employment offices to assess aptitudes of applicants for work. Some of the tests of the GATB are geared for a comprehension reading level of eighth grade, which is above the reading level of most retarded adults. While an employment counselor could use failures on GATB to give an indication of what the mentally retarded applicant *cannot* do, this information is not too helpful in deciding what he *can* do. The challenge of developing new psychological tests or adapting available ones to evaluate mentally retarded adults has stimulated some researchers. To mention but a few, the E. R. Johnstone Training and Research Center has been standardizing a test of vocational interests of the retarded;[9] Peck has developed the Texas Screening Battery for Mental Subnormals;[10] there has been some experimentation with the Illinois Test of Psycholinguistic Abilities[11] in evaluation and planning the training of retarded adults; Cain and Levine[12] are continuing their work on evaluating the social and vocational competency of severely retarded adults.

Second, there are few psychologists trained or experienced in evaluating the mentally retarded adult. Of those who do have such training and experience, most are employed in state institutions for the mentally retarded. It is a common experience of social agencies and professionals who wish to have a mentally retarded adult tested, to find that among the local psychologists there are few who feel adequate to perform this task. As community programs develop and as mental health centers and mental retardation centers emerge, there will be more psychologists trained in mental retardation and their role in evaluation will undoubtedly greatly increase.

SOCIAL EVALUATION

Social evaluation is most often done by social workers or vocational rehabilitation counselors during early contacts with the client, through interviews with parents, guardians, or the client himself. Information about social development in childhood and adolescence is of vital importance in understanding the present situation and problems. Social and economic factors often contribute significantly to the adjustment difficulties the mentally retarded adult faces.

Social evaluation calls for thoroughness, a process which may require extensive interviewing and in some instances home visits. Complex problems of long standing require careful study before they achieve clarity. The process of social evaluation may lead to the development of plans for future social services. It must always be kept in mind that the social evaluation may be the first time that the mentally retarded client and his family have been reached for intensive study.

Among the questions which will concern a social worker developing a social evaluation of a mentally retarded adult are these: What are the basic personality pattern and behavior dynamics of the mentally retarded adult? What is his role in his family and in his community setting? What are the family structure and dynamics? What is its socioeconomic status? What are the aspirations of family members for themselves and for the mentally retarded adult living with them? What is the background of the family's understanding of the mentally retarded adult's condition? What has been the impact on the family? In what areas will the family members need help if they are to help the mentally retarded adult? What assets and limitations exist in the retarded adult which can be worked with by a social worker?

Following is a social evaluation of a mentally retarded young adult, who was referred by the Division of Vocational Rehabilitation.*

Social Assessment Summary: Stephen P.

Family History

Stephen P. is twenty years old, the oldest of three children born to Mr. and Mrs. P. Mrs. P. passed away earlier this year and the only persons presently living in the household are Mr. P. and the three boys.

Mr. P. is forty-four, quite outspoken in his views, but very cooperative with the interviewer and seems to be vitally interested

_____

* Adapted from a case evaluated by the Structured Community Services for the Retarded, Milwaukee, Wisconsin.

in the welfare of his children. He admits that he has provided all of the necessary physical requirements for the children but that he seems somewhat inadequate in providing all of the necessary guidance which is often delegated to the female member of the family. He admits very candidly that he sorely misses the support of his wife in dealing with the three boys but that he feels he is doing the best he can under the circumstances. Mrs. P., who died of a coronary, had evidently suffered from heart disease for some time. It is obvious from being with Mr. P. that she was the more dominant partner of this union. He takes the boys bowling, attends basketball games, dances, et cetera with them. If anything, he may be overindulging the children and, in fact, admits that he may have "spoiled them rotten."

He views Stephen's retardation as an unfortunate incident and accepts the irreversibility of his affliction. His goals for Stephen are certainly realistic. He hopes to find some social outlet for Stephen, feeling that he has no companionship among his brothers nor among his brothers' friends. Consequently this youth is left pretty much to his own devices and has resorted to associating with older persons. This retardate is certainly not isolated by geography from others his own age but seems to be a quite passive young man who needs encouragement in order to participate more actively in activities with persons his own age.

Stephen's two younger brothers, twelve and sixteen, have little relationship with him. They neither engage in any active group participation with him nor do they introduce him to their circle of friends. During family activities in which Mr. P. participates, however, the family appears to be more closely knit. Mr. P. insists that Stephen participate in all family activities such as bowling. He accompanies the family on these activities. According to Mr. P., Stephen is unable to compete favorably with the other two boys in most areas.

The reaction of the children to the mother's recent death is varied. His brothers took the death rather hard, while Stephen was unable to show any visible grief. From the remarks he has since made, it is obvious that he sorely misses the presence of his mother in the home.

Personal History

Stephen was a full-term baby and was delivered without complication. At first no physical disabilities were apparent, and five days after delivery the infant went home with his mother. At age two, according to Mr. P., Stephen was playing with a young cousin who, in an attempt to kiss him, knocked him over, resulting in Stephen's hitting his head on the door. No apparent damage was immediately evident; however, that evening Stephen went into convulsions which necessitated immediate hospitalization. The tests determined that a blood clot had formed and that some of the child's motor control was hampered. He was unable to effectively use his left arm for a period of time. Tests determined that the degree of organic damage was not known. As a result of this accident it was necessary to retrain him through the normal developmental tasks, such as walking and weaning. The exact medical diagnosis was not known to the father, but at his absolute insistence, when Stephen was tested by the Veterans Administration psychologist, Mr. P. was told that his son's IQ was 68.

Mr. P. could not recall any friends who associate with this young man regularly. He is an "isolate" by definition, though gregarious when he gets to know someone more closely. Most of his time is spent watching television, approximately twenty hours per week. He also enjoys hiking. He plays passive games such as cards.

He graduated from Special "C" classes° at high school. He was not regarded as a school problem by his parents or by teachers.

He had only one period of competitive employment, as a farm laborer, approximately two years ago. He worked as a bean picker for one month. He quit at the insistence of his father when it was obvious that he was being ridiculed because of his mental retardation. At the present time he is engaged in a maintenance training program at the——Workshop. According to his father he has shown no interest in this type of work. He is more interested in employment where he can work alone.

He had a recent physical examination and is presently in good physical health. He was hospitalized for the concussion when he was two, for a tonsillectomy when he was five, and for an electroencephalogram when he was eight years old.

Previous Agencies and Institutions

He has availed himself of the university speech therapy department, attends the —— Reading Center. He was in the work study program with the —— Vocational Center during his last year of high school. According to Mr. P. he was withdrawn from this program by Mrs. P., who felt that her son was not as severely retarded as the other students.

Services Needed

Mr. P. sees Stephen's primary need as one of social-recreational.

° Classes for the mentally retarded.

This young man is an *isolate* and needs some social outlet. The evaluator is in general agreement with Mr. P.'s view; however, it is entirely probable that Stephen could benefit from some type of vocational training. He is currently engaged in a maintenance training program, and it is possible that he could be encouraged in some other area that he is more interested in for vocational training. Some type of bench work of a repetitive nature or some type of work where he could operate independently, but with the necessary supervision, is indicated.

(SUPERVISOR, SOCIAL EVALUATION)

MEDICAL EVALUATION

It has been estimated that "three of every four retarded individuals have significant medical problems. The retarded seem especially susceptible to infection and illnesses, especially to the complication of respiratory illness. . . . The physician must be alert to these considerations."[13]

The medical evaluation of the mentally retarded adult is concerned with the physician's diagnosis of disabilities or impairments, established as a result of medical examination and judgment. The report is expressed in anatomical or pathological terms and includes a prognosis as to the removal or amelioration of the condition. Major functional limitations are spelled out. The report should include a statement of the physical capacities as compared with normal persons of the same age and socioeconomic background.

Following is a report of the medical evaluation of a mentally retarded adult who was referred for possible placement in a foster home in the community. It will be noted that the physical examination shows few significant findings that would differentiate this retarded adult from other persons in the general population.

Medical Evaluation of Frank P. [*]

Personal History

The pregnancy, which was the mother's first, had been normal except for the last two months, at which time she had an increase

---

[*] From a case provided by Peter Cohen, M.D., Associate Professor of Pediatrics, University of California Medical Center, San Francisco.

in blood pressure. The labor was induced. Ether anesthesia was used, and the child was born without any difficulty although forceps were used for delivery. The baby breathed immediately. The mother noted bruises on the baby's scalp. Following the delivery the mother required several transfusions. The child's birth weight was 9 pounds 3 ounces. His motor development seemed to be normal. He held up his head at six weeks; sat alone at six months; first walked alone at fourteen months; however, he didn't say words until two and one-half years, and spoke sentences at four and one-half years. He was toilet trained by about eighteen months. He was noted to have a large head at age three months. Also, he had one seizure with an episode of fever early in life. He had the usual childhood illnesses: chicken pox, measles, mumps, and whooping cough. He had a T and A and a circumcision at age four.

It was obvious from early childhood that this young man was mentally retarded, and he attended special classes. After completing school at eighteen he was enrolled for awhile in a workshop for the retarded.

When his mother had a nervous breakdown and required hospitalization, it became necessary to place him in a private institution.

He has had many psychological tests, using the Stanford-Binet (Form L) with the following results: At five years an IQ of 45; at six years an IQ of 35; at twelve years an IQ below 30; at sixteen years an IQ of 25. When seen at a state hospital for a pre-admission examination at twenty-two years, he was given a Stanford-Binet again which showed an IQ of 24. According to the psychologist's report, there was no consistent pattern in his successes and failures in the tests except to indicate very little mental capacity.

Family History

There is one younger sibling who is in good health. The father and mother are apparently in good health also. A cousin of the father is said to have been in an institution since he was a child. Also, a maternal aunt is described as having a very large head but is intellectually normal.

Physical Examination

This thirty-one-year-old young man is fairly tall, well-developed and somewhat obese. He is very friendly and obviously interested in cooperating with the examiner and trying to answer his questions. It is apparent, however, that it is very difficult for him to comprehend most of what is asked of him. He appears particularly limited in areas that involve judgment. He has a large head (circumference is 61 cm), a large oval face, large ears which are turned somewhat anteriorly, and a long, curved nose.

Skin: Clear. No café au lait spots.

Glands: No lymphadenopathy.

Eyes: Pupils round and equal. No Brushfield spots. React to light and accommodation. EOM are normal. Fundi are normal.

Ears: Canals patent. Tympanic membranes normal.

Mouth: Teeth in good state of repair. Tonsils out.

Neck: Thyroid not palpable.

Chest: Normal configuration.

Heart: Not enlarged. No murmurs.

Lungs: Clear to percussion and auscultation.

Abdomen: Obese. Spleen and liver not palpable. No masses palpated.

Genitalia: Normal adult male. Circumcised. Testes in the scrotum.

Anus: Good sphincter tone. No hemorrhoids.

Extremities: Normal.

Neurological: Cranial nerves: normal.

　Motor: good tone.

　Sensory: intact.

　Balance: good.

　Coordination: good.

　Reflexes: deep reflexes active and equal. Abdominals active and equal. No clonus or Babinski.

Laboratory: Urinalysis: negative including $FeCl_3$ test.

　CBC: normal.

　Xray of the skull: except for the large size, nothing unusual was noted.

Impression: Mental retardation, moderate to severe. Arrested hydrocephalus.

Prognosis: Poor for independent living. His physical condition is comparable to a male of his age and social-cultural milieu, except for the head which is above average size. His social adjustment is primarily limited by his mental retardation.

In those cases where medical examination is directed towards possible employment, limitations of activities the person can perform or of environmental conditions he can tolerate should be stated.*

---

* See Figure 2.

DEPARTMENT OF PREVENTIVE MEDICINE AND REHABILITATION
UNIVERSITY HOSPITAL
ADULT EVALUATION CLINIC
PHYSICAL ABILITY RATING FORM

Blank = No Restriction
0 = No Ability
Written Numbers = Maximum Limits of Ability in Hours during............
Working Hours of 8-Hour Day

Name ....
                                                Age   Height   Weight

PHYSICAL FACTORS:

—— 1   1-5 lbs.
—— 2   6-10 lbs.
—— 3   11-25 lbs.   } Total Lifting Ability—
—— 4   26-50 lbs.   } Including Pushing and Pulling Effort
—— 5   51-100 lbs.
—— 6   100+ lbs.
—— 7   1-5 lbs.
—— 8   6-10 lbs.   } Carrying Ability—
—— 9   11-25 lbs.   } Carrying Ability means that portion of
——10   26-50 lbs.   } Total Lifting Ability which may be
——11   51-100 lbs. } used in Carrying
——12   100+ lbs.
——13   Right
——14   Left   } Fingering—Fine Dexterity
——15   Right
——16   Left   } Handling—Including Coarse Fingering
——17   Right
——18   Left   Below Shoulders
——19   Right   } Reaching
——20   Left   Above Shoulders
——21   Right
——22   Left   } Hammering or Throwing
——23   Sitting
——24   Total Time on Feet
——25   Standing or Moving About in Small Area
——26   Walking
——27   Running
——28   Jumping
——29   Stairs or Ramps   } Climbing
——30   Ladders or Scaffolds
——31   Right   } While Sitting   } Treading—
——32   Left   } Operating Foot Pedals
——33   Right   } While Standing
——34   Left
——35   Stooping—Low-Back Bending
——36   Crouching—Knee Bending
——37   Kneeling
——38   Crawling
——39   Reclining—Working Horizontally
——40   Twisting—Spine
——41   Waiting Time—Periods of Inactivity on Job
20/——42   Far-Corrected Snellen
20/——43   Near-Corrected Snellen   } Vision
——44   Color
——45   Depth
——46   Hearing
——47   Speaking
——48   ....   } Other Physical Factors
——49   ....

DEPARTMENT OF PREVENTIVE MEDICINE AND REHABILITATION
(Continued)
ENVIRONMENTAL FACTORS:
--50 Inside or Protected from Weather
--51 Fair Weather ⎰ Outside Without
--52 Wet Weather ⎱ Weather Protection
--53 Hot ⎫
--54 Cold ⎪ Due to Conditions
--55 Sudden Temperature Changes ⎬ Other than
--56 Humid ⎪ Weather
--57 Dry ⎭
--58 Operating or Around Moving Vehicles or Objects
--59 Hazardous Machinery
--60 Sharp Tools or Materials
--61 Cluttered Floors
--62 Slippery Floors
--63 High Places
--64 Electrical Hazards
--65 Exposure to Burns
--66 Explosives
--67 Radiant Energy (Kind): ....
--68 Poor Lighting
--69 Poor Ventilation
--70 Toxic Conditions (Kind): ....
--71 Wet Working Quarters
--72 Close or Cramped Quarters
--73 Vibration
--74 Noise
--75 Working With Others
--76 Working Around Others
--77 Working Alone
--78 Rotating Shifts—Zero if only day shift is suitable
--79 .... ⎰ Other Environmental
--80 .... ⎱ Factors
Remarks: ....
....
....

Figure 2. Physical ability rating form. From *Training Guides in Evaluation of Vocational Potential for Vocational Rehabilitation Staff*, 1966, p. 54. Courtesy of Vocational Rehabilitation Administration, U. S. Dept. of HEW.

PSYCHIATRIC EVALUATION

The role of psychiatric evaluation in mental retardation has only recently begun to emerge. The Group for the Advancement of Psychiatry[14] (GAP) has gone far to interest psychiatrists to accept mentally retarded persons for evaluation and treatment. Their statement on evaluation of the retarded is ". . . an adequate diagnosis is concerned with the implications of the specific symptomatology, an understanding of etiology, a realistic prognosis and a comprehensive program of care, treatment, and training."[15]

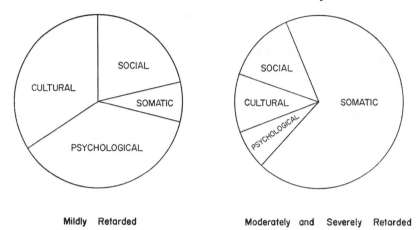

Mildly   Retarded   Moderately and Severely Retarded

(These   figures are   schematic and   are not intended   to represent
exact proportions.)

Figure 3.   Relative importance of etiologic factors in mental retardation.
From *Basic Considerations in Mental Retardation: A Preliminary Report,*
1959, p. 11. Courtesy of Group for Advancement of Psychiatry.

With respect to the etiology of mental retardation, GAP
has taken the position that severely retarded persons with an
IQ below 50 usually suffer concomitant organic brain-damage
involvement, or other conditions such as metabolic disorders or
infections, whereas psychological, social, and cultural factors
play only a small part in determining their over-all status. "On
the other hand the mental status of the mildly defective individual usually is less influenced by organic involvement than
by early cultural influences, social environment, and psychopathological problems."[16]   Figure 3 reproduces the GAP's chart
which indicates the relative importance of etiologic factors in
mental retardation. While one may disagree with this formulation of the causes of retardation, it does point up the contemporary psychiatrist's view that social factors play an important
role in bringing about mental retardation, especially among the
more able (mildly) retarded living in the community.

Following is a psychiatric evaluation of a mentally retarded
adult.

Psychiatric Evaluation of Fred S.*

Fred S. is a twenty-two-year-old young man who attended a special ungraded class for educable mentally retarded (EMR) through two semesters of high school. Since being exempted, he has remained at home. He lives with his mother, age forty-eight, who remains at home, supported by the public welfare department. His half brother, twenty-seven years old, is married and out of the home. His father, age fifty, has been out of the home since Fred was two years old, whereabouts unknown.

Chief Complaints

Mother concerned because Fred "has trouble growing up," acts more like a twelve or thirteen-year-old. No close friends. Stays at home, "too tied" to mother. Lacks physical strength and energy. Overly nervous and moody. Has trouble speaking in proper sentences.

Formulation of Problem

Fred shows evidence of mental deficiency (IQ 47, MA nine to ten years), and moderately disturbed behavior. During the birth process he incurred a transient cephalohematoma. Although this factor probably has psychological implications due to his mother's concern, it is unlikely that any permanent physical damage resulted. His slow motor and verbal development is remarkable. Although there are a few islands of behavior, such as the accomplishment of toilet training between two and three years, and dressing himself before age five, which may be used as examples in questioning the extent of his deficiency, it is likely that the overall picture of retardation suggests a moderate degree of deficiency.

According to mother's knowledge of Fred's father, both mental deficiency and emotional illness are present in the paternal family. Psychosis, alcoholism, and borderline psychotic states are present in mother's family. Reportedly, mother's IQ is slightly below average.

Fred's consistently poor school performance is most likely on the basis of mental deficiency, as well as emotional disorder. The degree of emotional illness alone does not seem to be severe enough to account for the severity of his past record. His physical weakness and lack of energy result from a combination of mental deficiency and lack of motivation.

The relationship between Fred's emotional difficulties and his mother's problems began to emerge most strikingly perhaps in

---

* Adapted from a case provided by Langley Porter Neuropsychiatric Institute, San Francisco.

mother's extreme overprotectiveness, bordering on a symbiotic psychotic relationship. Mother's background of severe deprivation is remarkable. Projection, isolation, denial, and paranoid ideation are mechanisms used excessively by both mother and Fred. His physically aggressive behavior over many years is noteworthy in light of mother's lack of anxiety regarding this, and her inability to curtail this behavior. It is also to be noted that both Fred and his half brother became dependent wards of the court when Fred was seven years old because of mother's physically aggressive behavior towards them.

The precipitating events leading to the present study are not clear. Mother's anxiety may have been mobilized by several events such as Fred's arrival at adulthood and the paucity of mature reactions and actions, his potential for sexual acting out, mother's fear of dying and leaving him alone in the care of relatives from whom she has isolated herself, recognition of her own helplessness and limitations in helping him, and perhaps the knowledge of the impending death from cancer of one of her sisters.

Certainly the evidence of emotional disorder is present in his prolonged difficulty in separating from mother, his long extended physically aggressive behavior toward other children, and relatively recent reversal of behavior to withdrawal, his immature regressive methods of warding off anxiety, such as rocking, head banging, and bed wetting, and his excessive use of projection and paranoid ideation to view the world. Clinically his mental deficiency appeared to be less severe than that indicated by his psychological tests.

Although the prognosis is guarded, his present containment of his impulses, his motivation to improve himself, his intact fine motor coordination, and his mother's request for outside help may permit Fred to follow through on a program of vocational and personal training leading to a more independent life. In addition to mastering basic training skills, psychotherapy and a supervised experience in social interaction would be helpful. Inclusion of mother in a program would lend a marked advantage toward realizing achievements with Fred.

Diagnosis

Mental deficiency: Idiopathic (moderate), with behavioral reaction, personality trait disturbance.

Stress: Mother's increasing concern over Fred's immaturity, dependence on her, and potential for sexual acting out as he enters adulthood.

Predisposition: Mental retardation from birth and personality disorder from early childhood.

Impairment: Moderate.

Disposition at This Time

Applied for and has been accepted in workshop for the handicapped, as recommended by us. To have follow-up visit in three weeks. Periodic mental retardation follow-up offered and accepted by family. Psychotherapy may be considered with family in the future.

No. of Visits	Patient	Mother
Social Service	—	1
Psychiatrist	4	4
Psychologist	3	—
Laboratory:		
EEG	1	—
Clinical	4	1
Xray	2	—
Total	14	6

(STAFF PSYCHIATRIST)

WORK EVALUATION BY VOCATIONAL REHABILITATION COUNSELOR

Study of the vocational potential of the retarded adult has been and continues to be a basic concern of the vocational rehabilitation agencies on the state and federal levels. In the Federal-state program for vocational rehabilitation (see Chapter VI) the vocational rehabilitation counselor, using available information, makes the determination as to whether the individual is eligible for vocational rehabilitation services. Among the questions which are involved in such an evaluation are these: What is the retarded adult's educational background? How far did he go in school? What grades were received? What subjects were taken? What special interests were shown? What is his work history? What jobs were held, salary received, working conditions, social adjustment on the job, reasons for leaving? What are his work habits and work attitudes? What are his vocational aspirations and vocational expectations? What is his motivation to achieve them? What opinions of his actual work are held by his former employers and co-workers? What does his family think of his vocational potential? What is the occupational level of the immediate family? Would he profit from evaluation and training in a workshop for the handicapped?

What kind of jobs are available for him, and what is the labor market outlook for persons with his capabilities and limitations?

Vocational Evaluation of Donna T. *

Because of the similar needs and the limited community resources for mentally retarded clients, the counselor felt that a program should be developed which would allow for the greatest exposure of the clients to the community. It was also felt that there should be a continuous assessment of each client's vocational potential over a long period of time. In order to accomplish these goals, a system was developed to secure the necessary diagnostic material and evaluation of the individual's vocational potential, and to arrange a maximum number of community contacts.

The following case illustrates the way this system was employed with a mentally retarded client.

Donna T. applied for our service at the age of eighteen. She had just graduated from special classes in a local school district. She was small in height, alert, and appeared to be cooperative. She came from a family which consisted of her mother, her brother, and herself. Her only previous work experience was that of a baby-sitter on a part-time basis. The client stated her only interest was to be a baby-sitter or a dressmaker. She could travel around the city and she also could make small change. The school reports indicated that her academic work was very poor. Test scores from the schools showed that she had been given the Stanford-Binet on several occasions and that each time she measured mildly mentally retarded with an IQ varying from 62 to 72.

The client was interviewed and then given a general medical examination. This was followed by a series of psychological tests including the Raven's Progressive Matrices (estimated IQ 68-70), Wechsler Adult Intelligence Scale (IQ 70), and Employment Aptitude Survey (estimated IQ 74). Later a psychiatrist interviewed the client and her mother. The report from the psychiatrist indicated that the client was mildly mentally retarded, but otherwise normal. After these reports were received, the decision was made to work with the client. This decision was based on the following facts: the client was mentally retarded; she was motivated; she appeared to have some work potential; her mother was supporting this program.

The client was first placed in a Goodwill Industries workshop

---

* Adapted from a case from the files of the California Department of Rehabilitation.

for evaluation and training. The experience lasted for a relatively short period of time. The client had many problems adapting to the world of work. The staff at the workshop felt that she had problems attending to the job and problems of taking suggestions from her supervisor. Finally, the workshop staff and the rehabilitation counselor agreed that the client should leave the shop.

The client was next placed for further evaluation in a different workshop which provided more personal and social adjustment services, in addition to work experience. In this workshop the client was included in a small therapy group made up of other mentally retarded clients and conducted by a psychiatrist. The client attended the group to help her establish close contact with her peers, help her discuss freely and understand her vocational and family problems, help her establish an identity that was separate and distinct from her family structure, and help her develop motivation towards a vocational goal.

The client did much better in this workshop. She was able to get along with her supervisors and was able to remain at her job station without wandering around the shop. At this point, the client was encouraged to join a recreation group which many of the other clients were attending. This group was sponsored by the city recreation department for mentally retarded individuals in the community. She attended the weekly programs for some time and enjoyed the events. After four months her work reached a point of maximum production within the shop. At the evaluation session, the staff recommended that she should be placed in an on-the-job training assignment in some industry. An on-the-job training opportunity was available in a laundry, and the counselor transferred her there.

During the first several months in this training and evaluation program, a number of problems developed around her misunderstanding of her role in the world of work, and misunderstanding by her trainers of her limitations. The counselor saw her at regular intervals and was able to work out some of these problems with the client and with her laundry supervisor. As she was working in the laundry, she was no longer able to attend the therapy group or the recreation program.

Because of her special needs, she was invited to join the group program at the DVR office which the counselor conducted for clients who had left workshops and were on regular on-the-job training programs in the community. She was able to attend, and this group proved to be very helpful to her. The subjects for discussion in the group were training, getting along with an employer, doing a job better, and getting along with peers. The problems occurring on the job were discussed in the group with the other clients who had similar problems. In this way, she was able to evaluate and to work through many of her problems, and reach a better understanding as to why she was in an on-the-job training program.

After a three-month period, she was considered by her employers to be an adequate person for employment. They asked if they could hire her permanently as an employee. She was hired by the laundry at $1.61 per hour for a forty-hour week. Since then she has developed into a permanent employee.

WORK EVALUATION IN WORKSHOPS FOR THE HANDICAPPED

A recent trend in vocational evaluation of the retarded adult is to use a workshop for the handicapped for evaluation purposes. A workshop* "is a work-oriented rehabilitation facility, with a controlled working environment and individual vocational goals, which utilizes work experience and related services for assisting the handicapped person to progress toward normal living and a productive vocational status."[17] One of the most important functions of the workshop is "the work evaluation or tryout period, during which the client's capacities are put to practical test and his potential evaluated before a vocational objective is set and a work-conditioning and training program is charted."[18]

Usually the client is referred by a vocational rehabilitation counselor to the workshop, where the staff, consisting of director, social caseworker, counselor, psychologist, workshop manager, and floor supervisor (see Figure 4), is already experienced in doing work evaluations in the workshop setting. The major advantages in using the workshop for evaluation are the realistic

---

* This book uses the terms *workshop* and *workshop for the handicapped* in preference to the more widely used designation *sheltered workshop*. It is the author's contention that the use of the term sheltered workshop perpetuates and reinforces older concepts of the workshop as a *sheltering* facility. Current thinking favors emphasis on the evaluative and rehabilitative functions of the workshop, as reflected in such usages as *Association of Rehabilitation Workshops, Curriculum in Rehabilitation Workshop Administration,* and *Work Training Center.*

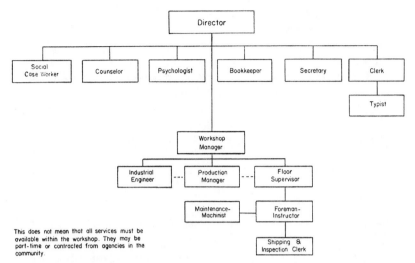

Figure 4. A basic staffing pattern for workshops for the handicapped. From *Sheltered Workshops—A Handbook*, revised 1966. Courtesy of National Association of Sheltered Workshops and Homebound Programs.

work setting, the trained staff, and the opportunity to vary such factors as supervision, rate of productivity, and types of work activities. After the evaluation period a staff conference is held to pool thinking about the client, and to set up a plan for further training and counseling.

Some workshops have set up special vocational evaluation units, which are separated from the main work areas. Most workshops, however, tend to incorporate the clients being evaluated into the regular work force in order to assess his work habits and skills under realistic working conditions.

Following is a sample of work evaluation of a mentally retarded adult in a workshop for the handicapped.

*Workshop Evaluation of Joseph F.**
Work Adjustment Evaluation

To: DVR Counselor   Period: May to June 1966
Joseph F——, Age 22 years
    Wechsler-Bellevue (WAIS)

———————
* Adapted from a case report of a client evaluated by the San Francisco Community Rehabilitation Workshop. This report was made available through the courtesy of the California Department of Rehabilitation.

Full Scale IQ 77
Performance Scale IQ 79
Verbal Scale IQ 78

Attendance

During this period, there were no absences and one lateness. He was absent two mornings for scheduled appointments.

Work Performed

Contractor	Rate*	Job Description
Romo	.7, .8, .9	Assembly of hair curlers, the body to the slide. Requires dexterity and judgment.
Donnelly Packing	.6, .7	Inserting two envelopes of instant breakfast, plus a descriptive insert, into an envelope which is self-sealing.
ADA	Est. .7	Stapling.
Schilling Spices	.6	Stapling a spice packet to a card.
Fibreboard	.5	Labeling.
Arcade Bandage	.4	Packaging of various sizes of bandage strips. Seal boxes and pack in bulk. Requirements: judgment, finger dexterity, neatness.

He was slow at the beginning of each of these assignments but picked up speed when reminded.

Quality of Work

He had problems on one of the jobs, ADA stapling; his work station was sloppy and disorganized. On this particular job his staples were askew, but when he was corrected he performed adequately. Quality on other jobs was within quality standards.

Reactions to Supervision

Client was immature and childish in response to correction—"Aw Gee, Mr. Johnson." He had difficulty dealing with firmness; therefore, a "light touch" was found to be the best approach. He had to be constantly reminded about over-socialization.

Work Attitudes

Despite many aspects of immaturity, client often expressed concern about his production rates. His greatest problem is one of self-discipline. He responds to the work situation as though "this is a fun place to come." It has been difficult getting through to him that what he is doing is important. There remains a problem with accuracy and organization whenever a task is demanding in nature.

---

* A rate of 1.0 indicates performance at 100 per cent level of productivity of a nonhandicapped worker doing the same job; a rate of .9 indicates performance at 90 per cent level of productivity of a nonhandicapped worker doing the same job; a rate of .8 indicates performance at 80 per cent et cetera.

There has been some rise in his production rates when he is aware that it is piece-rated.

His foreman feels that he could function on a simple clerical job, but his problems again would be in the area of self-discipline and social maturity. He works best with people who are not his own age.

Plan

Client will continue for one additional month under the supervision of Mr. Johnson, the foreman. He should be given clerical work whenever possible.

Present at Meeting

DVR counselor, work supervisor, shop director, shop counselor.

(SHOP COUNSELOR)

DIAGNOSTIC TEAM APPROACH TO COMPREHENSIVE EVALUATION

The diagnostic team approach to comprehensive evaluation of the mentally retarded adult requires not only a group of skilled specialists but also the facilities to carry out the evaluation appropriately. Comprehensive evaluations may be conducted in rehabilitation centers, clinics, or workshops. To conduct such an evaluation "involves an integration of the evaluative skills of disciplines including medicine, psychology, social work, education, nursing, rehabilitation counseling, and related areas. The diagnostic team approach is an organized, systematized, supervised procedure, coordinated and conducted by professional personnel whose basic skills, philosophies, and concepts are evaluative in nature. The term further suggests the employment of established and tried methods of collecting, interpreting, and analyzing predictive data through a process which is culminated in a staffing conference which finalizes, interprets, and integrates the collected data in the preparation of meaningful, practical and definitive recommendations."[19]

Following is the summary of a diagnostic team report of comprehensive evaluation of a mentally retarded adult, including general medical evaluation, psychological testing, psychiatric consultation, pre-vocational workshop, job sampling, job tryouts, and vocational training.

Vocational Evaluation Staffing Reports: Aaron K.*

K——, Aaron   April 12, 1966

Mr. K., a nineteen-year-old man, enrolled at the center March 14, 1966, for an evaluation program. His disability is listed as mental retardation. There is also some question regarding the possibility of epilepsy. The referral information reveals he failed the eighth grade and that he has no work history. The tentative vocational objective was body and fender repair or some type of mechanical work. Prior to enrollment, in October 1965, the WAIS was administered on which he obtained a Verbal IQ of 77, a Performance IQ of 68 and a Full Scale IQ of 72. The Kent EGY yielded an approximate IQ of 75. Some additional testing was undertaken here at the center. This included the Beta which revealed an IQ of 73 and the Otis Employment Test which revealed an IQ of 69. His academic achievement abilities in reading and arithmetic were measured at 5.3 and 6.0 grade level respectively (see Psychometric Data Report).

Psychometric Data Report

Name: K——, Aaron   Sex: M   Age: 19
Education Level: 8th Grade

SCORES

NAME OF TEST	RS	IQ	%ile	NORM GROUP	INTERPRETATION AND COMMENT
Revised Beta Examination	47	78		Chronological age	Inferior
Otis Employment Test	11	69	5	Unselected Adult Population	Very Inferior
California Reading Test				Elementary	
Vocabulary					5.1 Grade Equivalent
Comprehension					5.3 Grade Equivalent
TOTAL READING					5.3 Grade Equivalent
California Arithmetic Test				Elementary	
Reasoning					5.6 Grade Equivalent
Fundamentals					6.0 Grade Equivalent
TOTAL ARITHMETIC					6.0 Grade Equivalent
WRAT Arithmetic	21				4.9 Grade Equivalent

TESTS ADMINISTERED AT HOT SPRINGS REHABILITATION CENTER, EVALUATION UNIT

By (PSYCHOLOGIST)   March 14 to 16, 1966

Mr. K.'s evaluation program consisted of general medical evaluation, psychological testing, and work evaluation. Because of his youth and the nature of his disabilities, it was the opinion of the staff that his initial evaluation should be conducted in the prevocational workshop performing simple, repetitive work activities.

———

* From a case evaluated at the Hot Springs Rehabilitation Center, Hot Springs, Arkansas.

It was felt this would provide him with time to make an adjustment to the center and hopefully provide a more valid evaluation of his vocational aptitudes and abilities. The general medical evaluation suggested a possibility of epilepsy. Mr. K. has encountered blackout spells for approximately the past two years. This was based on a psychiatrist's consultation at which time it was expressed that the student might have an epileptic equivalent, but there was some uncertainty of this. It was the recommendation of the consultant that he be restricted from working in high places or around dangerous machinery.

Work Evaluation

Mr. K. made a favorable impression during the initial contact and he appeared to be interested in a program here at the center. It was felt he would need some time in the pre-vocational area due to his immaturity, the nature of the disability, and the lack of work experience before entering into the job-sample area. During the past thirty-day period, he has been performing routine work activities consisting of sorting, packaging, cleaning, and other similar work for the purpose of developing adequate work habits, orientation to work, and providing time for him to adjust from the home setting to the center routine. Mr. K. has made a satisfactory adjustment to his pre-vocational program and has been a fairly consistent worker in the shop; however, on occasions he has presented some minor problems. These are primarily related to his reaction to supervision and interpersonal relations with his peer group. He displays an aggressive work personality which would be viewed as a positive feature in keeping with his vocational interest in the mechanical area. He is able to learn practical work assignments fast, retains well, and, in general, appears to function quite well in practical work areas. At this time it appears he has made sufficient progress to enroll him in the job-sample area for further observation and testing in practical work areas such as the mechanical field, up-holstery, body and fender, and laundry. In working with Mr. K. he appears to respond more effectively to fairly direct supervision and probably will need a structured program with well-defined behavioral limits. There have been no blackout periods observed while in the area. Mr. K. impresses one with the attitude of bettering himself, and from the observations and contacts I have had with him, I feel he will make a good candidate for training.

Recommendations

Transfer to the job-sample area. Test in the practical area. Establish a fairly structured program.

Counselor

In the initial interview, Mr. K. appeared to be intimidated by the center setting. It is felt this reaction was a result of the size of the center and the large number of students. In the initial session, we discussed his blackout spells and he stated these do occur; however, they last only a few seconds. The referring information indicates that these could be a result of an improper diet and malnutrition. Regarding his vocational interest, he stated he was interested in auto mechanics, body and fender repair, and woodworking, but he implied he would be quite receptive to any type of training program recommended. Throughout his program he was a very quiet and reserved individual, who leaves the impression of being younger than his chronological age. I concur with the evaluator that he is now ready to engage in job-sample testing to assess his vocational strengths and weaknesses.

Summary

Based on tests and observations, it is the opinion of the staff that Mr. K. has made an acceptable adjustment to the center and that we can now more adequately assess his vocational capabilities than at the time of initial enrollment. He makes a fairly good impression and has displayed an expressed interest in the center program. He is a fairly consistent and aggressive worker, yet, as reported, there have been some minor problems related to his reaction to supervision and to his peer group. It has been our experience that he responds best to direct and matter-of-fact type of supervision. Too, we found that he functions quite well in practical situations such as body and fender repair, general mechanics, upholstery, and other semiskilled areas. We feel that, because of his low intellectual and academic levels, he should avoid attempting any more-skilled areas.

Recommendation

Transfer to the job-sample test area for more specific testing in practical areas such as outlined above and to include job tryouts if necessary.

(COUNSELOR, EVALUATION SERVICES)

K——, Aaron   May 10, 1966

Mr. K., a nineteen-year-old man, from Arkansas, enrolled in the center on March 14, 1966, for a thirty-day evaluation program. At the conclusion of his initial stay in the job-sample test area, the recommendation of the committee was that his program be extended for an additional thirty days in order for him to make a better adjustment to the center, for acquisition of better work habits, and hopefully to arrive at a definite vocational decision. It was suggested his extended thirty-day program be devoted primarily to participation in job-sample test areas of a semiskilled nature and actual job tryouts. Mr. K. has completed his extended program and is being discussed this date in a regular evaluation conference as scheduled.

Work Evaluation

Mr. K. required a great deal of supervision throughout his evaluation period, but has not presented any major problems. He functions well with his co-workers in a work situation and has adjusted well to the shop. Initially, he did not seem to fully understand the shop requirements or the purpose of his evaluation program. His initial interest was in auto mechanics which reflected his lack of understanding of the demands of competitive employment. He has evidenced a good deal of difficulty in reading and applying instructions in the semiskilled areas, such as mechanics and upholstery, but appeared able to understand and apply verbal instructions well in the less-skilled areas. His work habits were only fair in the shop. He reported to work on time and presented a neat appearance, but he tended to sit down when the opportunity presented. He had difficulty organizing his work in the more complex areas and was unable to proceed in a systematic manner. His working speed was of a moderate nature in the areas in which he performed. He displayed satisfactory manipulative skills in the use of common hand tools and did not experience any difficulty with gross coordination. He was unable to sit and work for any extended period and displayed a very low frustration tolerance for sedentary work. The results of the mechanical tests did not indicate any ability or aptitude for mechanics. He displayed no previous experience or knowledge of machinery on the theory portion of the mechanical tests and exhibited poor ability in the selection and use of tools on the practical phases. He was unable to read and apply the instructions in the upholstery area and needed verbal instructions for all phases of testing in this area. He was not capable of constructing a spring and webbing assembly, although he was given verbal instructions and demonstrations. He could not grasp the significance of the various specialized tools in this area.

He became very nervous while using the sewing machine and could not continue the construction of a cushion in the upholstery area. His best performance was in such areas as painting and body and fender repair. Because of his expressed interest in body and fender repair, a tryout was arranged for him in this area. After working in this area, he expressed a desire for training in body and fender repair. The instructor stated he was a capable and willing worker and that he appeared highly motivated for training in this area. The tests and job-sample results also indicate he has the ability to be successfully trained in the lower levels of vocational activities, such as laundry, food service, painting and at the helper level in body and fender repair. It appears he has now found an area he is interested in and is willing to work hard at it. It is my recommendation that he be enrolled in body and fender repair at the helper level. He appears to be a typical nineteen-year-old individual, and will probably be guilty of breaking minor regulations because of his immaturity; however, I do not feel there will be any major difficulties during training.

Counselor

Mr. K. has evidently made an acceptable adjustment to the center as there have been no reports regarding any deviant behavior. Initially, he experienced some difficulty as far as arriving at a realistic vocational decision; however, recently in discussing the possibility of body and fender training, he expressed a desire to be enrolled in this training area. As was reported by the evaluator, he possesses the necessary ability and aptitude for this type of work. He has been rather immature on occasions although there have been no real problems, and I can anticipate none, other than occasional childlike antics during his center program. He has mentioned needing work clothing if he is enrolled in vocational training. This information will be passed on to the new center counselor if he remains for training.

Summary

For the past thirty days, Mr. K. has participated in job-sample tests in the evaluation workshop and a job tryout in the body and fender area. As the evaluator reported, he displayed very little ability for the mechanical areas and became frustrated when using the sewing machine in the upholstery field. It was reported that while in the evaluation workshop he became rather frustrated, confused, and extremely upset when placed in work activities of a sedentary nature. The results of job-sample tests in the body and fender area indicate he possesses some aptitude for this type of work and a tryout was initiated in this area as a means to further assess his motivation, interest, and potential for this type work. The reports indicate that he is highly motivated, interested, and a willing and cooperative worker. It was also the instructor's opinion that he could be successfully trained in body and fender repair training. The committee is of the opinion that the possibility of special education should be explored while in training and if the instructor feels this can be of benefit, that this service be initiated. No problems other than his immaturity are expected during a formalized vocational training program.

Recommendations

Enrollment in body and fender repair, effective May 11, 1966, enrollment in special education and transfer to Miss R. G. as center counselor aide.

(COUNSELOR, EVALUATION SERVICES)

QUESTIONS FOR DISCUSSION

1. What are the limitations of currently used intelligence tests for determining the intelligence of mentally retarded adults? Show examples to support your position.

2. What kind of report would you expect from a social worker in order to help evaluate the social competency of a mentally retarded adult?

3. What information would you want a physician to provide in order to help you to evaluate the physical aspects of a mentally retarded adult?

4. A nineteen-year-old woman with an IQ of 55, who recently graduated from classes for the educable mentally retarded, is very depressed. She attacked her mother with a kitchen knife and then attempted suicide by cutting her own wrists. How can her problems be evaluated?

5. Prepare a comprehensive evaluation of a mentally retarded man, twenty-five years of age, who is referred to a rehabilitation center for vocational evaluation.

REFERENCES

1. Wechsler, David: *The Measurement of Adult Intelligence.* Baltimore, Williams and Wilkins, 1944.
2. *Ibid.*
3. Lorge, Irving, and Burgemeister, Bessie: *The Columbia Mental Maturity Scale.* New York, World Book Co., 1954.
4. Raven, J. C.: *Raven's Progressive Matrices.* London, England, H. K. Lewis and Co., Ltd., 1947.
5. Klopfer, Bruno, and Kelley, Douglas: *The Rorschach Technique.* New York, World Book Co., 1946.

6. Murray, Henry A.: *Thematic Apperception Tests Manual.* Cambridge, Mass., Harvard, 1943.
7. Doll, Edgar A.: *The Vineland Social Maturity Scale: Manual of Instructions.* Minneapolis, Educational Test Bureau, 1947.
8. U. S. Dept. of Labor, U. S. Employment Service: *Guide to the Use of the General Aptitude Test Battery.* (*Restricted.*) Washington, U. S. Gov. Printing Office, 1952.
9. Parnicky, Joseph J.; Kahn, Harris, and Burdette, Arthur: Preliminary efforts at determining the significance of retardates' vocational interests. *Amer J Ment Defic, 70:*393-398, 1965.
10. Peck, J. R.; Stephens, W. B., and Fooshee, D. K.: *The Texas Screening Battery for Subnormals: Manual.* Austin, Texas, Texas Screening Battery, 1964.
11. McCarthy, J. J., and Kirk, Samuel A.: *Illinois Test of Psycholinguistic Abilities: Experimental Edition.* Urbana, U. of Ill., 1961.
12. Cain, Leo F., and Levine, Samuel: *Effects of Community and Institutional Programs on Trainable Mentally Retarded Children.* Washington, Publications Sales Section, NEA, 1961.
13. American Medical Association: *Mental Retardation: A Handbook for the Primary Physician.* Chicago, AMA, 1965, p. 55. (Reprinted from the *J Amer Med Ass, 191:*183-232, 1965.)
14. Group for the Advancement of Psychiatry: *Basic Considerations in Mental Retardation: A Preliminary Report.* New York, Group for the Advancement of Psychiatry, 1959, p. 5.
15. *Ibid.,* p. 10.
16. *Loc. cit.*
17. National Association of Sheltered Workshops and Homebound Programs, Inc.: *Sheltered Workshops—A Handbook,* revised 1966. Washington, National Association of Sheltered Worshops and Homebound Programs, Inc., 1966, p. 1.
18. *Ibid.,* p. 24.
19. U. S. Dept. of Health, Education, and Welfare: *Training Guides in Evaluation of Vocational Potential for Vocational Rehabilitation Staff.* (Third Institute on Rehabilitation Services, May 23-27, 1965.) Rehabilitation Services Series, 66-23. Washington, U. S. Gov. Printing Office, 1966, p. 35.

Chapter IV

WHAT ARE THE NEEDS OF THE RETARDED ADULT IN THE COMMUNITY?

The NEEDS OF ALL human beings—which include the mentally retarded—may be classified as physiological and psychosocial.

PHYSIOLOGICAL NEEDS

The physiological* needs are common to all living organisms. The behavior of even the simplest forms of life is directed towards achieving such basic goals as survival of the individual and reproduction of the species. More complex organisms show more complex efforts to fulfill their needs to survive and to reproduce. Humans need food, clothing, and shelter to survive. Reproduction of the species is a physiological need, which in humans is governed by socially and culturally determined factors.

The mentally retarded adult's physiological needs to survive are the same as those of any other person. The retarded individual, however, being less mentally competent and often less physically able than his normal counterpart, has a greater struggle to fulfill his survival needs.

With respect to reproductive needs, it was widely believed not too many years ago, that mentally retarded persons if permitted to reproduce would give birth to mentally defective children. The eugenic sterilization movement of the early twentieth century had as its goal the protection of "society through preventing the production of defective offspring."[1] In view of the absence of scientific verification of the assumptions of the eugenic movement, sterilization for racial eugenic pur-

---

* Also known as bodily needs, tissue needs, organic needs, viscerogenic needs.

73

poses has been discontinued. Current thinking concerning sterilization of the mentally retarded is that "the prospect of a significant reduction in the amount of mental deficiency from this source seems relatively meagre and not wholly practically realizable."[2] Further studies of the reproductive needs of retarded adults should be undertaken since so little seems to be known about this subject.

PSYCHOSOCIAL NEEDS

Psychosocial needs[3] arise in the process of social living. They may be broadly grouped as needs for *security* and needs for *adequacy* (Table V).

TABLE V
SOME PSYCHOSOCIAL NEEDS

SECURITY NEEDS	ADEQUACY NEEDS
Companionship (affiliation)	Achievement (feelings of worth)
Love (for self and for others)	Prestige (status)
Acquisition (possessions)	Independence Strivings

Needs for security arise from human needs for companionship and love, as well as from needs to acquire possessions and property. These needs arise early in life. Normally the need for love goes through phases: self-love, love of parents, love of friends and others outside the home, and in adulthood, love of spouse and love of children.

Needs to be adequate encompass needs to achieve status and prestige, as well as needs to control others. Strivings for independence are a form of need to be adequate. Such strivings go through stages: a relatively slight need to be independent from parents while one is a child, the so-called *adolescent rebellion* from parental controls, and the achievement of total independence from parents in adulthood.

Failure to satisfy psychosocial needs is likely to lead to failure in community living. In the case of the retarded adult, in addition to the usual obstacles which stand in the way of fulfillment of psychosocial needs, other obstacles are often added: a long history of failure in competition with normal and bright associates, general slowness in learning, poor communication skills, social and cultural deprivation.

Retarded adults are often unable to satisfy their needs to

achieve security, adequacy, and self-esteem; to gratify their curiosity, and to test reality. Some develop heightened needs for affection and social approval. Others may withdraw excessively or may react to their frustrations by hostility and aggressive behavior.

An important contribution to understanding human needs has been made by Maslow[4] in his formulation of the concept of a *hierarchy of needs*. His arrangement of needs on a hierarchical basis is presented in Table VI. All persons have physiological

TABLE VI
HIERARCHY OF HUMAN NEEDS*

LEVELS	NEED	MANIFESTATION OF NEED
I	Physiological	Hunger
		Sex
		Thirst
II	Safety	Protection from dangers
III	Love	Affection and love for others
		Belonging to family
		Belonging to group
IV	Esteem	Independence
		Freedom
		Recognition by others
V	Self-actualization	Self-fulfillment
		Achieving one's potential

* Adapted from Maslow.[4]

needs and psychosocial needs. *Higher* needs emerge as the more *basic* needs are satisfied. In any person the hunger needs, for example, must be satisfied before needs for gaining prestige and esteem of others can emerge. While this particular sequence of levels in a hierarchy of needs may not be generally accepted, in a mentally retarded adult there may well exist certain needs which must be satisfied before other needs can emerge. Only a careful study of the individual can reveal which needs are most important and should be satisfied first.

THE EXPRESSED NEEDS OF THE MENTALLY RETARDED ADULT

There has been little systematic study of the retarded adult's expressed needs. The ideal way to determine these needs would be to obtain the information directly from the retarded adult himself and wherever possible this method should be used. There are many limitations to such an approach. Many retarded adults have poor comprehension or distorted ideas of what their needs are, based on incorrect knowledge or on inadequate judgment. There are many who cannot express themselves verbally and cannot state what they need. In many instances it is the parents or guardians who express what they believe the retarded adult needs, and this may represent what the parent needs rather than what the retarded person needs.

In Table VII are listed some of the needs of seventy-two

TABLE VII

NEEDS EXPRESSED BY APPLICANTS TO AN INFORMATION AND REFERRAL SERVICE FOR THE MENTALLY RETARDED*

Category	Statement of Need†
Evaluation	
Comprehensive	"Future plans for son"
Medical	"Clarification of diagnosis"
Psychological; social	"Any information you can give in regard to patient's ability to adjust to her present situation (marriage)"
Vocational	"Vocational evaluation"
	"Reevaluation of vocational potential and counseling"
	"Evaluation and work plan"
	"Referral for vocational planning"
Educational	"Diagnostic evaluation for possible training school or additional schooling"
Financial assistance	
	"Financial assistance"
	"Locating funds for residential school"
ATD	"Advice re: ATD and Social Security—appropriate referral"
Social security	
Residential	
arrangements	"Home placement for sister so she will be taken care of. Parents deceased"
	"Place for patient to go where he could live and be productive with a little job; mother and sister are sick, atmosphere not good"
	"Activities to take patient out of home and lead to out-of-home placement"
	"Find a nice home"
Foster home; family care home	"Private foster care when parents are no longer able to care for him"
	"State institution . . . or foster home"
	"Placement in foster home"
	"I would like to place her in a boarding school or foster home temporarily until she becomes adjusted"
Boarding house	"Help in finding home where patient will receive stimulation, physical care, and opportunity to continue on his job"
Private institution	"Permanent placement or money to pay for [denominational] home"
State institution	"Assistance in placing son in state hospital"
	"Readmission to state hospital"
	"Placement or school"
Clinical services	
Medical	"Medical advice"
	"Treatment to control seizures"
	"Resources for sterilization (patient on third pregnancy)"
Psychiatric	"Referral for psychiatric treatment"

CATEGORY	STATEMENT OF NEED†
	"Psychiatric treatment for son (father denies retardation)"
	"Referral for psychiatric help; counseling for patient and family"
Psychotherapy;	"Supportive therapy"
casework;	"Counseling"
personal	"[Department of Social Services] social worker requested
counseling;	information on intensive counseling to help patient relate
family	to others"
counseling	"Help with behavior problems"
	"Counseling to improve family relations"
	"Counseling to provide guidance re: handling boys"
	"Family counseling in planning for son"
	"Help in planning for daughter after graduation from classes for trainable retarded children"

Vocational services

Evaluation	(See under *Evaluation;* Vocational)
Counseling	"Assist with vocational planning; goal—a paying job"
Training	"Some sort of trade"
	"Job training"
	"Help with vocational training"
	"Placement of daughter in vocational training"
On-the-job training	"On-the-job training or job placement"
	"Training place for a job, or a job"
Short-term workshop	"Training job in a center"
Job placement	"Vocational placement"
	"Help patient find a job"
	"Find a job"
	"Some kind of work"
	"Work for son"
	"Patient seeking employment"
	"Job in a big plant"
	"Would like to baby-sit, take children to park"
Long-term workshop	"Sheltered workshop program"
	"Finding day school or workshop"
	"Day program and/or workshop (sheltered)"

Socio-recreative programming

Activity center	"Day program for something to do"
	"We would like for you to help find a place where he can maybe learn some more things"
	"Occupy self"
	"Something for her to do if something could be found"
	"Needs to be kept busy"
	"Activities to take patient out of home, and lead to out-of-home placement"
Socialization	"Recreation and socialization for daughter"
	"Social experience"
	"Needs other 'children' to socialize and learn from"
	"Socialization"
	"Social interest, one-to-one relationship"

Education

School (public;	"Education or school for son; has never been to school"
private)	"Help patient get back to school (not achieving, was suspended)"
	"School; to learn to write, at least his own name"
	"School, even a home teacher"
	"Help patient get education and training, or get into Job Corps"
	"I would like to have the names of schools that offer

CATEGORY	STATEMENT OF NEED†
	manual training classes for mentally retarded" (sister called)
	"To place my son in public school or funds to keep him in his private school"
	"[I would like] patient sent to a private institution so he will be content to accomplish an education"
Tutoring	"Home teaching"
	"Learning how to set up budget"
Transportation	"Some type of regular activity which includes transportation"
"Respite" and day care	"A foster home for patient, Christmas and school holidays and weekends, until placement in state hospital (now on waiting list)"
Assistance to parents at home	
Baby-sitting	"To have someone take care of my daughter weekends and on some other occasions"
Legal aid	"Legal advice"
Miscellaneous	"Referral to appropriate sources"
	"Worker wants to know anything new available"
	"Any information you can give; patient moving to Chicago"

* From records of 72 applicants (ages 16 to 57) to San Francisco Information and Referral Service for the Mentally Retarded, 1965 to 1966.

† Many of these clients expressed the same needs. Some clients expressed more than one need.

applicants who requested help from a community information and referral service for the mentally retarded.* These statements were entered in the case record by the social worker after the first interview with the applicant who was usually accompanied by his parents or responsible relative. The ages of these applicants ranged from sixteen to fifty-seven years, with two-thirds of the group below twenty-four years of age. Many of these statements were made by the retarded applicant's parents; some were the formulation of the intake social worker; some were statements made by the referring agency or by a referring professional worker, and a few were in the words of the applicant himself. Despite the fact that the statements in Table VII may not express clearly the retarded adult's needs—owing to the limitations mentioned—these statements give a truer picture of needs than would be obtained from popular assumptions. It will be noted that the statements of need have been grouped to suggest community services which might be used by the applicants to meet their needs.

---

* From the records of the San Francisco Information and Referral Service for the Mentally Retarded.

TRANSLATING EXPRESSED NEEDS INTO
COMMUNITY SERVICES

Even if all the needs of mentally retraded adults were known (which they are not) there would be many problems in translating this information into actual community services to meet these needs. First, in each person at any given time, some needs are more urgent than others. For example, the retarded adult who cannot satisfy his hunger pangs is not likely to seek the esteem of others until after his hunger is appeased. The chronically ill retarded adult must first take care of his health problems before he can look for work to fulfill his need to achieve independence.

Second, there is considerable variation among retarded adults in their needs for different services. Some need help in earning a living, while others need help in finding recreation and congenial friends.

Third, there are great differences in their needs for particular services. Large numbers need help in finding satisfactory residential arrangements, while relatively few need legal aid, and only at infrequent intervals.

Fourth, specially interested persons or groups may have a strong influence on what direction is taken to meet the needs of retarded adults at a given time. Sometimes this reflects the needs of sponsors rather than of the retarded adults themselves. This may or may not operate to the advantage of the retarded and must be carefully evaluated in each situation. For example, in one community a group of parents of severely retarded adults, led by a parent who was a bowling fan, developed an active bowling team which went on to compete in bowling tournaments. At the same time these parents totally neglected the need for personal-adjustment counseling manifested by some of the team members.

Finally, available funds, staff, facilities, and legal restrictions have an important determining effect on how the needs of retarded adults are met. Public and private agencies usually have clearly defined limits on their services and can use their funds only as previously budgeted. For these reasons it is clear that many needs of retarded adults, even though clearly identified, may well remain unfulfilled.

Following are a few instances of how specific needs are met in different ways in the community.

John F., a twenty-five-year-old man who had attended public school classes for the trainable mentally retarded, was interviewed by the information and referral service worker. When he was first interviewed, he said, "I want a job." Over a period of several interviews it became clear that what he really meant was that he needed a place where he could be with his friends and have a more active and interesting social life. While he used the word "job," the concept of work was very far from his interests. There was little doubt that he could not hold a job in competitive employment. He was referred to the day care center for the mentally retarded. There he had an opportunity to engage in social activities, a small amount of work during the day, and recreation experiences, such as visits, trips, and social dancing.

A mentally retarded adult needed financial support to meet his daily requirements for food and shelter. He turned to the county welfare department which was legally mandated to meet this particular need. In this case his need for food, clothing, and shelter was met by a public agency, the county welfare department.

The parents of a severely mentally retarded woman needed a baby-sitter to relieve them of the pressures of constant attendance on their child so that they could have a little more freedom for recreation. Their need for a baby-sitter was satisfied by a privately operated baby-sitter service whenever this was needed. Fortunately they were affluent enough to pay the necessary fees.

Everett S., a mentally retarded adult, needed training to obtain a janitorial position. For him this was a reasonable vocational goal. A program for training him as a janitor was developed through the local adult education school in cooperation with the Department of Vocational Rehabilitation. This program was also used for training other retarded and physically handicapped persons for janitorial jobs. He is now employed as a janitor.

A mentally retarded adult and his stepfather went to their family doctor and indicated that the retarded adult had so many problems disturbing him that he could not look for a job.

After physical examination, the physician found that the problem, not being a physical one, was beyond his scope. He wanted to refer his patient to a vocational evaluation center, but the nearest one was in a distant city. Awareness of the needs of his mentally retarded adult patient stimulated the physician to work with other interested people and organizations to establish a comprehensive evaluation program for the retarded in his community.

What would have happened to these retarded adults and their families if there had been no way to meet their needs in the community? What would have become of John F. if he had been placed in a job without study of his vocational limitations? What if the county welfare department did not have enough funds to meet the retarded adult's needs? What would the parents have done if they had no funds to hire a baby-sitter? What if there were no adult education program to train Everett S.? What if the physician had not been interested in establishing a comprehensive evaluation program in his community?

QUESTIONS FOR DISCUSSION

1. How does a description of needs of living organisms and of human beings help us to understand the needs of mentally retarded adults?

2. You are an intake social worker in a public welfare agency who interviews mentally retarded adults and their families applying for help. What kinds of help would you expect them to seek?

3. A vocational rehabilitation counselor interviews mentally retarded adults who are applying for vocational rehabilitation services. What needs do you think the clients would express?

4. The family of a thirty-four-year-old mentally retarded man with an IQ of 40 is disturbed because he is wandering away from home and hides in vacant houses for several hours at a time. Can you speculate about what some of his needs may be? What questions would you ask the family?

REFERENCES

1. Guyer, Michael F.: Birth control. *Encyclopaedia Britannica,* 1958, 3:650c.
2. Doll, Edgar A.: Mental retardation. *Encyclopaedia Britannica,* 1958, 15:260b.
3. Murray, Henry A.: *Explorations in Personality.* New York, Oxford U. Press, 1938.
4. Maslow, Abraham H.: A theory of human motivation. *Psychol Rev,* 50:370-396, 1943.

Chapter V

HOW ARE SOME NEEDS OF THE RETARDED ADULT MET IN THE COMMUNITY?

IF THE RETARDED adult's physiological and psychosocial needs are adequately met in the community, there is every reason to believe that he will be able to get along in the community and will be able to remain outside of an institution.

RESIDENTIAL NEEDS

Living Independently

Many single and married mildly and borderline retarded adults are able to live by themselves in an apartment, a house, or a single room, as normal people do. Wherever this is possible, this arrangement should be encouraged. However, it must be noted that retarded adults, in order to make a good adjustment in this type of living arrangement, may require help in such matters as finding proper housing, shopping for food and clothing, proper diet, preparation of meals, budgeting their funds, social and recreational experiences, and personal counseling.

Large numbers of retarded adults live in low socioeconomic areas (deprived communities, poverty areas) and are not differentiated from others in these communities. Retarded adults suffer the same deficiencies of diet, health, and social deprivation as the others surrounding them. Even to make a marginal adjustment and to satisfy their basic needs for food, clothing, and shelter, retarded adults living independently need more help than those around them.

The foregoing is not to imply that all retarded adults living on their own reside in poverty-stricken areas. Some live in middle-class urban and suburban communities or in rural areas.

The kind of help they need is little different from that needed by those retarded living in a poverty area, with slight modifications due to the different environmental settings.

Living at Home

Most retarded adults in the community live with their parents as long as their parents can take care of them. This arrangement meets their needs for food, clothing, and shelter. At first glance this may appear satisfactory for all retarded persons. However, this living arrangement is normally the way children live at home until they become adult, at which time they usually make homes for themselves. The retarded adult living at home is thus functioning as a child well into adulthood.

Living at home may be a good solution for a moderately or severely retarded adult who is immature and needs close supervision. If he is very disabled and living with understanding parents who devote a considerable amount of time to helping him, he will not only be happier and better adjusted, but he will also be less likely to need much help from community agencies until his parents—because of illness or age—are no longer able to care for him. Another similarly handicapped retarded adult, living in a home where parents and siblings openly reject him, will be extremely unhappy and disturbed and may have to be placed out of his home for his own and his family's good. In the past the only alternative for such difficult situations was to place the retarded adult in a state institution.

Many mildly and borderline retarded adults who continue to live at home even though they would be able to care for themselves, are overprotected and may become overdependent on their parents. When their parents are no longer able to provide for them, these retarded adults will be unable to function independently and will have to be cared for by others unless they have had special training.

Family Care and Foster Care

Family care home is a term used in some states to characterize the home in which a patient is placed after release from a state hospital for the mentally ill or the mentally retarded. *Foster home* is used to refer to a home in which any person, including a retarded adult, is placed if he has no home or if his home is found to be inadequate. Because of their similarity, these terms are often used interchangeably.

Under this living arrangement, the caretaker family or foster parents are paid to assume responsibility for board and lodging of the retarded adult. In some instances foster parents are paid extra fees to cover expenses such as clothing, medical, and dental bills. In other instances, the foster parent is expected to bring the retarded adult to a medical or dental clinic for care and to obtain clothing and incidental expenses from the social worker in the agency which made the placement.

The great advantage of placing a retarded adult who is an ex-patient of the state hospital in a family care or foster home is that the home provides supervision during the transition from the institution to community life. One of the disadvantages of a foster home is its temporary character, since the foster parents may terminate the client's stay in the home at any time if they are unable or unwilling to care for him. Furthermore, foster parents are not trained to deal with the special problems presented by the retarded adult. Finally, it is very difficult to find suitable foster homes for retarded adults, since most prospective foster parents prefer to take younger children. The wide variations among foster homes make it imperative that the right home be found for each retarded adult who needs foster care.

Halfway House

Another residential arrangement for the retarded adult is the halfway house. This is a facility which provides the patient on leave from a state institution for the retarded with a transition to normal community living by housing him temporarily in a supervised residence.

Halfway houses for retarded adults serve two general functions, to test the readiness of the patient to leave the institution and to train the patient to adjust to community life. If a patient is sent to a halfway house and he cannot tolerate the pressures of community living, it usually is necessary for him to return to the institution. Once he has demonstrated that he is ready for community life, the supervision and counseling provided by the halfway house staff can assist him in achieving greater independence.

The number of patients in a halfway house may include as many as twelve to twenty-five persons, supervised by the staff. Ideally this staff should be experienced, trained house parents who understand and can deal with the many problems facing the released institutional patient. In addition, medical, psychological, psychiatric, and social services should be available when needed.

The advantage of the halfway house is that the staff helps the retarded adult patient fit into the stream of community living, often after a long period of institutionalization. Members of the house may be encouraged to shop for food in the local markets, at first under supervision, later, independently. Some learn to do the cooking and house cleaning. Living with a group of persons with a similar background provides opportunities for group interaction and socialization. As the ex-patient begins to travel around the community, perhaps looking for a job, he can bring his questions and problems back to the staff and to his fellow housemates for discussion and clarification. The staff and the others may in turn encourage him to find recreational outlets and to be comfortable in normal heterosexual associations.

Two major difficulties have arisen in relation to halfway houses for ex-patients of institutions for the retarded. One is the need for well-trained staff to operate such facilities. As in so many other community mental retardation programs, unless the staff is attracted to the program and paid in relation to the importance of the assignment, it may be necessary to employ persons with inadequate training and experience, thus lowering the level of service. An even more serious danger lies in the possibility that a halfway house may turn into "just another institution," isolated from the rest of the community. The essentially transitional character of the halfway house must at all times be maintained. This means that provisions must be made from the start to admit those who are likely to move on to greater independence in community life. If an ex-patient is found to be in need of extended supervision in a more protected environment, he should be moved from the halfway house into an appropriate family care home or foster home.

There are only a few halfway houses for retarded adults, the majority being for the mentally ill. Examples are the Devereux Schools in Devon, Pennsylvania,[1] and the Mary McDowell Settlement House in Chicago.[2] The Conard House in San Francisco[3] has been experimenting with some success in mingling mentally retarded, emotionally ill ex-patients, and normal non-handicapped adults in the same residence.

VOCATIONAL NEEDS

This is a society in which most persons are either engaged in, or being prepared for, gainful employment. Retarded adults who are not employed feel degraded, isolated, and unable to adjust to normal living. This is why many retardates and their families seek help in finding suitable jobs. In seeking and holding gainful employment in the competitive labor market, the retarded adult is heavily penalized. His problems arise from his limitations in general intellectual functioning, impairment in adaptive behavior, and related physical handicaps. By and large, employers, in seeking to fill a job, would rather hire a person who is not mentally retarded even though the retarded person could do the job as well or better.

The More Able Retarded Adult

For those *more able* retarded adults (see Chapter VI) who are capable of obtaining gainful employment in the competitive labor market but are not now employed, every effort must be made to place them in regular employment. Those more able retarded adults who need training before they can be gainfully employed should be given every assistance to make this possible.

The Less Able Retarded Adult

There are many *less able* retarded adults (see Chapter VII) who are not capable of obtaining gainful employment in the competitive labor market even after every effort has been made to help them do so. Many, however, are capable of full-time or

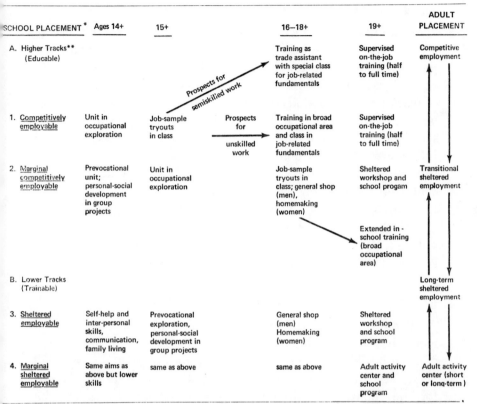

SCHOOL PLACEMENT *	Ages 14+	15+			16–18+	19+	ADULT PLACEMENT
A. Higher Tracks** (Educable)					Training as trade assistant with special class for job-related fundamentals	Supervised on-the-job training (half to full time)	Competitive employment
1. Competitively employable	Unit in occupational exploration	Job-sample tryouts in class	Prospects for unskilled work		Training in broad occupational area and class in job-related fundamentals	Supervised on-the-job training (half to full time)	
2. Marginal competitively employable	Prevocational unit; personal-social development in group projects	Unit in occupational exploration			Job-sample tryouts in class; general shop (men), homemaking (women)	Sheltered workshop and school progam	Transitional sheltered employment
						Extended in-school training (broad occupational area)	
B. Lower Tracks (Trainable)							Long-term sheltered employment
3. Sheltered employable	Self-help and inter-personal skills, communication, family living	Prevocational exploration, personal-social development in group projects			General shop (men) Homemaking (women)	Sheltered workshop and school program	
4. Marginal sheltered employable	Same aims as above but lower skills	same as above			same as above	Adult activity center and school program	Adult activity center (short or long-term)

*Program assumes foundation of personal and social skills, and their continuing development into adulthood. The program includes occupational exploration, self-evaluation and plan for adult-preparation, individual counseling, group counseling, parent counseling, vocational training, ½—school + ½—work experience, evaluation and plan for adult-readiness, job placement, follow-up, and counseling for adult living.
**Interchange of student from one "track" to another may be made whenever desirable.

Figure 5. Outline of plan to provide maximum vocational opportunities for mentally retarded adolescents and adults. From "Providing full vocational opportunities for retarded adolescents and adults," by DiMichael, Salvatore G.: *J Rehab*, 20:11, 1964. Courtesy of Salvatore G. DiMichael and *Journal of Rehabilitation*.

part-time employment, but not in the competitive labor market. These persons need a place where they can work at their own pace within their limitations and can be provided with other rehabilitative services such as counseling, recreation, socialization, and training in independent living. This is best done in a long-term workshop for the handicapped.

The Least Able Retarded Adult

In addition to *more able* and *less able* retarded adults, there are the *least able* retarded adults (see Chapter VIII). These are persons who, owing to severe mental retardation often coupled with physical handicaps, are only capable of doing limited types of work for short periods of time or cannot engage in productive work of any kind. They need primarily training in self-care, socialization and recreation experiences under supervision, and if they are capable of doing so, opportunities to engage in closely supervised simple work activities. This is best done in an activity center for the severely handicapped.

DiMichael[4] has outlined a plan (Fig. 5) for providing full vocational opportunities to retarded adolescents and adults of differing levels of competency. The plan emphasizes flexibility of programming according to individual capacities and needs.

MARRIAGE ADJUSTMENT

There is only limited information relative to marriage among mentally retarded adults, and of the nature of family life associated with such marriage. Follow-up studies of mentally retarded persons, whether they were formerly patients in state institutions for the retarded or students in public school classes for the mentally retarded, have substantiated that considerable numbers married and settled down in the community. Few studies, however, have thrown light on their marriage adjustment, other than to determine whether the marriage continued or ended in divorce or separation. In the Delaware study by Jastak, MacPhee, and Whiteman, there was evidence that the retarded* were not substantially different from the nonretarded in their marital status. Table VIII[5] reproduces data from their study relative to the marital status, number of marriages, age at first marriage, and number of separations in present marriage of a representative sample of 123 retarded persons compared with 123 nonretarded persons. While there are slight differences between the two

---

* Jastak, MacPhee, and Whiteman defined retarded differently from the definition used in this book.

TABLE VIII

MARITAL STATUS AND BACKGROUND OF RETARDED AND
NONRETARDED RESPONDENTS (UNWEIGHTED NUMBERS)

Marital Status and Background Variable	Number Retarded	Nonretarded	Percentage Retarded	Nonretarded
Marital Status				
Single	33	34	26.8	27.6
Married	68	79	55.3	64.2
Married (under Common Law)	8	4	6.5	3.2
Divorced	1	1	0.8	0.8
Widowed	8	3	6.5	2.4
Separated	3	2	2.4	1.6
Not Reported	2	0	1.6	0.0
Total	123	123	100.0	100.0
Number of Marriages				
1	70	74	77.7	83.1
2	15	13	16.7	14.6
3	1	0	1.1	0.0
Not Reported	4	2	4.4	2.3
Total	90	89	100.0	100.0
(of those who are or have been married)				
Age at First Marriage				
14-18	29	19	32.2	21.3
19-21	26	28	28.9	31.4
22-25	18	16	20.0	18.0
26-29	3	11	3.3	12.4
30-35	6	9	6.7	10.1
36 or older	2	3	2.2	3.4
Not Reported	6	3	6.7	3.4
Total	90	89	100.0	100.0
(of those who are or have been married)				
Number of Separations in Present Marriage*				
0	72	77	80.0	86.5
1	8	6	8.9	6.7
2	3	2	3.4	2.3
3 or more	2	2	2.2	2.3
Not Reported	5	2	5.5	2.3
Total	90	89	100.0	100.0
(of those who are or have been married)				

* Or last marriage, if divorced or widowed.
    From Jastak, Joseph F.; MacPhee, Halsey M., and Whiteman, Martin: *Mental Retardation, Its Nature and Incidence: A Population Survey of the State of Delaware,* 1963, p. 165. Courtesy of U. of Delaware, Newark, Delaware.

groups, the over-all impression from examination of this table is of similarity between the retarded and the nonretarded. Jastak, MacPhee, and Whiteman[6] concluded the following:

A significantly greater proportion of the nonretarded are married legally and live with their legal marriage partners. Common-law marriages and the death of a spouse are more frequent among the retarded.

The marital adjustment of those who are married in the two groups does not show significant divergences in terms of frequency of separation or divorce. This condition obtains despite the fact that those in the retarded group had married at a relatively younger age and had been married for a longer time than the nonretarded when they were interviewed.

There is urgent need for research into the married life of retarded adults. Do retarded persons marry other retardates or do they marry nonretarded persons? How stable are their marriages? How large are their families? What is the intelligence level of their children? What effect does marriage have on the retardate's self-image as a worker and as a contributing member of society? What differences exist between married retardates and married nonretarded persons of the same age and socioeconomic status? Such studies are yet to be made.

John M. and Doris M. are mentally retarded adults who are married. They met while they were clients in a workshop for the handicapped. John is a short, well-developed man of thirty-three years, with not too noticeable features of Down's syndrome. He had been a patient in a state institution for the mentally retarded for a number of years. During that time he had shown good ability to get along with other people and to manage himself creditably.

When the opportunity arose to transfer him from the institution to the community, he was sent to a large city. There he was placed in a family care home. He was supervised by a social worker and eventually was assigned by a vocational rehabilitation counselor to a workshop. While there, he demonstrated that he could work consistently, and plans were gradually formulated to place him in some type of janitorial work. When he finished his training in the workshop, he was placed as a janitor's helper in a large office building.

Doris M. is twenty-nine years of age, slightly obese, without noticeable features of mental retardation, a graduate of classes for the educable mentally retarded. She did fairly well in school and seemed able to manage some of her own affairs, although she lived at home and had little independence from her parents.

John is a very gentlemanly person with pleasant manners. When he first came to the workshop he needed dentures and his speech was hard to understand. After a while the dentures were provided. This had a beneficial effect on his verbal communication as well as on his appearance. He was now able to form many consonant sounds which he could not do without dentures.

John became friendly with Doris and she responded likewise. They met at workshop socials and she invited him to visit at her home. Their friendship gradually intensified, and after about a year they planned to be married. There was much antagonism to this idea from Doris' family, as they felt that she might not be capable of living independently and raising a family. On the other hand, John, in spite of his years of institutionalization, felt that he could be a good husband and provider. As John proved himself to be steady, trustworthy, and able to hold a job, the resistance of Doris' parents gradually subsided. The social worker had many interviews with John, Doris, and her parents to help them with plans. After extended discussion, Doris and John both agreed that she should undergo an operation which would eliminate the possibility of pregnancy. To accomplish this, it was necessary to consult with a psychiatrist, who agreed with all concerned that sterilization in this case was clearly indicated and made the necessary arrangements.

They now live in their own apartment near her family. John works as a janitor's helper, earning $100 per month, with supplementation to his salary provided by the welfare department. The apartment is neat and clean. Doris' mother drops in every day or two to see that everything is running smoothly. Doris continues to attend the workshop on a part-time basis twice a week, where she receives some training in homemaking and does some industrial work. The fee for her attendance at the workshop is paid by the welfare department as part of her rehabilitation plan.

The above case illustrates points often overlooked. There are situations where appropriate preparation, training, and continued understanding help make it possible for mildly or moderately retarded adults to have as good a marital adjustment as non-retarded persons in the same socioeconomic circumstances.

Another point is the importance of personal and family counseling and active cooperation of the parents of the retarded adults who plan marriage and independent residence. The case illustrates involvement of social worker, vocational rehabilitation counselor, workshop staff, psychiatrist, and cooperative parents in making it possible for adult retardates to establish a successful marriage. It also shows how the right of retarded adults to make their own decisions is respected.

HEALTH AND MEDICAL NEEDS

An authoritative medical source has indicated that "three of every four retarded individuals have significant medical problems."[7] While this figure is not derived from census information but reflects the experience of practicing physicians, it does suggest that mentally retarded adults are more prone to illness and disabling conditions than those who are not retarded. To some degree this higher incidence of medical problems may be related to constitutional factors associated with birth deformities and poor physical development. To some degree it may be associated with social-cultural factors such as poor nutrition and inadequate medical care in lower socioeconomic communities, where many mentally retarded adults live.

Militating against adequate medical care for the mentally retarded adult is the belief held by many persons, including some physicians, that remedial medical services are not too helpful for the retarded. This attitude has had adverse effects on the mentally retarded especially where remedial efforts in childhood could have prevented more serious conditions later in life. To consider mental retardation as the reason for withholding appropriate medical care inevitably is a breach of human rights and makes for denial of much needed services. The position of the American Medical Association is now clear and positive. "Fortunately, the old concept of bracing, corrective surgery, and other remediation as useless expenditures for the retarded is now being replaced by more enlightened concepts which the physician may help promote."[8]

Another prevalent assumption which has undergone considerable change is that retarded adults are prone to die earlier than others in the population. This belief stems in part from earlier statistics of state institutions for the retarded which reported that many retarded patients succumbed early in life from respiratory and epidemic diseases. With the advent of antibiotics and more sophisticated medical science, retarded individuals, except those with marked birth defects, should be able to live a normal span of life.

The President's Panel on Mental Retardation noted that "the retarded child is subject to all the diseases and health hazards to which the intellectually normal child is heir. In addition his problems of retardation are frequently complicated by such serious disorders as speech, hearing, sight and dental defects."[9] This comment implies that not only retarded *children,* but even more so retarded *adults,* may require special attention to their medical problems, especially if the conditions were not treated in childhood. It also suggests that so far as retarded adults are concerned, serious disorders may keep them from carrying on their activities.

> Susan S. is a 30-year-old retarded woman who was born prematurely. She attended public school special education classes, doing rather poorly since she had to be out of school much of the time because of ill-health. She left school at sixteen years of age. She lives in a public housing project with her elderly parents, who spend most of their time at home. Their sole support is social security benefits, while Susan receives ATD[10] support. She needs constant medical attention and dental care. She spends many hours waiting in the clinics for appointments since she can be seen only in the county hospital. Her medical needs have consistently made it impossible for her to obtain employment or to be trained for an occupation.

COUNSELING AND THERAPY NEEDS

Emotional disturbances manifested in psychopathological behavior adversely influence the normal person's adjustment to society. This is also true of the mentally retarded. As Heber[11] has put it, "In view of the intellective limitations in the capacity of the retarded person to gratify basic needs in a socially approved manner within a highly competitive culture it would be rather remarkable if the mentally retarded did not show a heightened susceptibility to personal and social maladjustment." Professional help, whether it be called personal counseling, therapy, guidance, or casework, is frequently necessary to help the retarded adult deal with his personal frustrations and social conflicts.

Many counselors and therapists have hesitated to work with mentally retarded adults in individual treatment or group approaches either from lack of knowledge about, or interest in, the retarded client or because of a misconception that the retarded cannot profit from such help. With reference to psychiatrists as therapists, for example, the Group for the Advancement of Psychiatry in a self-critical vein has stated, "While it is self-evident that mental retardation should be of major concern to psychiatry, psychiatrists know little about it and often show, at best, minimal interest in the problem."[12] Some reports have suggested that the retarded, owing to limited intelligence and poor communication skills, are less able than normals to express frustrations and conflicts to their therapists and therefore are unable to achieve insight necessary for amelioration of their emotional difficulties.

Although negative attitudes towards counseling and therapy of the retarded have effectively limited therapeutic efforts of many professionals, in recent years most of the published reports have indicated that successful results have been obtained in individual and group therapy with retardates. A recent questionnaire survey[13] was conducted among sixty-four members of the psychology section of the American Association on Mental Deficiency, who held either a Ph.D. or an Ed.D. degree, resided in the United States or Canada, held the status of Fellow in the association, and who spent most of their professional time in therapy of retardates. It was reported that the areas in which mentally retarded persons benefitted from counseling and psychotherapy were the following: ". . . institutional adaptation, motivation for learning, peer group associations, familial relationships, control of unacceptable behavior, resolution of conflicts with authority figures, return to the home, personality modification, return to the community, and improving employability."[14] This study also found that the therapists considered the relationship between level of intelligence and the value of counseling and psychotherapy to be significant. "The following relationship is suggested: the higher the level of intelligence the greater the value of counseling and psychotherapy."[15]

It is interesting to note that counseling and psychotherapy were reported in this study to be beneficial to most retarded clients except the severely and profoundly retarded. This is different from earlier beliefs that no mentally retarded person could profit from therapy. As for the severely mentally retarded, it is possible that their emotional disturbances can be helped by therapy in a form appropriate to their level of communication and comprehension. This would require modification of techniques and willingness to accept therapeutic progress in smaller increments than is currently the case. There is no logical reason why such a change in standards should not be adopted in therapy of the severely retarded, when this is precisely the approach used in special education of the severely mentally retarded.

Case of Sarah M.*

Miss Sarah M. is a thirty-two-year-old single woman who "graduated" from ungraded classes and in the public schools. She works as a file clerk in a large insurance office. Both parents in their early 60's are living and well. She came to the medical center for an ear examination and for help with emotional problems.

She has been known to the medical center since the age of thirty-two months with diagnoses of mental retardation, congenital torticollis, allergic rhinitis, and talipes equinovarus, and has had a number of surgical procedures. At the age of five years she obtained an IQ of 75. Later testing at the age of 12 years revealed an IQ of 73. At the time of later testing, the patient was described as negativistic, as not sustaining effort, and as needing much urging.

At the initial interview, she impressed the intake worker as being quite tense and at times close to tears. Speech production seemed to require special energy on her part. She related her problems to anxiety attacks around the anticipation of any out-of-the-ordinary situations involving her, which led to vomiting attacks. The specific situation which caused her to seek treatment was the recent development of a relationship with a young man who has asked her for dates. She said she vomited last night following a telephone call from him and she anticipates difficulty on a date she has accepted for tonight.

She indicated that she wished help mainly with relief from the symptoms of nervousness leading to her vomiting attacks. She raised the question of the help of tranquilizers, having found that one given to her by a friend had helped.

Following graduation from high school, she worked in a hospital business office, disliking everything about it—the work, the pay, the employees. During this period she was tense and had diarrhea every day. She left this job after six months. For the next few years she was unemployed or held part-time jobs. She has been employed at her present job for the past three years.

Her social activity now consists of going with girls to public

---

* Adapted from a case of the Adult Psychiatry Clinic, University of California Medical Center, San Francisco.

dances where she occasionally meets an interested young man who dates her. She gets tense, nauseated, and vomits, proportionally to her attraction to the interested party. Her mother is "aggravating." She cross-examines her when she comes home from dates, a practice she feels nerve-wracking, almost to the point of vomiting.

After ten sessions of treatment it was noted that she is a highly motivated patient who is attempting to conquer her present difficulties. She demonstrated dependency in her interview sessions. She expects to settle down with a husband and to lead a happy home life.

At her nineteenth session she reports that she had been to a dance and has danced with one fellow all night. He asked to drive her home and she accepted. They drove home directly. She was tense most of the evening and wanted to heave, but controlled herself. She was asked by the therapist whether there had been any change in her symptoms from when she first dated. She answered, "They have worsened." She was asked if she had thought more about what might be causing her symptoms. She said that she had and guessed it was fear of not being able to be free with her mother or with her dates.

During the twenty-fourth interview she was very agitated. She asked if she should continue with the interviews. She said that she wondered if she could try alone. Sometimes she feels she gets nothing from the interviews, while at other times she feels benefitted. She becomes agitated and her voice quivers on the verge of crying. She had two alternative plans in mind: to quit the clinic for two months, or, to continue for the next few months without change.

At the thirtieth interview, it was noted that she walked into the interview smiling, talking in a much more relaxed manner and sat down comfortably in the chair. Her hands remained in her lap throughout most of the talk and she had noticeably fewer nervous habits today. She felt she was definitely more confident in herself and that she had learned to be more independent in her activities. She still had episodes of anxiety, although not frequently.

At her thirty-second interview she was very nervous, gulped saliva, and spoke tensely. She had attended a dance on Saturday night, had disturbing feelings, and had to leave the dance. She was very discouraged. However, she did feel that she was making progress. She was aware, as she talked, that the episode would pass, and she looked forward to happier times.

At her thirty-fourth interview she described an "attack" which had occurred at a dance. This was resolved by her vomiting in the bathroom, and then returning to the dance as though nothing had happened. She felt she had made great progress in dealing with her anxiety.

At the thirty-fifth interview she stated that she now has the ability to talk about her problems and understands which direction to take. This relieves much of her tension.

The case was closed after the thirty-fifth interview as "much improved." The patient was instructed to return for treatment if she felt she needed further help.

A follow-up contact after two years indicated that she was happily married and was expecting her first child.

Group Therapy

In view of the broad interpretation of *group therapy,* many retarded adults may be said to be receiving group therapy in a variety of settings. These include social group work conducted in a recreational setting, family therapy in which the retarded adult is a member of a group including himself, his parents, siblings, and the therapist, more conventional group therapy in which retarded adults meet regularly with a therapist to discuss their personal and social problems. Reports of the different kinds of group therapy with retarded adults reflect generally beneficial results.

Schapps[16] made an interesting report of group therapy with mentally retarded adults, with the general goal of helping group members resolve some of their problems in relation to achieving a vocational objective. The therapy was carried out by a well-trained social worker, meeting for one hour a week over a ten-month period in the Work-Training Center,[17] a project for rehabilitating mentally retarded adults in a workshop setting. The following is taken from her report.

In July we started with six men and four women. All were unmarried except for one man who lives with his wife and two sons. Two were Negroes, the remainder white; all religions were represented; IQ's ranged from 49 to 82 with six in the 60's, two in the 50's; chronological ages nineteen to forty-eight years. One man dropped out almost immediately; another took leave for medical care, and three others were added.

At the first meeting the director made the following

announcement to those selected: "Everyone selected is a good worker who should be able to hold a job someday but doesn't seem to be ready yet. This is because some are nervous about holding a job, some aren't interested, some don't want to leave the workshop. In these meetings, everyone can say what he likes—just so he does not hurt someone else—and nobody will stop him, but no one will force anyone to say anything unless he wants to."

Over the months, one of our members changed his position from "What do you think of an employer who does that to me?" to "What was the matter with me that made the employer act that way?" Another is now able to say in the group, "I felt like telling him off, but I held it in." He knows that the group is the place he doesn't have to "hold it in" and has learned social control.

Illustrative of some of the content of the group sessions is a summary of the performance of one of the members.

John is twenty-four years old, the younger of two children. His brother has everything he has not—success in every endeavor, high honor in the service and university, a junior executive in a large firm, a marriage, and children. John's parents are employed middle-class white-collar workers. They are angry and impatient at their son's limitations, which they do not accept. John is overweight, is 5' 7" tall. He has splayed hands and feet and a visual defect. He is a good-looking young man, who gives such a good first impression that it is only upon further acquaintance that his limitations are discovered. The local vocational rehabilitation services gave him service over a period of two years and finally closed the case because they considered him "not feasible" for job placement. On his Wechsler Adult Intelligence Scale, his scores are Verbal Scale IQ 68; Performance Scale IQ 44; Full Scale IQ 62. Since employment is most apt to be in an occupation where performance skills are important, this young man's dilemma is easily seen.

By the close of the second session the therapist had discovered that John's anxiety revealed itself in discussive talk, a tendency to monopolize with long monologues, a need to continuously quote his parents, at the same time indicating clearly that if he had any ideas of his own, they had never been expressed.

By the end of September, one member of the group had grasped the idea that when you work on a job, you work as an adult and that rest periods are for play and fun, which is all right. However, John resisted the idea that an adult could play "Ring around the rosy," and it was difficult for him to find any acceptance of childish needs in himself, which dictated so much of what he did. During October, John began to express the conflict that he was now feeling. He said, "Psychologists say to my parents, 'Don't prod him,' but if they don't, I won't do what I should. You have to keep after me. I don't do nothing. I just sit back."

During October, John began to clarify for himself the meaning of mental retardation. During earlier sessions, he had mentioned unrealistic vocational goals for himself, such as being a biologist, but by this time, he had decided that it would be all right to be a janitor. He even accepted the fact that there were others in the group who could be janitors and who could work wtih their hands doing electrical and other maintenance work that might be difficult for him. He was able to develop this theme with a good deal of reality.

On February 3, John came to the meeting after not having been selected for a job. His greatest concern was what his parents would think, and he fell easily into the dependent role by suggesting that his father might come and complain at the discrimination against him since he had not obtained the job. Then he suddenly realized what he was saying and added, "My parents have been pushing me all my life." By the end of the session, the group had helped him to evaluate his childlike fears and he seemed to feel it would be possible to decide not to create an issue at home and that he could handle his disappointment in an adult way.

At the March 10 meeting, John was saying, "That's my trouble—I talk too much—if I would only keep still, I would be better off." Later in this session, he said, "I am anxious to get out and get a job that is steady. I am grateful for the training, but some day I will get up enough confidence and go out and get a job and not rely on my parents. When you look back and see what a meat head I was—well, this is my chance to go forward—never go backward."

In the early sessions, John leaned forward with great intensity, his face flushed; tears often came to his eyes. Lately, he has been able to relax and to talk in a more purposeful way. Occasionally, he smiles at and enjoys the contributions of others. By the forty-first session, he had had a job for two months as part-time janitor at $1.50 per hour. He is now beginning to question his status in the family, although his ambivalence is clear. One member said to him in the fortieth session, "What John's got to do is get out from his folks—I've been away years-on-top-of-years. Never did depend on my folks—did it by myself. I left and went on my own. That's what you need to do, John." John's response was, "I will be frank with you—as long as my folks are living, I will be living with them."

Our therapeutic goal with John has been achieved. He has a job. However, it is not sufficient to support himself and he still has not achieved independent status even though he is paying income taxes, buying most of his own clothing, and paying a share of the expenses at home.

Work as Therapy

The following material is adapted from a paper presented by the author at the California State Psychological Association Convention in 1966.

In order to clarify a few points as to the role of work as therapy with the mentally retarded adult, two cases studied in a workshop for the handicapped have been selected for presentation and discussion. One was a patient on leave from the state hospital for the retarded; the other a graduate of the public school classes for the retarded.

Case of Bernard L.

Bernard L. was a tall, slender, reddish-haired young man of twenty-four who became a patient at the state hospital for the retarded when he was eight years old. He dressed neatly, was well groomed, and sported a neat mustache. When he was placed in our program two years ago by the vocational rehabilitation counselor for evaluation, training, and counseling, he lived in a family care home with several other young men also on leave from state hospitals.

While in the hospital he had escaped many times, walking or riding for long distances. He could not explain why he did so, but it was believed that in his fantasy life he was seeking his mother who had abandoned him many years before.

Early in his enrollment in the program he exhibited many of the same tendencies, being absent without leave and wandering. Once he was picked up as a vagrant in a distant city and was in jail for two days until his background and status became known to the police. He was also having trouble with his family caretaker, and with one or two of his fellow housemates.

Prior to admission to the program he had no work history other than helping out in the state hospital. Shortly after admission, it was learned that he was capable of doing packaging and assembly work at a productivity level equivalent to half that of a nonhandicapped worker doing the same work. He was soon being paid at that rate, when he worked. Being paid such a salary created problems at first, since now he had money which could be used to purchase things, as well as to finance his urge to wander away. He was almost totally devoid of any skills in using money wisely, preferring to buy unrealistically, such as expensive radios and television sets which he stored in his room or gave away as gifts. He also ran up a bill for his minimum fee of one dollar per month to the workshop, which he had agreed to pay when he was admitted.

As the months went by it became clear that his skills were improving to the point where he could be employed full time on a job at a minimum wage, if he could give up his fantasy of seeking his mother and if he could assume greater responsibility for his own actions in such matters as budgeting and spending money appropriately. By this time, episodes of wandering had almost disappeared.

Several months ago a crisis developed. He was having serious difficulties with his family caretaker and it appeared that he might have to be returned to the state hospital. He had become angry with the workshop staff for making him face up to his obligations to pay his fee—which would have been no hardship to him. He was also showing that he could carry on more complex assembly and packaging operations, especially if allowed to work by himself. Suddenly he began to absent himself from the program.

By staff agreement, the workshop supervisor interviewed him and told him that he was doing so well on the job that he would be given a trial promotion to assistant leadman (an enrollee who helped other enrollees do their work). It was also made clear that he must meet his obligations to the agency, in order to hold his job, including paying his fee and coming regularly.

This was the turning point. He returned to work, paid his bills, and no longer absented himself. A few weeks later he was doing so well at his work as an assistant leadman, that the vocational rehabilitation counselor arranged to get him a temporary job in a small restaurant as a busboy and kitchen helper. This job has turned out to be a permanent full-time one, for which he is being paid the minimum wage of $1.25 per hour. He occasionally returns to the workshop on his day off to happily tell about his job, and about how much he is earning. The restaurant in which he works would not retain him if he were not able to work steadily and meet his obligations as a worker. Unfortunately, there is no information about how he spends his salary.

Case of Grace R.

The second case is that of Grace R., a twenty-year-old woman, looking and dressing like a young adolescent girl, with socks, little girl dresses, starched ruffled petticoats. She had attended public school classes for the trainable mentally retarded, and had been "graduated" at the age of eighteen years. School reports indicated that she obtained Stanford-Binet IQ's in the 40's, and that she had been a well-adjusted pupil. For reasons not explained, during the summer following graduation she became very disturbed and tried to attack her mother with a knife. She was admitted to the state hospital for the mentally ill for observation. She was released with a diagnosis of schizophrenic reaction, undifferentiated.

When she was first admitted to the workshop about two years ago, her behavior was immature and unpredictable. She could not stick to her regular assignment but insisted on going to other parts of the program. She related to only one staff member. She kept on the fringe of all groups and would not participate. Her hostility to certain staff members and enrollees was shown by unexpected punches or kicks delivered in such a way as not to be noticed until after she had moved past her victim. She also possessed a choice vocabulary of "cuss words" which she used frequently and loudly. At times she was observed moving her lips as though talking to someone, but whether this was hallucinating was not known.

The area of the program she did best was production work, where her skills were good. When tests of her productivity were performed, it was found that she was capable of doing work up to 50 to 60 per cent of the productivity level of nonhandicapped workers doing the same job. Poor concentration, however, meant that she was functioning well below her potential even at this rate of productivity.

As months went by a noticeable change took place in her work habits. When she was having trouble with others, she no longer resorted to physical aggression but restricted herself to calling them names. She was now better able to accept limitations, and her wandering finally ceased.

Then she was placed on a temporary "loan" to another workshop, located in the same building. There she had a full workday in the company of handicapped workers who were distinctly more able in their work. She performed this assignment quite well for the agreed period of two weeks. When she returned, there was a sharp improvement in her self-assurance and her actual productivity. She could now be given any task in the workshop and would do it almost to the level of a nonhandicapped worker. Some who knew her when she first came to our program commented, "Look at the change in Grace!" Whereas the earlier staff plan was to keep her from withdrawing into herself and help her become more mature, now with her newly developed self-image as a worker, the goal was to place her in a workshop where she could work full time under industrial demands, with only limited supervision.

The cases of Bernard L. and Grace R. illustrate several points in relation to work as therapy for the mentally retarded adult.

1. In a community where all are either engaged in work or being prepared for work, retarded adults who do not work feel degraded, isolated, and unable to adjust to normal living.

2. As far as work is concerned, the retarded adult is severely penalized. His problems arise from basic retardation in mental development and limitations in social competency. He needs to resolve his feelings of inadequacy and insecurity derived from a lifelong history of failure in competing with others around him.

3. In a workshop setting where there is an understanding of the total life experience of the retarded adult enrollee, productive work is used as an important element in treatment. Opportunities are provided for each enrollee to realize his work potentials. In certain cases there is a dramatic demonstration that work is indeed therapeutic for the mentally retarded adult.

EDUCATIONAL NEEDS

Adult education is available for all adults, including the mentally retarded. In theory, adult education classes are thrown open to all. Unfortunately when this is done, it creates the same difficulties that were manifested years ago when the mentally retarded child was placed in the same class with all other children—the level of the class was too difficult and the retarded child fell behind the other students. In the public schools this has been dealt with by providing special curriculum and smaller classes for the mentally retarded. Under similar circumstances the retarded adult in a regular adult education class finds the class too difficult, falls behind, and inevitably drops out or is dropped. While there are no statistics on this point, it is likely that the number of retarded adults who are attending regular adult education classes is far below the number who need adult education.

One approach to meeting their educational needs is to set up special classes for retarded adults. This also meets with many difficulties, since there may not be enough adult retarded interested in a given subject to make a full class or the range of comprehension and expression among the retarded students may be too wide to make it possible to provide group instruction.

Another approach has been used in some communities. Adult education provides teachers who train mentally retarded adults in basic work skills and attitudes, and carry on necessary remedial academic work in a workshop setting. Since this approach has many implications, the following history in one community, San Francisco, is of interest.

The earliest reported use of adult education for providing staff in any workshop in the United States was the San

Francisco Aid Retarded Children Work-Training Center for the Mentally Retarded, which was founded in 1951. In 1953 the Adult Education Division of the San Francisco Unified Schools assigned one full-time instructor to the workshop. Additional instructors have since been added. The services provided by the adult education teacher include observation of the work habits and work skills of each trainee, study of his capabilities and limitations, and individual supervision so that he can master the job of working within the workshop. Individual instruction is given in academic work which is involved in the workshop experience.

While adult education could have a significant and wide-spread role in training mentally retarded adults, there are problems which must be worked through before this can be accomplished. First, unless there is universal acceptance that smaller classes are needed for retarded adults and that necessary funds must be made available for this purpose, there will be only a few school districts willing to use tax-supported funds to meet the deficits created by such classes. A second problem is the shortage of teachers trained to work with mentally retarded adults. While it is hoped that such training will be available, it has not as yet been instituted to this writer's knowledge. Third, the respective roles of adult education, with its interest in educating the whole person, and vocational rehabilitation, with its interest in vocational aspects, must be reconciled so that there is a mutual working together. This cooperative relationship is especially important in workshops where vocational rehabilitation and adult education could jointly provide the best services for the most clients.

RECREATIONAL NEEDS

Recreation has been defined as "any activity engaged in voluntarily just for the pleasure and satisfaction that it brings to the participant."[18] What is considered recreational by one person may be boring and even fatiguing to another. It is therefore necessary to provide a variety of recreation programs to meet individual needs.

Because of its essentially voluntary nature, recreation in the past has been viewed as one of the *frills,* not to be confused with the *necessary* tasks of earning a living and achieving progress through work. In recent years it has become more evident, with growing amounts of leisure time for workers as the work week grows shorter, that recreation is a great need throughout the population and recreational opportunities must be provided for all. In fact, public recreation (free) and commercial recreation (for profit) are large industries.

The need for recreation among retarded adults is no different, and may be greater. Having a shorter workday and a larger amount of free time, many retarded adults need a greater variety and number of appropriate recreational activities. Present recreation programs for retarded adults are nonexistent or inadequate, despite some recent progress.

The mother of a moderately retarded man, thirty years of age, was interested in arranging opportunities for her son to meet with other men and women on a social basis. She discussed the matter with two or three other parents of young-adult retarded persons and was assured that they were anxious to do the same for their children. They worked out an arrangement with a local church to use its social hall for a monthly party to be held on Friday evenings. The parties were open by invitation to other retarded adults. Since many of them had had some experience in social dancing, the only missing ingredient was a band. This was finally found in a group of volunteers headed by the brother of one of the retardates. Once a month about thirty retarded adults came to the party; many parents brought them and took them home afterwards. While the party was on, these parents held a meeting in another part of the church to discuss matters of mutual interest, especially in relation to the social and recreational program for their retarded children.

In a large city there were more than 150 foster homes licensed to care for mentally retarded adults on leave from the state institution for the retarded. Many of the ex-patients were unable or unwilling to go to public recreation centers near their homes, as they found little available for them. A group of foster parents formed a committee which approached the City Parks and Recreation Department for help. They were told that they could have the use of a room in a recreation center, just as any other nonprofit group could, but that no staff would be available. The family caretakers decided to conduct the recreation program themselves. They arranged games, clubs, arts and crafts, and a variety of entertainment. This activity was so successful that after a year the Parks and Recreation Department applied for and received city funds to add two regular employees to the recreation staff, one to work with mentally retarded adults, and one to work with all other handicapped persons.

Camping

Outdoor camping is a recreational activity which has been greatly stimulated by easy automobile transportation and by the development of different types of camping facilities to meet different needs. Summer camps and day camps for the moderately and severely retarded have been very successful. These provide socialization experiences in living together informally and opportunities to get closer to nature and to participate in athletics. Camping makes it possible for retarded adults living in crowded slums to enlarge their limited environment.

Since the 1950's, member units of the National Association for Retarded Children have been leaders in setting up summer camps for retarded persons of all ages. Community groups such as service clubs (Lions, Kiwanis, Civitan) have sponsored camp programs or have contributed funds for needy retarded persons to attend camps.

The basic goals in camping for the mentally retarded are relatively the same as those for the nonretarded.

The aims and objectives (education as well as recreation) are to guide and counsel for health and happiness, promote proper habits and attitudes, wholesome fun, joy of achievement, self-reliance, team play, and leadership.[19]

Edward at Camp*

Edward B. is the son of an upper-class family whose father is in sales work in a metropolitan city in California. The parents are refined, intelligent people. He has a twin sister, who is a successful teacher of educable mentally retarded children. He is twenty-five years of age and attended school until he was nine. Schooling was very spasmodic—he was in and out of many schools—because of his

---

* Adapted from a case report by Rita Mattei, Director, San Francisco Aid Retarded Children Summer Camp, and Director of Special Education, Santa Cruz City Schools, California.

severe mental retardation (IQ 33) and extremely aggressive behavior. He has remained at home all of his life.

He was introduced to the camp director through a telephone call from his mother, who stated that he was very difficult, very aggressive, hit people, kicked, threw things, and would not eat with anyone. Edward was accepted at camp—with the understanding that he would be watched, worked with, and that the parents would be called if necessary.

Edward arrived at camp on the camp bus. His size—a man—and his surly appearance—in spite of being clean and obviously well cared for—made the director and counselor wonder. True to form, the first meal was chaotic. The counselor was kicked, other campers were kicked and hit, and things were difficult. The second meal was partially successful with Edward sitting alone at an individual table some ten feet from the table where the counselor and other campers sat. Before each meal his table was moved closer until it adjoined the other table—this at the end of ten days. During this time, the counselor was shoved and kicked at various times, but each day the intervals between episodes became longer.

Edward never smiled and rarely spoke to anyone other than his counselor, to whom he began to relate, but only with words of distress at hitting people. He would be removed from the scene of any incident and walked to his cabin where he remained until quiet prevailed. He would then return to the group. The last three days of camp, no one was shoved; he went to all activities, and finally on the last day he sat at the table with his group. He returned home on the camp bus.

Two days later came a letter from his mother relating that it was almost a miracle—Edward had sat at the family table for dinner on the night of his return from camp. At this writing three and one-half years later—he has enjoyed every meal with the family.

His second year at camp found him sitting on the edge of the swimming pool—an activity that brought only rebellion during his previous camp experience. During this second year he also found pleasure in all activities with only three incidents of aggression. He began to relate to the director and showed much pleasure at meeting her and other counselors at a camp reunion a month after camp.

During his third camp session, he went willingly and freely into the pool and participated in all activities; he communicated with all campers and counselors. His home life has become pleasant, and his ease at being with people is readily noticed. He talks about camp and his camp friends, and he wonders why it is such a long time before camp will start again.

The number of camps for the mentally retarded has been increasing steadily as the need is so great and the results so good. Most of these camps have served moderately and severely retarded children and adults, as these were the persons who stood out in the community as being mentally retarded and in need of help. Unfortunately, these camps rarely have reached the much larger number of mildly and borderline retarded adults who are also in need of this type of experience. There is the same urgency to meet the recreational needs of this less visible group of adult retardates.

Creative Activities

For many retarded adults important recreational experiences are painting, making craft objects, singing, dancing, or playing a musical instrument. These represent modes of self-expression by which individuals can release some of their feelings and gain pleasure from their own productions. The finished work, or the appreciative audience for a performance, gives great personal satisfaction even if the skill is crude and the actual result immature. This does not mean that their creative activities need necessarily be inferior productions. It is possible for retarded adults to paint pictures which express strong feelings with great beauty, and to sing songs with eloquence and conviction.

Spectator Sports

An important form of recreation with many implications for mentally retarded adults is *spectator sports*. This involves viewing sports on television, listening to games over the radio, or watching games at the ball park. There have been many who have argued that being a spectator is less beneficial than being an active participant, but there is little evidence to support any generalizations on this subject. What is important is that the retarded adult as a spectator is essentially no different from any other spectator. When he watches his favorite football team on television, tunes in a portable radio to hear the World Series, or attends a wrestling match, he is no different from millions of other citizens. While he should be encouraged to actively participate in sports within his physical and mental limits, being a spectator may be a most satisfying form of recreation.

RELIGIOUS ACTIVITY

Little is known about the participation of the retarded adult in religious worship and in religious education. As in other areas, major efforts have been focussed on work with retarded children.

Prior to the 1950's, individual clergymen may have been serving some retarded adults, but almost nothing on their efforts was published. Since the founding of the National Association for Retarded Children in 1951, there has been a rapid increase of religious activity. The focus is on religious education, a program generally limited to children. Work with retarded adults is very limited. Following is a brief description of one of the few church programs for handicapped adults in which retarded adults were included.

A Program in Oakland*

An example of a special program serving handicapped adults, and including some mentally retarded, has been in operation at First Christian Church of Oakland.

In 1960, this church realized that the 635 persons then on the list of the county cerebral palsy center had no church that was really interested in them as individuals. A brilliant thirty-five-year-old man who was severely handicapped by cerebral palsy had been a member of this church for a long time, and a handicapped social group, of which he was an officer, used the church building several times a year. At his suggestion the congregation, through its religious education department, made a study and interviewed a number of handicapped persons. It was decided to organize a special Sunday morning class. The room chosen soon became too small, and the church re-modeled a larger room on the main floor. At present

---

* From a report by Thomas P. Weir, Redwood City, California.

twenty persons are members and seven of the group show signs of mental retardation. They live in many areas of the East Bay. Some members of the church take turns driving two Red Cross station wagons that are usually available on Sunday mornings. Some members pick up a few others in their own cars. A few class members come to this downtown church on their own.

The first teacher of the class was a person who had had some public school teaching experience with retarded children. In the five years the class has been in operation, a retired school superintendent and a speech therapist in the congregation have also led the class at various times.

The majority of the class have been handicapped by cerebral palsy, and sometimes they have shown impatience with those who are retarded, but such problems have been resolved in the spirit of Christian understanding and friendship.

After the class meets for one hour, it is time for the 11 A.M. worship service. They come into the sanctuary, which is on the same floor level as their room, and take seats near the front. The church has removed one row of seats so that there would be more room for those in wheelchairs.

It has been frankly acknowledged from the first that some would be coming from other church backgrounds, that all would be welcomed, and that no pressure would be put on anyone to join this church. Some who were not members anywhere have joined, a couple have decided to transfer, and a number still keep their old affiliation, but all are considered a real part of the congregation.

Once a month there is a coffee hour after the church service. At their own suggestion, this class acts as hosts once a year. Several class members also serve on church committees.

For the past two summers the class has held day retreats in a hillside park, and one year had an overnight retreat at the Easter Seal Camp in the Santa Cruz mountains. Such events have required the enlisting of many adults in the church to help, and the college-age young people have been especially active in assisting. Several of these young people have told this writer when he was working with this church, that the presence of this class has caused them to seriously consider vocations in teaching and social work where they might work with handicapped individuals.

Table IX lists needs of retarded adults and their families for community services. It also gives an indication of the need for these services by more able, less able, and least able retarded adults.

TABLE IX

NEEDS OF MENTALLY RETARDED ADULTS (MORE ABLE, LESS ABLE, AND LEAST ABLE) IN THE COMMUNITY

CATEGORY	SPECIFIC NEEDS	CLASSIFICATION* MORE ABLE	LESS ABLE	LEAST ABLE
Residential	Living independently	†	‡	‡
	Living with own family	†	†	†
	Boarding house	†	†	‡
	Foster home	‡	†	‡
	Small institution	‡	‡	†
Vocational	Vocational evaluation	†	†	†
	Vocational rehabilitation services	†	‡	‡
	Work training			
	On-the-job training	†	†	‡
	Short-term workshop	†	§	‡
	Job placement in competitive employment	†	‡	‡
	Sheltered employment	†	†	‡
	Long-term workshop	‡	†	‡
	Activity center (minimal work)	‡	‡	‡
Marital	Marriage counseling	†	†	‡
Health	Marriage with financial support	§	†	‡
	Medical care	†	†	†
	Dental care	†	†	†
	Physical restoration, appliances	†	†	†
	Occupational and physical therapy	†	†	†
	Public health nursing	‡	§	†
Counseling	Psychotherapy, casework, social group work, personal counseling	†	†	§
	Family counseling	§	†	†
	Vocational counseling	†	†	‡
	Educational counseling	†	†	‡
Educational and training	Vocational training	†	†	‡
	Academic training			
	Subject matter (content)	†	‡	‡
	Basic (reading, writing, arithmetic)	†	†	‡
	Independent living			
	Homemaking	‡	†	§
	Personal grooming	§	†	†
	Use of public transportation	‡	†	§
	Speech therapy	†	†	†

Socio-recreative	Individual activities			
	Spectator sports (watching television, movies)	†	†	†
	Active sports (hiking, bicycling)	†	†	‡
	Reading	†	§	‡
	Creative activities (art, music, hobbies)	†	†	§
	Group activities			
	Spectator activities (sporting events, concerts)	†	†	§
	Active sports (playing baseball, football)	†	†	‡
	Camping and picnicking	†	†	†
	Indoor activities (clubs, games, parties, dances)	†	†	§
	Visits (to relatives, museums, sightseeing)	†	†	§
	Creative activities (chorus, dramatics)	†	†	‡
Religious	Church going	†	†	§
	Religious classes	§	§	§
	Social activities	†	†	§
Transportation	Public transportation (busses, subway)	†	§	‡
	Nonpublic transportation (taxi, family car)	‡	§	†
Legal aid	Guardianship	‡	§	†
	Legal assistance	†	†	†

* Classifications:
  † Needed by most or all retarded adults in this classification.
  ‡ Needed by none or few retarded adults in this classification.
  § Needed by some retarded adults in this classification.

QUESTIONS FOR DISCUSSION

1. A forty-year-old mentally retarded woman is about to be placed in the community from a state institution. What would be the best living arrangement for her?

2. What are some of the advantages and disadvantages of a halfway house for mentally retarded adults?

3. A forty-eight-year-old mentally retarded man with very poor teeth needs extensive dental care. Where should he go to get help and what help could he get?

4. A thirty-one-year-old moderately mentally retarded man is demonstrating many emotional disturbances, including fears, tantrums, and some aggressive behavior. What agencies should be contacted for help?

5. A mentally retarded young adult woman of twenty years with an IQ of 70 has been told that if she can master alphabetical filing she can get a job in the office of the telephone company. Whom would she contact to get training for this job?

6. A group of teen-age volunteers wishes to help severely

retarded adults make weekly visits to a nearby park. How could this be worked out?

7. For a number of years the local Aid Retarded Children (ARC) has been conducting a monthly dance on Friday nights in a church, primarily for mentally retarded teen-agers and adults. The ARC is anxious to encourage more mentally retarded persons to attend. How should they go about doing this?

REFERENCES

1. Kukoda, Louis J.; Jacobs, Abraham, and French, Edward L.: *Vocational Rehabilitation in a Residential Treatment Center*. Devon, Pa., Devereux Schools, 1964, pp. 21-23.

2. Woloshin, Arthur A.: *Progress Report, Illinois Mental Health Center, Mary McDowell Settlement House*. Proj. No. RD-470. Chicago, Dept. of Mental Health, 1964.

3. Mikels, Elaine, and Gumrukcu, Patricia: For the former mental patient: a therapeutic community hostel. *J Rehab*, 29:20-21, 1963.

4. DiMichael, Salvatore: Providing full vocational opportunities for retarded adolescents and adults. *J Rehab*, 20:11, 1964.

5. Jastak, Joseph F.; MacPhee, Halsey M., and Whiteman, Martin: *Mental Retardation, Its Nature and Incidence. A Population Survey of the State of Delaware*. Newark, Del., U. of Delaware, 1963, p. 165.

6. *Ibid.*, p. 138.

7. American Medical Association: *Mental Retardation: A Handbook for the Primary Physician*. Chicago, AMA, 1965, p. 55. (Reprinted from the *J Amer Med Ass*, 191:183-232, 1965).

8. *Ibid.*, p. 56.

9. President's Panel on Mental Retardation: *A Proposed Program for National Action to Combat Mental Retardation*. Washington, U. S. Gov. Printing Office, 1962, p. 86.

10. State of California, Dept. of Social Welfare: *Aid to Needy Disabled Program* (circular). Sacramento, Office of State Printing, October 1965.

11. Heber, Rick: Personality. In Stevens, Harvey A., and Heber, Rick (Eds.): *Mental Retardation: A Review of Research*. Chicago, U. of Chicago, 1964, p. 146.

12. Group for the Advancement of Psychiatry: *Basic Considerations in Mental Retardation: A Preliminary Report*. New York, Group for the Advancement of Psychiatry, 1959, p. 5.

13. Woody, Robert H., and Billy, Joel J.: Counseling and psychotherapy

for the mentally retarded: a survey of opinion and practice. *Ment Retard,* 4:20-23, 1966.
14. *Ibid.,* p. 23.
15. *Ibid.,* p. 22.
16. Schapps, Myra: Reaching out to the mentally retarded. *Soc Casework Papers.* In *Current Trends and Services for the Mentally Retarded.* Papers from the 86th Annual Forum of the National Conference on Social Welfare, San Francisco, 1959. New York, National Association for Retarded Children, 1960, pp. 46-58.
17. Katz, Elias (Ed.): *Final Report. Work-Training Center for the Mentally Retarded.* (For Vocational Rehabilitation Administration, Project No. 205.) San Francisco, Aid Retarded Children, 1961.
18. Lehman, Harvey C.: Recreation. *Encyclopaedia Britannica,* 19:17-18b, 1958.
19. Ginglend, David, and Gould, Kay: *Day Camping for the Mentally Retarded.* New York, National Association for Retarded Children, 1962, p. 38.

Chapter VI

HOW ARE THE VOCATIONAL NEEDS OF THE MORE ABLE RETARDED ADULT MET IN THE COMMUNITY?

T HE MORE ABLE retarded adult is one who, after receiving vocational rehabilitation services, is able to engage in *gainful employment.**

Until the passage of the Vocational Rehabilitation Amendments of 1965, "State rehabilitation agencies were expected to determine, after diagnosis but before any rehabilitation services were rendered, whether or not a handicapped person could become employable after rehabilitation services. For large numbers of handicapped persons, with severe disabilities or complicated problems or both, this is virtually impossible. As a result, many of these handicapped individuals did not receive services."[1] After the passage of these 1965 amendments, a handicapped person could be provided vocational evaluation services up to a maximum of six months, and in the case of the mentally retarded, to a maximum of eighteen months. "Within this period the State agency can observe his response to services and determine whether further services could be expected to result in employment."[2]

There is little question that this liberalization of vocational rehabilitation services opens opportunities to more adequately *evaluate* the retarded adult over a longer period of time. It does not officially change the criterion that the applicant must be able

---

* The term *gainful employment* is widely used but not clearly defined. Persons engaged in gainful employment are usually considered to be those who are making a successful adjustment to full-time employment in the competitive labor market, with earnings sufficiently high as not to require public or private subsidy.

to achieve the goal of gainful employment. Only those retarded clients who are believed to be capable of achieving gainful employment are entitled to these vocational rehabilitation services.

If at any time during the evaluation period the retarded person is found not feasible for employment, the case may be closed. The retarded client whose case is closed because he is not feasible for gainful employment receives no further vocational rehabilitation services. He is a less able mentally retarded adult.*

FEDERAL-STATE VOCATIONAL REHABILITATION PROGRAMS AND THE MORE ABLE RETARDED ADULT

The present-day vocational rehabilitation program came into existence in the 1920's as a means of helping veterans disabled by World War I, as well as those who had been injured in industry and in other ways. Grants were made by the Federal Vocational Rehabilitation Agency to each state, which in turn appropriated matching funds. Counseling and physical restoration services were provided to eligible handicapped clients by vocational rehabilitation counselors employed by the state vocational rehabilitation agency. The major emphasis in most states was on vocational rehabilitation of the physically handicapped who could be placed on jobs. In some states a high priority was placed on rehabilitating welfare recipients so that they would not need public assistance. The Barden-LaFollette Act of 1943[3] included mental retardation and mental illness among the eligible handicaps, but few mentally retarded clients were accepted for vocational rehabilitation services.

With the passage of the Vocational Rehabilitation Amendments of 1954,[4] the modern Vocational Rehabilitation Administration (formerly Office of Vocational Rehabilitation) took on new dimensions. Services to the mentally retarded were substantially increased and improved. Many more retarded clients were accepted. In addition, a greatly expanded program of demonstration and research was authorized. This included short-

---

* See Chapter VII.

term (two to four years) financial support for community demonstration projects of workshops for the mentally retarded and other handicapped adults. Many of these projects have been absorbed into the community as ongoing services. These projects have also provided a stimulus for other groups, in communities faced with similar problems, to develop their own workshops.

Vocational rehabilitation has been characterized as a combination of services provided to a physically or mentally disabled person, as needed, to fit him for employment and productive useful living. . . . The range of services includes:

Full evaluation, including medical diagnosis, to learn the nature and degree of disability and to help evaluate the individual's work capacities

Counseling and guidance in achieving good vocational adjustment

Medical, surgical, psychiatric, and hospital care and related therapy to reduce or remove the disability

Artificial limbs and other prosthetic and orthotic devices needed to increase work ability

Training, including training for a vocation, prevocational and personal adjustment training, and remedial education

Service in comprehensive or specialized rehabilitation facilities including sheltered workshops and adjustment centers

Maintenance and transportation during rehabilitation

Tools, equipment, and licenses to work on a job or in establishing a small business

Placement in a job suited to the individual's highest physical and mental capacities and postplacement follow-up to see to it that the placement is satisfactory to the employee and the employer.[5]

Figure 6 indicates the types and amounts of service provided for vocational rehabilitation clients in 1964.

The steps taken to carry out the vocational rehabilitation agency's mission may be summarized as follows:

1. An interview with a counselor helps determine how the disability handicaps the applicant and whether there is a reasonable chance of getting and holding a job after rehabilitation.

2. Medical and other examinations are arranged to determine the need for treatment and the ability to work.

3. If the examinations show a need for medical, surgical, or

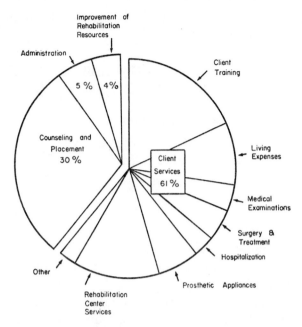

Figure 6. What state rehabilitation agencies do for clients ($139 million spent in 1964). From *Restoring Disabled People to Jobs and Useful Living*, October 1965, p. 5. Courtesy of Vocational Rehabilitation Administration, U. S. Dept. of HEW.

psychiatric services to remove or reduce a disability, these may be provided.

4. If the disability problem requires artificial appliances such as limbs, braces, hearing aids, or optical aids, these may be purchased, fitted, and adjusted. Clients are carefully trained in their use and their adaptation to a trade or business.

5. A place in the working world often requires training, so it may be necessary to supply schooling, on-the-job learning, tools and equipment, supplies and licenses, and related services when these are part of preparation for a job.

6. All during the rehabilitation process, a counselor continues individual counseling, guidance, and aid to the client in adjustment to handicaps, the service program, and the attainment of a specific job goal.

7. Some rehabilitation help, including examination, guidance, counseling, training, and placement, can be given eligible clients without cost. Expenses for medical services, living allowances,

transportation, books, tools, supplies, and equipment are arranged based on the client's ability to pay.[6]

AVAILABLE VOCATIONAL REHABILITATION SERVICES FOR THE MORE ABLE RETARDED ADULTS

Comprehensive Vocational Evaluation

How does one go about evaluating the vocational potential of the more able retarded adult? In Chapter III evaluation is described. Comprehensive vocational evaluation includes the following:

Medical Examination

A *medical examination* should determine physical capacities and limitations affecting vocational potential. Unfortunately, a limited physical examination is usually conducted providing only a meager picture of the client's total medical status. Forms for evaluating physical capacities and limitations* have been available for many years, but few physicians make use of them. It would be highly desirable if a complete physical evaluation as suggested in these forms would be the rule, rather than the exception.

Psychological Evaluation

Assuming a complete physical examination has been made, a psychological evaluation should be conducted by a psychologist trained to evaluate this type of handicapped person. This evaluation includes both standardized and clinical evaluations of intellectual functioning, social maturity, educational achievement, personality organization, and mechanisms of adjustment. Such information is indispensable in understanding whether the mentally retarded adult has the personal resources and capabilities to pursue a given vocational goal. In addition, any appropriate performance tests which might be necessary to gain some idea of the individual's dexterity or special skills and aptitudes could be incorporated into the study.

---

* See Figure 2, pp. 54-55.

Social Evaluation

Of extreme importance is the social evaluation by a social worker or a vocational rehabilitation counselor. Such a study requires extensive reporting on the composition of the family, the family members and ancestors, early personal, educational, and social developmental history, and the history of work experience. It must be remembered that many retarded adults do not have any significant work history, so it becomes important to know about even limited work experience, whether part-time or intermittent, and the reasons for success or failure on the job.

Work Evaluation

Work evaluation involves careful study of work habits, work skills, productivity rates, and attitudes towards supervisors and co-workers, carried on in a realistic work setting. Such evaluations are conducted in workshops which have a special evaluation staff, in rehabilitation centers with a vocational evaluation unit, and in on-the-job training programs. Vocational capacities and competencies are not easily tested in a brief period, nor in terms of a specific test, but require extended observation and review in order to obtain a clear image of the individual's vocational potential.

Case Review

All aspects of such comprehensive vocational evaluations need not be done under one roof during a short period of time, although this is often the case. The findings are brought together by the group making the study at a joint conference or case review during which the material is integrated and a total picture of the client emerges.

An example of a program which was geared to carrying on comprehensive vocational evaluation of more able retarded adults was the Work-Training Center project.[7] Prior to the client's admission, a physical examination was conducted. During the initial evaluation period of eight weeks, he was studied by the director, a psychologist, a social worker, the training staff, and work supervisors; he was observed in the workshop and on other occasions. Members of the family were interviewed, and every effort was made to determine relationships between family attitudes and the client's behavior manifested in the daily program. The process of evaluation of vocational potentials was carried on by the total staff at regular staff reviews, as well as by informal discussions whenever possible, such as during coffee breaks or lunch periods. Those who were studied in this manner were enabled to receive rehabilitation services which were closely geared to their needs. Those who could not profit from the program were terminated. Every effort was made to find help for them elsewhere.

Vocational Training

Vocational training means training in work habits, work skills, and attitudes toward work. Such vocational training can be conducted in classroom settings with vocational instructors or in on-the-job training stations where the employer supervises the trainee on the job.

Those who have provided vocational training to retarded adults are in agreement that the major training problems are not only in relation to the development of work skills required in carrying on specific jobs, but also in the development of good work habits such as punctuality, personal cleanliness, and orderliness. Stress is placed on positive attitudes towards employers, co-workers, immediate supervisors, and towards the job itself. The greatest number of failures on work assignments among retarded adults may be traced to failures in work habits and attitudes, rather than to poor work skills.

Job Placement

The purpose of job placement for the more able retarded adult is to help him get a full-time job with sufficient remuneration to make it possible for him to support himself in the community. The task of job placement is usually assumed by the vocational rehabilitation counselor. In some state employment service offices special staff members are available for selective placement of retarded job applicants. Unfortunately few state employment service offices have employment counselors trained to work with retarded adults.

Generally speaking, most employers tend to reject mentally retarded persons for jobs. As a consequence, special efforts must be made either to encourage the employer to accept the retarded for those jobs which they can do, or to develop new jobs which retarded persons can perform.[8]

In a number of occupations, including retail clerking, dry cleaning, meat cutting, and laundry work,* labor unions, business management, the Vocational Rehabilitation Administration, and the National Association for Retarded Children have joined to develop new job opportunities for mentally retarded adults. Most of these new programs involve training and on-the-job experiences leading to job placement. The following describes one such program.[9]

1500 New Jobs for the Retarded

A major national breakthrough in employment of the mentally retarded has been announced in California by Katharine T. Small, President, Exceptional Children's Foundation, Los Angeles.

The U. S. Department of Labor and the National Association for Retarded Children, of which ECF is a member, signed a contract authorizing placement of 1500 retarded persons in on-the-job training in the nation's retail chains.

According to the contract, signed by Secretary of Labor W. Willard Wirtz and NARC President Thomas A. Tucker, trainees will be paid the existing minimum wage. Employers will be reimbursed by the government for half this amount.

Upon successful completion of training, the mentally retarded workers will attain equal pay and status with fellow employees.

Tucker said, "I would point out that over a period of ten years the trainees who enter the program we have signed today will have paid back, in taxes on the wages they have earned as equal-status employees, double what it cost to train them."

"This contract," Mrs. Small said, "signifies an awakening to the challenge of the untapped source which the country's 2,000,000 able, though unemployed, retarded represent.

"Here in Los Angeles the retarded have already begun successful on-the-job training with laundries and dry cleaners.

"The retarded have the capabilities of learning a job and staying with it despite the fact that it might become boring to many other

---

* See Appendix B.

people. This makes them ideal employees for many kinds of work, as business is beginning to discover."

She said the Exceptional Children's Foundation would welcome inquiries from employers who feel they have work that might be suitable.

Under the aegis of the President's Committee to Employ the Handicapped and with active support of Vocational Rehabilitation Administration and National Association for Retarded Children, a program has been developed to open civil service careers to retarded adults who cannot pass the required written examinations. Under this plan the retarded adult's vocational rehabilitation counselor certifies him as being capable of performing the job. The written examination is waived, and the retarded adult is appointed. From then on he must demonstrate to the supervisor's satisfaction that he can fill the job. This plan is being extended to state civil service levels, and probably will eventually be extended to municipal and county governmental jurisdictions.

Governor Directs State Agencies to Employ Retarded

In an executive order issued March 1, 1966, Governor Nelson A. Rockefeller has directed all state agencies to follow newly established procedures for employing qualified mentally retarded persons in the state civil service system.

The order also establishes an annual Governor's Award to be given to the state agency showing the most outstanding "effort and accomplishment" in the program.

Indicating New York State's determination to insure "a brighter future for the retarded" through provision for "fullest development of each individual's capacity," the Governor outlined the following procedures designed to promote opportunities for employment:

1. The Division of Vocational Rehabilitation of the State Education Department shall extend its service program for all handicapped persons and serve as the certifying agency for employment of the retarded.

2. The Interdepartmental Health and Hospital Council Committee on Mental Retardation shall provide state departments and agencies with a list of positions which have been evaluated as being potentially appropriate for employment of the retarded.

3. Each department or agency will, upon receipt of the list of

positions, determine the number of vacancies and submit the information to the Committee on Mental Retardation.

4. Each department and agency shall notify the nearest office of the Division of Vocational Rehabilitation when vacancies occur in jobs listed as appropriate for the retarded.

5. The Committee on [Mental] Retardation will forward to the Division on Rehabilitation the list of vacant positions, and state agencies will be responsible for establishing vocational training workshops for jobs reported as frequently vacant, so that curriculum may be developed in special classes, state schools, and workshops to train the retarded for skills needed for employment.

6. Each state agency and department will take part in training institutes planned periodically to assure maximum employment opportunities for the mentally retarded.

The program, the result of a nine-month study begun last June under a directive from the governor, was developed by the Inter-departmental Health and Hospital Council, the Governor's Council on Rehabilitation, and the Governor's Committee on Employ the Handicapped, in cooperation with the civil service department and the Department of Mental Hygiene.[10]

Vocational Counseling

Vocational counseling is the process of helping the client move in the direction of obtaining and holding a job.[11]

> In the Federal-state program the rehabilitation counselor is the key staff member, making the determination as to whether the individual is eligible, arranging with the individual the development of a plan for his rehabilitation, managing the arrangements for the necessary services, counseling and guiding the individual, and staying with him through successful placement on the job.[12]

Vocational counseling involves knowledge not only of the client and the community in which he lives, but the counselor must also be fully aware of his own attitudes, especially since they may affect his client's success. There is little question that the enthusiastic yet realistic counselor with faith in the potentials of the mentally retarded adults in his case load will obtain excellent results as compared with the counselor who feels that all mentally retarded adults should be kept out of the labor market. It is important to realize that there are many counselors in the United States who still subscribe to the latter negative point of view.

Follow-up of Rehabilitated Retarded Clients

Under present practices in most states, the postplacement follow-up of the retarded client who has been placed on a job is limited to a designated period of time, usually three to six months. After this follow-up period, the client who has kept his job is considered successfully rehabilitated. His case is closed, and he ceases to be a client. Successful closures are reported in state and national statistics, e.g., "135,000 disabled persons were vocationally rehabilitated in fiscal year 1965."[13]

It has been noted by many vocational rehabilitation counselors that to close retarded clients prematurely and to discontinue follow-up services create serious problems in many cases. As Richman[14] has put it in relation to the retarded client, "The experience of the rehabilitation agency and other service organizations has indicated that lack of social competence constitutes the major block to social-vocational effectiveness."

After the retardate is employed for a while, social and personal adjustment problems do not automatically disappear. Changes in employers or working conditions, as well as personal feelings of inadequacy, may bring about emotional disturbances and loss of job.

As a consequence, the idea of extended follow-up of retarded clients is being pursued by some counselors. This involves closing the case administratively, after the usual period, so that the client can be recorded as a successful rehabilitation. However, the door is left open for the client to return periodically, as well as for the counselor to periodically visit and review the current status as long as this may be needed. Such a preventive approach may be helpful in those cases where the client is making a vocational adjustment but may need occasional help.

Records and Reports

An important aspect of vocational rehabilitation services has to do with records and information which must be communicated to others. The kinds of information which have been found to be most helpful to those who are to continue working with the retarded adult after the evaluation are not only the descriptions of behavior and the reports of competencies, skills, and levels of ability, but also recommendations as to future planning an future steps to be taken. Of special value are cumulative narrative records of changes in the client as he moves through the vocational rehabilitation counseling process. The many cases presented in this book point up the significance of extensive documentation as a basis for arriving at meaningful decisions in the best interest of the client.

THE ROLE OF WORKSHOPS FOR THE HANDICAPPED IN REHABILITATING MORE ABLE RETARDED ADULTS

Workshops for the handicapped* are programs offering specialized services to handicapped persons, including work evaluation, work adjustment, work training, personal counseling, work experience, job placement, and follow-up. This embraces a wide variety of agencies engaged in different types of work, such as salvage operations, contract work for other businesses and industry, prime manufacturing, and service occupations. Some workshops include all types of handicapped persons ranging from the most able to the least able, while others are limited to a single category, e.g., more able retarded young adult (see Table X).

For present purposes, workshops for the handicapped are classified as *transitional*† or *long-term,* depending on the workshop's objectives. In the transitional workshop, the goal is to place the client in competitive employment after a relatively short period of evaluation and training. Since the more able retarded adult is one who is eligible for vocational rehabilitation services leading to gainful employment in the competitive labor market, the transitional workshop is well suited to meet his vocational training needs.

Following is a case of a more able retarded adult who was rehabilitated through the efforts of a transitional workshop.[15]

---

* Also known as *sheltered workshops, rehabilitation workshops, work training centers, occupational centers.*

† Also called *short-term.*

TABLE X

LOCATION OF WORKSHOPS FOR THE HANDICAPPED (1965)°

California	79	Arizona	8
New York	75	Utah	8
Pennsylvania	74	Arkansas	7
Ohio	58	Oregon	7
Illinois	36	Kentucky	7
Michigan	33	South Dakota	5
Texas	27	New Mexico	5
New Jersey	26	West Virginia	5
Indiana	25	Delaware	4
Washington	24	District of Columbia	4
Wisconsin	23	Nebraska	4
Connecticut	20	Hawaii	4
Minnesota	20	South Carolina	4
Massachusetts	19	New Hampshire	3
Tennessee	17	Rhode Island	3
Colorado	15	Maine	2
Missouri	15	Vermont	2
Virginia	15	Mississippi	2
Alabama	14	North Dakota	2
Maryland	13	Wyoming	2
Florida	11	Idaho	2
Louisiana	10	Montana	1
Oklahoma	10	Alaska	0
Georgia	10	Nevada	0
Iowa	9	Puerto Rico	0
Kansas	9		—
North Carolina	9	Total	787

SIZE OF SHOPS

The average number of clients per workshop is approximately 56; however, almost half of the workshops have fewer than 30 clients. Workshops for the mentally retarded typically have from 20 to 30 clients; shops for the blind typically have from 50 to 60 clients, but many have more than 100 clients. Many of the *general* shops are relatively large, particularly those affiliated with Goodwill Industries of America, which has about 145 independently chartered workshops throughout the country, several with more than 100 clients, some with more than 500 clients.

° Certified by U. S. Department of Labor, April 30, 1965. From U. S. Dept. of HEW, Summary of 1965 provisions (of Vocational Rehabilitation Amendments of 1965), *Rehab Rec*, 6(Nov-Dec 1965): p. 11.

Case Study: Alice

Alice was eighteen and a half years old when she entered the VAC (Vocational Adjustment Center). Her father's occupation was listed as laborer, the mother's as housewife, and there was a younger brother still in school. The family unit was judged to be relatively well integrated, with rather warm internal relationships. According to a report from the Bureau of Child Study, Chicago Public Schools, Alice was transferred from regular classes to the ungraded division after kindergarten and one semester in Grade 1C. She remained in ungraded classes until the eighth grade. Various examinations administered by the Bureau of Child Study during this period yielded IQ's ranging from 62 to 73, and scholastic achievement at

IQ expectancy. While stressing that Alice's rate of mental growth was slow, these reports continuously point out that Alice was making a very good adjustment, seemed well behaved and eager to please, and appeared to have a warm and accepting family.

When Alice was approaching seventeen, she was referred to the Illinois Division of Vocational Rehabilitation by the school authorities, with a view to vocational rehabilitation. She was seen there by the psychiatric rehabilitation consultant who felt that, while strongly motivated for work, there was a good deal of "free floating anxiety and apprehension." There was a medical finding of congenital hypothyroidism, which was judged to be under excellent control and did not interfere with general functioning. Psychological testing revealed an IQ of 71 but a rather positive personality development, with a good deal of striving and strong motivation. From the interview, there was an impression of a well trained and conforming young woman of limited endowment, who had almost no social life except that available in the family circle, and who seemed quite frightened and apprehensive at the prospect of seeking employment.

Alice was accepted for service, and entered the VAC in September of 1953. From the beginning it was noted that she had positive work habits and was capable of working at above average rates. The chief initial problem was distractibility. Alice was apparently so overjoyed at being with young people in a productive situation that she sometimes quite lost herself in conversing and socializing, and her output suffered wide swings as a consequence. She was worked with in this area, and soon learned to control her impulse to socialize and use it in a positive way. During the last few weeks of her stay at the center, she worked quite well and consistently, used supervision constructively, and was able to concentrate her attention on the work to be done. She was deemed fully employable (A) and was recommended for any kind of light, factory assembly occupation.

Alice's subsequent employment history is interesting. After two very brief placements, from which she was discharged as too slow, she was placed on a similar factory job, one month after leaving the center. This job she held for ten months. After being laid off again for talking on the job, she was at once placed again and was working at the end of the one-year follow-up period. The placement counselor noted, in closing the case, that Alice's general adjustment seemed much improved. She had made several friends, had begun to date and gives the impression of being a happy, well adjusted young person.

In summary, Alice has changed from a rather isolated, fearful, and rather anxious young person, who had no real knowledge of what it takes to be an acceptable employee. While she still has problems in the areas of impulse control (excessive talking on the job) and limited ability, she can find work and keep it for relatively long periods. She was classified in follow-up as "B" (worked most of time, but on several jobs) and deemed to be a case of reasonably successful rehabilitation. It is the judgment of the VAC staff that without the benign atmosphere of the VAC, in which she was helped to work out some of her problems, she might otherwise have encountered a number of quite unsuccessful work experiences in the ordinary labor market, and that her fears and anxieties would have been intensified, rather than diminished.

A major step forward in expanding the role of transitional workshops for meeting the needs of more able retarded adults was made when the Vocational Rehabilitation Amendments of 1965 were passed.[16] The new law made possible a multifaceted approach designed to substantially increase the number and improve the quality of workshops for all disabled persons. First, training service projects were authorized in workshops providing "training in job skills, work evaluation, work testing, tools, equipment, job tryout, and related services; and the payment of a training allowance to the handicapped trainee at a rate up to $25 per week plus $10 for each dependent (but not to exceed $65 per week per trainee)."[17] Second, workshop improvement grants are funded, "to help workshops analyze, improve, and increase their professional services, to similarly elevate their business operations, and to generally make more efficient and effective the total operations of the workshop."[18] Third, technical assistance is provided to workshops for the "help of experts in business management, shop layout, professional services, sales management, and the many other facets of a total workshop operation."[19] Fourth, a National Policy and Performance Council is established, "responsible for advising the Secretary of Health, Education and Welfare on the policies and criteria"[20] in making the grants for workshop improvement and training services projects. Such a broad approach to the development of workshops will have highly beneficial effects on vocational rehabilitation of the more able retarded adult.

Following are brief summaries of the successful rehabilitation of retarded young adults in the workshop and employment program of Abilities, Inc.,[21] of New York, a workshop for the handicapped which has in the past been highly successful in employing and placing physically handicapped adults.

Case No. 7

Gary is a nineteen-year-old mentally retarded youngster who obtained a Full Scale IQ of 78 on the Wechsler Adult Intelligence Scale. He has a severe speech impediment and limited verbal comprehension and communication. Gary made excellent progress in the work evaluation program and was referred for full-time employment in the glass engraving department at Abilities. He adjusted well to the work situation and was helpful in inspection, packaging, and some limited areas of production control within the glass engraving department. He was a very highly motivated youngster, well accepted by co-workers and supervisory personnel. His training supervisor requested that the Division of Vocational Rehabilitation initiate speech therapy for Gary. He has consequently received speech help since October 1964 and shown remarkable progress. Prior to Gary's employment at Abilities, he was placed on probation by the juvenile court because of allegedly breaking and entering a private home. Contact with his probation officer as well as contact with his supervisors in Abilities indicate that Gary is making satisfactory progress with no more difficulties with authority. When the work load in the glass engraving department diminished he was transferred to the mechanical assembly department where he was completely accepted and functioned at standard for production. He is currently being paid at the rate of $1.45 per hour.

Case No. 3

Elaine was referred for a work evaluation in clerical skills on June 22, 1964. She is a nineteen-year-old mentally retarded youngster with a Full Scale IQ of 70 on the Wechsler-Bellevue Intelligence Scale. Initially, Elaine was distractible, restless, and poorly motivated. As soon as she was excluded from training in typing—for which she has neither aptitude nor motivation—her work and behavior improved. She was placed in an on-the-job training program in the student banking division at Abilities on September 14, 1964. She learned all of the seven job procedures in the banking department consisting of signing in of the schools, slicing deposits, checking cash in deposit envelopes, posting, making change, returning specific deposit books to source, and alpha and numerical card filing.

She functions on all these skills at the same rate of productivity required by the normal worker. She is a very conscientious worker who readily grasps and understands the job skills. Socially, Elaine tended to be overexuberant and hyperactive; however, with counseling her social functioning has become acceptable. She started on the banking job at $1.25 per hour and now makes $1.32 per hour as a full-time employee at Abilities.

QUESTIONS FOR DISCUSSION

1. What significant contributions to the vocational rehabilitation of the mentally retarded adult were made by the 1965 Vocational Rehabilitation Amendments?

2. A vocational rehabilitation counselor after interviewing a nineteen-year-old woman, a recent graduate of public school classes for the mentally retarded, comes to the conclusion that she needs a complete vocational evaluation. How would he go about getting this for her? What kinds of reports would be helpful to him?

3. A Manpower and Development Training Administration (MDTA) program has been established to train mentally retarded adults for work as janitors. How should the instructor organize the course to most effectively train these students for jobs as janitors?

4. A vocational rehabilitation counselor placed a mentally retarded adult in an on-the-job training assignment in a factory making leather bags. What experiences would he expect the employer to provide for his client?

5. A thirty-eight-year-old mentally retarded man, who was placed by the state employment office in a job as a busboy in a cafeteria, is looking for a job in a restaurant closer to his home. How does he go about getting such a job?

6. A vocational rehabilitation counselor placed a twenty-two-year-old man on a job in a garment factory, moving clothes racks from one part of the building to the other. Should he or should he not visit his client regularly? Why?

7. A forty-seven-year-old mentally retarded man has been working in a warehouse all his life, except for the past year since

his employer's business changed hands. He is in a transitional workshop for the handicapped, training as a warehouseman's assistant and has good prospects of getting a job in this kind of work. What training should the workshop be providing to help him to do a better job when he gets placed?

REFERENCES

1. U. S. Dept. of HEW: Summary of 1965 Provisions (of Vocational Rehabilitation Amendments of 1965). *Rehab Rec*, 6:6-14, 1965, p. 9.
2. *Loc. cit.*
3. U. S. Dept. of HEW: *Restoring Disabled People to Jobs and Useful Living.* Committee on Education and Labor, House of Representatives, 89th Congress, 1st Session. Washington, U. S. Gov. Printing Office, October 1965, p. 6.
4. *Ibid.*
5. *Ibid.*, p. 2.
6. State of California, Dept. of Rehabilitation: *Through the Open Door* (circular). Sacramento, Office of State Printing, 1965.
7. Katz, Elias (Ed.): *Final Report, Work-Training Center for the Mentally Retarded.* (For Vocational Rehabilitation Administration, Project No. 205.) San Francisco, Aid Retarded Children, 1961, p. 20ff.
8. Peterson, R. O., and Jones, E. M.: *Guide to Jobs for the Mentally Retarded.* Pittsburgh, Am Inst for Research, 1964.
9. State of California, Dept. of Mental Hygiene: "1500 new jobs for the retarded." *Calif Ment Health Prog (Sacramento)*, 7(May), 1966.
10. State of New York, Dept. of Mental Hygiene: "Governor directs state agencies to employ retarded." *Ment Hyg News (Albany, NY)*, 36(Mar.), 1966.
11. Ogg, Elizabeth: *Rehabilitation Counselor: Helper of the Handicapped.* New York, Public Affairs Pamphlets, 381 Park Avenue South, 1966, pp. 20-22.
12. U. S. Dept. of HEW: *Restoring Disabled People to Jobs and Useful Living. Ibid.*, p. 3.
13. *Ibid.*, p. 2.
14. Richman, Sol: *Counseling and Placement of the Mentally Retarded.* Paper presented at Annual Convention of Am Assn on Mental Deficiency, May 1966, p. 9.
15. Quoted in Fraenkel, William A.: *The Mentally Retarded and Their Vocational Rehabilitation: A Resource Handbook.* New York, Nat

Assn for Retarded Children, 1961, pp. 58-60. From Gellman, William: *Adjusting People to Work.* Chicago, Jewish Vocational Service and Employment Center, 1957.

16. U. S. Dept. of HEW: Summary of 1965 Provisions (of Vocational Rehabilitation Amendments of 1965). *Rehab Rec, 6*:6-14, 1965.
17. *Ibid.,* p. 13.
18. *Ibid.,* p. 13.
19. *Ibid.,* p. 13.
20. *Ibid.,* p. 13.
21. Human Resources. *Final Progress Report: The Development of New Techniques and the Training of Mentally Retarded and Severely Physically Disabled Adults in Commercial and Industrial Skills.* For U. S. Dept. of Labor, Office of Manpower, Automation and Training, and Bureau of Apprenticeship and Training. Project MDS-23-64. Albertson, Long Island, New York, Human Resources, August 1965.

Chapter VII

HOW ARE THE NEEDS OF THE LESS ABLE RETARDED ADULT MET IN LONG-TERM WORKSHOPS?

T HE LESS ABLE mentally retarded adult is one who, after vocational evaluation, has been found to be ineligible (not feasible) for further vocational rehabilitation services, because he could not be gainfully employed even if such services were extended to him. As pointed out in Chapter VI, persons engaged in gainful employment are usually considered to be those making a successful adjustment in full-time competitive employment, with earnings sufficiently high as not to require public or private subsidy.

Some less able retarded adults can work a full day, but their productivity or social adjustment is well below acceptable standards in competitive employment. Many of the less able retarded adults are not able to work more than a few hours a day because of various reasons, such as short attention span, physical handicap, emotional disturbance, immaturity, or poor training. Those who cannot work a full day may need social and recreational experiences or training in self-care to fill their time meaningfully. These objectives can best be accomplished in a long-term workshop.

Case of Arthur F.

Arthur F., a thirty-year-old less able retarded man, has been a client in a workshop for the past ten years. He has an IQ of 57, has mild cerebral palsy affecting his left arm and left leg. His speech is clear and appropriate. He is neatly dressed and groomed. His father works as a trucker in the food industry. His mother volunteers her time to another agency one day a week. When he was first referred to the program, his vocational rehabilitation counselor thought that he might eventually get a job in the trucking industry. His evaluation in the workshop was financed by the state vocational rehabilitation agency. As part of the evaluation, two attempts were made to place him on jobs, but each time he failed because of slow responses and physical weakness. His case was closed after four months as not feasible, since it appeared that he would not be able to be placed in gainful employment.

Since that time he has been a long-term client in the same workshop. The cost to the workshop of providing him with ongoing supervision and other activities is no longer paid by the Vocational Rehabilitation Agency, but by the workshop, which is financed by whatever funds can be obtained (fees from parents of clients, United Community Fund support, cake sales, overage from contract work performed*).

In the workshop which Arthur attends full time, he is able to work four hours a day. For this work he is paid about 20 per cent of the minimum wage, since his production rate is about 20 per cent that of a nonhandicapped worker doing the same type work. He spends the rest of his day in training in homemaking activities and engages in leisure time activities under supervision twice weekly. He looks forward to going to the workshop daily and missed only a few days because of illness during the past few years. He will probably remain in this workshop indefinitely.

The designation of less able retarded adult must not be conceived as a permanent, unchanging classification. Experience has demonstrated that over a period of time, with appropriate training, counseling, and work opportunities, some of the less able retarded adults can develop into what is termed more able retarded adults, capable of being gainfully employed. Following is a case which illustrates such a change in a retarded adult.

Case of Helen M.†

Helen M., a twenty-eight-year-old female, came to California with her family when she was ten years old. The public schools did not accept her in regular classes, so she was referred to a special

---

* *Overage from contract work performed* usually refers to the amount remaining from the gross receipts of contract work performed by clients in the workshop after their salaries are paid.

† Adapted from a case report of the Exceptional Children's Foundation, Los Angeles, through the courtesy of the Mental Retardation Services Board of Los Angeles County.

education school. When transferred to a junior high school, emotional problems caused her to drop from school. In 1958 she enrolled in special training classes in the Exceptional Children's Foundation (ECF), where she attended four years. Her teacher reported that she could read at the seventh-grade level, write well, and perform addition, subtraction, multiplication, and division. She was rated very independent in the classroom. She was seen as kind, always willing to help, very industrious, and generally a "very fine citizen."

In 1962 the parents considered filing an application for state hospital placement. Since they were getting along in years—the father 68 and the mother 73—they were concerned how Helen could manage without them.

In October 1962, Helen was referred to ECF for workshop services. Intellectual testing revealed a Full Scale IQ of 53. The examining psychologist observed that Helen was rather poorly groomed, wearing clothes appropriate to a teen-ager rather than to a twenty-four-year-old woman. She wore her hair straight and in bangs and used no makeup. Psychiatric evaluation indicated that her mental retardation was accompanied by neurological damage and brain-function defect. She was considered incapable of social judgment. The psychiatrist believed that Helen could never be expected to be self-supporting or to be capable of self-management.

At the time of her referral to the ECF workshop, her father's income fell to $4,000 to $5,000 a year. The mother reported that Helen preferred to be by herself or with the family, stating that she did not make friends easily. However, she was able to travel by herself on public transportation, frequently going to the movies and on shopping tours.

She was enrolled in the workshop in October of 1962. In 1963 she began receiving Aid to the Disabled (ATD) benefits. In February 1964, she was taken under the WTC program.* In December 1964, the workshop psychologist reported that Helen was a good steady worker, remaining with a task until it was completed. However, her production level was far below industrial standards. She was accurate and capable of some of the more complex work tasks. However, she could not work under pressure, tending to become emotional and to go to pieces under stress. Generally, she functioned well in the workshop setting, but the workshop psychologist predicted that she would always be a worker in a sheltered workshop. In 1965 Helen was thought to have reached her maximum potential

---

* A special assistance program—workshops are paid a fee for services to ATD clients. DVR counselor coordinates program for ATD client.

and was considered rehabilitated at the workshop level. During the first nine months of the fiscal year 1964-1965, Helen earned a little over $500.

In March of 1966, the DVR counselor coordinating the WTC program placed Helen in an industrial laundry in an inspection and shake-out position. On this job she earned $1.49 per hour. Her employer expressed great satisfaction with her work, making the following comments: "She is one of the best girls I have. She is always on time, she keeps going all day long. She is accepted by others, quiet, willing, doesn't wander. When the bell rings, she is working, the others take ten minutes to settle down. If I had more like her, I would need fewer people. She's wonderful."

Helen's story illustrates how a case that appears to need long-term sheltered-workshop employment can graduate to outside employment when the right job is found for her. When placed on the WTC program, Helen received the special attention of a DVR counselor. This led to her job placement in the industrial laundry. It would be unlikely that a case such as Helen's would have received the attention of a DVR counselor through the standard channels, for she scored low on intelligence tests and would undoubtedly have been considered a terminal workshop client on the basis of early psychiatric evaluations.

EVALUATION OF SOCIAL AND VOCATIONAL POTENTIALS

The problem of assessing the social and vocational capabilities and limitations of the less able retarded adult has not received much study. Two substantial Federal research and demonstration projects, the Independent Living Rehabilitation Program (ILRP) in San Francisco,[1] and the Occupational Day Training Center in New York City,[2] explored evaluation of vocational and social aspects of less able retarded adults who had been found not feasible for vocational rehabilitation services, since they could not engage in gainful employment.

One of these programs[3] which explored procedures for meeting the needs of less able retarded adults summarized the evaluation aspects as follows:

The general objective of the program is to develop and

demonstrate a nonresidential community rehabilitation program which would meet the personal, vocational, and social needs of seriously handicapped mentally retarded young adults [who were not feasible for vocational rehabilitation services] so that they might achieve higher levels of self-care, self-support, and independence in daily living. This goal is achieved by evaluating the present strengths and potentials of the clients and providing appropriate training, social services, parent counseling, vocational counseling, and socialization experiences.

Although evaluation of the enrollee is an ongoing concern of the staff, the first eight weeks after admission are an intensive evaluation period. The purpose of this period is to study the new enrollee at work, at play, in social groups, and in individual interviews, to engage participation by the parents or guardians, and to arrive at a staff decision as to whether or not the enrollee would profit from continuing in the program for the stated maximum of two years' attendance.

From the first day, the enrollee is given a daily schedule, which is followed along with all other enrollees, and is assigned to a social worker for case work interviews. During this period the parent or responsible relative is seen regularly by the social worker.

At the end of the eight week initial evaluation period, a staff case review is conducted. At this session, the social worker presents a summary of the history. All staff members who have worked with the enrollee present orally their observations and evaluations as to the strengths and limitations of the enrollee and his family. A staff decision is made as to whether the enrollee should be referred elsewhere or should continue in the program.

To illustrate the social and vocational evaluation of a less able retarded client who was helped in the ILRP, two reports on the client, Mary J., are presented, one by her social worker and one by her work supervisors.

Case of Mary J.*

Mary J., an attractive twenty-four-year-old woman came to our attention when her mother responded to local newspaper publicity describing the program. She had last attended public school classes for the trainable retarded. Her school reports indicated behavior problems manifested by withdrawal and shyness. She seemed awkward in her physical movements and her social approaches. We learned that Mary had a history of behavioral conflicts which appeared to stem from friction within the household. Much of this conflict could be related to the family's inability to understand her. This resulted in inappropriate expectations, disagreement as to standard-setting and poor communication with family.

Her participation during her first year at the program illustrated the withdrawn behavior described by school reports. Further observation illustrated attempts to make friends using childish mechanisms. She seldom spoke to staff but would follow staff about. She had a similar relationship with peers. Her work was slow though accurate. The initial diagnostic impression as reported by the psychologist was "Mental retardation, severe (Stanford-Binet IQ 46); emotional disturbance, severe."

The staff formulated a treatment plan which was directed toward teaching her skills she could use at home, toward helping develop social relationships both with staff and peers and toward helping the family resolve those conflcits which centered around their relationships with her. Work with her involved encouragement to participate, an expression of staff faith that she could participate, as well as a lack of pressure that she do more than follow the minimal rules of the program. Social work with her parents as a family group and then as a part of a larger parent group enabled them to recognize their daughter's strengths and limitations and to place realistic demands on participation at home. As they learned to do this they discovered they felt more comfortable with her, and she found she was able to derive greater satisfaction from family participation.

Her participation in the workshop program and social group work programs started to increase as her parents learned to resolve some of their questions. She became more verbal with staff and peers and began to work more quickly at tasks. As she found she she could participate in activities and could form friendships, the staff approach to her took on a new direction. Staff began to indicate

* Adapted from a case report by Arthur Segal,[4] M.S.W., Field Work Supervisor, School of Social Welfare, University of California, Berkeley; formerly Chief of Social Services, Independent Living Rehabilitation Program.

to her their discomfort with her immature attention-getting devices and indicated some adult methods which might be used. Her response indicated that she too was uncomfortable with her childish relationships with staff and would prefer the more adult kind. Though for eighteen months she did not want to see a social worker, one day she asked for an appointment. The interview and those succeeding it were productively used to help Mary take the next steps. This involved reviewing the process of the two years in the program and planning for entrance into a long-term sheltered workshop.

The move into the long-term workshop was made with relative ease. Another psychological evaluation administered at this time provided a diagnostic impression of "mental retardation, moderate," with a rise in IQ scores of about fifteen points over the earlier score. She continues to improve, and her new work supervisors have reported to our staff that she is a good worker.

*Report on Mary J.**

Like other new enrollees to the program, when Mary J. was admitted, she was assigned a daily schedule including two hours in the workshop, one hour in homemaking activities, one hour in leisure-time activities, one hour in the lounge (a social group work and recreational activity), and one-half hour for lunch, a five and one-half hour day. During the initial eight-week evaluation period in the workshop, she was tried on different contract work, such jobs as packing paint brushes in a carton, inserting leaflets and sealing the envelopes, assembling ball-point pens, and packing leather heeltips in a box. On time-study tests she was able to perform at 50 per cent of the norms for nonhandicapped workers doing this type of work. Her performance was slow, steady, and accurate. Instructions had to be repeated several times before she could follow them correctly, but once she mastered the tasks she was able to do them without supervision. She rarely spoke, and then only when questions were put directly to her. On several occasions to test her ability to function under increased pressure, the work supervisor tried to get her to speed up her work. This resulted in her getting nervous and caused her production rate to drop off.

When this reaction to work pressures was discussed in the staff case review at the end of the initial evaluation period, the social worker felt that her problems might be related to her background of rejection and pressuring by parents and by being threatened by authority figures represented in this situation by the work supervisor,

---

* Adapted by the author from work supervisors' reports.

rather than inability to work more rapidly. It was agreed that for the time being she should be allowed to gain confidence in her ability by being successful at jobs which she could do at her present rate of productivity. It was noted that she had considerable knowledge of homemaking activities, such as housecleaning, bedmaking, cooking, and did not seem to be profiting from further training in these areas.

It was reported that in the leisure-time activities she was more relaxed and was beginning to express herself with the instructor and with other enrollees. The general consensus was that with extended training it might be possible for her to become a client in a long-term workshop.

Therefore her schedule was changed to more adequately prepare her for this goal, by eliminating the homemaking activities and using this time to increase her workshop hours to three hours per day. Because the leisure-time activities were proving so beneficial, these were continued unchanged.

After about fifteen months in the program, she began to indicate to her work supervisor that she preferred working longer hours. Since this would mean that she would have to give up the hour of leisure-time activities, the decision was left up to her. She thought a great deal about this because she enjoyed the leisure-time activities. Finally she decided to work four hours daily, thus cutting out the leisure-time activities. Shortly thereafter, arrangements were made to transfer her to a long-term workshop where she could work an eight-hour day. Prior to her transfer, she was given work assignments more closely approximating those she would be doing in the long-term workshop.

Several points are worth emphasizing. First, the evaluation of this less able retarded adult was conceived as comprehensive, covering areas of personal and social functioning beyond the vocational aspects. Second, it took time to make a thorough evaluation. In her case, even a period of one year was scarcely sufficient to adequately evaluate all her complex personal, social, and vocational needs. Third, an individualized, flexible schedule was established to meet her needs. Fourth, her parents participated actively, with the result that both the staff and parents gained a better understanding of her needs and shared in the development of future plans. Fifth, she actively engaged in participating in decisions affecting herself. For example, she made her own decision about dropping an activity which she enjoyed, in order to work longer hours.

THE ROLE OF WORKSHOPS IN RELATION TO LESS ABLE RETARDED ADULTS

Workshops offer specialized services to handicapped persons, including work evaluation, work adjustment, work training, counseling, work experience, job placement, and follow-up. These workshops are *transitional* or *long-term* depending on the workshop objectives.

Long-term workshops refer to those programs where less able retarded adults who cannot meet the demands of competitive employment can be remuneratively employed indefinitely. In the case of very slow workers this salary may be as low as ten cents per hour, where their rate of productivity is only a small fraction of that of a nonhandicapped worker. In the case of more rapid workers among the less able retarded adult group, the salary might be as high as eighty-five cents per hour or more. Some may be able to work only part time, while others can work a full day of eight hours.

In some of these workshops, recreation, training in grooming, and personal and family counseling are provided to meet client needs (See Table XI). There are many workshops where the only concern is *work*. Recreational and social services are omitted, even though the clients need such services.

Financial assistance by family or social agencies is needed to supplement the less able retarded adult's earnings if he is to survive in the community. If a retarded adult in a long-term workshop proves able to be employed in competitive employment, it is essential that he should not remain in the workshop but should be moved out into a regular job as soon as possible. Indeed, by definition, such a person would be called a more able retarded adult, with all the term implies.

The following brief description of a long-term workshop

TABLE XI
SAMPLE DAILY SCHEDULE IN A LONG-TERM REHABILITATIVE WORKSHOP FOR LESS ABLE RETARDED ADULTS, ILLUSTRATING FLEXIBLE ASSIGNMENTS ACCORDING TO CLIENT NEEDS

NAME	AGE	IQ	9:00-10:00	10:15-11:15	11:15-12:15	12:45-1:45	2:00-3:00	NOTES
Mary R.	27	52	Work	Work		LT	HM	
Rose	31	60	HM	Work		Work	Work	1 hour Warehouse training
Randy	22	67	Work	Work		Work	HM	
Cynthia	37	48	Work	Work		HM	LT	
Bob	26	55	LT	HM		Work	Work	
Jerry	20	53	Work	Work	LOUNGE / LUNCH	Work	Work	2 hours Janitorial training
Tom	39	56	LT	LT		Work	Work	
Harry	33	50	HM	Work		Work	Work	
Marcia	23	42	Work	Work		LT	LT	
Jim	42	48	Work	LT		LT	HM	Emotionally disturbed
Joan	31	58	HM	Work		Work	Work	
Sandy	32	58	Work	Work		Work	Work	1 hour Janitorial training
Perry	23	45	Work	LT		HM	LT	Cerebral palsy No HM
Shirley	18	38	LT	Work		Work	Work	
Jane	26	61	Work	HM		Work	Work	
Mary S.	29	59	HM	Work		Work	Work	Preparing for marriage
John	34	69	HM	HM		LT	HM	
Betty	24	47	Work	Work		Work	Work	
Roy	32	53	LT	LT		Work	HM	
Emily	24	66	Work	Work		Work	Work	Preparing for job training
Tod	28	60	LT	LT		LT	Work	Visually handicapped
Terry	19	52	Work	Work		Work	HM	
Mike	19	47	HM	HM		HM	LT	
Lucy	26	45	Work	Work		Work	Work	1 hour messenger training
Fay	29	56	Work	Work		Work	Work	
Alan	37	39	HM	LT		Work	Work	

All clients were found to be nonfeasible by vocational rehabilitation agency. Clients must be able to work at least two hours daily. All clients together during coffee breaks, lunch, and lounge.

Work—assignment to workshop for contract work.

LT—leisure-time activity—quiet games, crafts, art work, hobbies.

HM—homemaking activity—kitchen, food preparation, household chores, bedmaking.

Lounge—group work, active games, music, dancing, gymnasium, swimming.

Warehouse, janitorial and messenger training for those who show promise of achieving gainful employment.

Those needing personal counseling, training in grooming, independent travel experiences, or special tutoring are scheduled individually or in small groups.

highlights the mingling of work activities and recreational activities.*

In the East Bay Association for Retarded Children (EBARC) Work-Training Center we are serving two purposes: an actual training center to prepare individuals to satisfy employment requirements outside the workshop and a permanent employment center for those not as capable. In doing this we try to provide for these people some degree of economic sufficiency and provide a social outlet which aids them in continuing to be happy, secure people.

Our schedule has changed somewhat over the past few years because enrollees have built up more job endurance and job perseverance, as we have been able to have more work periods and cut down to some extent on the recreation periods. Our schedule consists of a half hour of counting proceeds from sales, checking orders, telephoning to obtain correct time, checking of date. We then have our work period until noon with a midmorning break. After lunch we have some recreation and then continue work again until three o'clock. On Monday, Wednesday, and Friday we have ceramics and on Tuesday and Thursday we have craft work with dancing and singing for recreation . . .

We were cognizant of the fact that for the most part our trainees had never had the opportunity for diversified recreational activities during their formative years. There were many and varied reasons for this, such as social nonacceptance, community unawareness, parent sensitivity, and feeling of inadequacy within themselves. Visualize a severely retarded person attending a public bowling alley for the first time with the frightening thought of actively participating. Compare the same retarded person in the

---

* Personal communication from Mrs. Frances Costa, Director, EBARC Work-Training Center. Although this description is based on reports from the period about 1955-1963, many long-term workshops operate in this manner at present.

same situation participating with a group of his own peers. Makes a difference to all of us—doesn't it? . . .

Every month each person whose birthday falls in that month is feted at one party on a Friday afternoon. This calls for a large cake with everyone's name on it, coke to drink, a present for each one, and dancing if requested. These parties are subsidized by the trainees themselves, each one contributing one dollar a month from the sales of ceramic work . . .

A few years ago it was decided to develop a swimming program. Sororities and clubs pay the cost of the swimming program at the Y.W.C.A. and the Red Cross provides the transportation. We also enlist the help of Red Cross water safety instructors as volunteers. Many of our trainees have moved step by step from the shallow water to the deep water. Their self-confidence has also increased and they go back to work relaxed and ready to work compatibly on the job.

Project work consists of furniture refinishing or woodwork for boys, sewing for girls—rug making and ceramic work for both. Articles are made on order or for sale and proceeds go to enrollees at the end of the month . . . Information regarding the type of work we offer has been sent to a drug firm and we hope to receive work from them . . . Other firms in the vicinity have been approached and have promised us work if it is of a nature that the enrollees can do satisfactorily.

Among the important features in reports from long-term workshops is the evidence that though there may be no dramatic change, there is slow but steady improvement in the general adjustment and productivity of many clients.

Following is a case report of a less able retarded young adult who was admitted to a long-term workshop. He had been previously found ineligible by the State Division of Vocational Rehabilitation.

The Education of a "Non-educable"[5]*

Stephen is twenty years old. Three years ago in 1959 when he reached the age of seventeen, he was discharged from school. Since his IQ is 40 compared to the normal [average] 100, Stephen was thereafter condemned to a life without stimulation, activity, or companionship. He could listen to the radio, watch television or —sit.

His mother learned that the New York City Chapter of the Association for the Help of Retarded Children had opened an Occupation Day Training Center at 222 East 5th Street for severely *retarded young* adults like Stephen. She applied and brought Stephen to the center for a screening interview.

To determine his eligibility, Stephen underwent a series of exhaustive tests by a psychiatric social worker, a psychologist, a medical doctor, the supervisor of training and the instructors. Finally the director of the center conferred with the entire group to discuss and assess the results of the tests.

The battery of tests proved that there was a strong probability that Stephen could benefit from attending the Occupation Day Training Center. This is the sole criterion for admission, provided the center has an opening. Soon Stephen would enter a new world, one that hadn't existed anywhere until the center opened. Living skills are stressed at the center. Young men and women are taught to plan and prepare meals, set the table, and clean up the kitchen. They repeatedly practice lighting a match, turning on the gas stove, using a can opener, pouring milk and hot liquids, cutting and preparing sandwiches, and wrapping them in wax paper. They take turns washing dishes and silverware; scrubbing tables, sinks, and stoves; sweeping floors; emptying garbage; making beds; washing and ironing clothes.

The social worker was aware that it was imperative for Stephen to have this special environment and productive training. Many trainees at the center would have to be placed in institutions if they were unable to attend.

When a retarded adult is discharged from school at the age of seventeen or eighteen, the family faces a crisis. Suddenly the physically mature, mentally retarded child is without service and requires constant care. Dependent on others for his simplest personal

---

* Adapted from a case of the Occupation Day Training Center, New York City Association for the Help of Retarded Children.

needs, a member of the family must stay home and care for him. Most of the trainees, including Stephen, had never been permitted to cross a street alone. Less than one third of the males were able to shave themselves. A survey proved that parents tend to think more of institutionalization as the child grows older.

The Occupation Day Training Center is attempting to reverse the trend, to make it possible for a family to keep a retarded young adult in the community. It serves the severely retarded person who cannot achieve the level of a trainee in a sheltered workshop, nor lead an active social life outside of the shop.

Before being admitted, the trainees at the center were dependent on others for the most essential daily living activities such as travel, grooming, and housekeeping.

Their IQ's average 40 and below.

Three months after his interview, an opening was found, and Stephen waited outside his house for one of the private buses to pick him up and bring him to the Occupation Day Training Center to begin his training.

The first day was confusing. Stephen watched a grooming session where two instructors were teaching several trainees how to shave with electric razors. The new trainee could hardly believe that he too might master this skill some day.

He was included in a group of trainees that prepared lunch, made sandwiches, set the table, cleared it off, then washed and dried the dishes under the supervision of an instructor. During recreation period, another trainee (a young man with mongolism) offered to teach Stephen to play checkers. A move toward friendship with an equal had been made. He watched some of the others play table tennis although he made no attempt to join in the game. Thus ended Stephen's first day.

Team work is emphasized in training. By working in groups, the trainees supply moral support for one another. Together they perform tasks in a short period of time that would appear far too difficult if a single trainee were given more time to do the same job. The construction of equipment, maintenance and renovation of the center, including the interior painting of the entire building, were done by trainees with the active assistance of the staff. By week's end Stephen was participating in all scheduled training sessions.

There is constant activity in every part of every room in the building. While one group may fold, insert, and stamp a mailing piece for a business firm, another paints wall-divider screens in fresh bright colors. The Daughters of Israel Day Nursery has given the center the use of the building, rent free. Once it was drab with dirty walls and floors, and an ill-kept, outmoded kitchen. It had an air of decay characteristic of a building after a long period of disuse.

The Occupation Day Training Center is now a bright cheerful place with freshly varnished floors and immaculate work, dining, and kitchen areas. Grooming tables have been built to teach young men to shave and young women to apply makeup and fix their hair becomingly.

Trainees were often dressed inappropriately for their age. Retardates close to thirty years old were dressed like young teen-agers. Their inappropriate dress and poor grooming attracted public attention. Community reaction was unfavorable and even the professional staff was uncomfortable when appearing in public with some trainees.

Following discussions with parents, grooming lessons and regular fashion shows, dramatic improvement was effected. Most trainees at the center are indistinguishable from their normal neighbors. They are able, inconspicuously, to avail themselves of community resources. Many eat in public restaurants, participate in social and athletic neighborhood activities, enjoy entertainment, and travel independently to and from the center.

The parents can contribute to a trainee's progress in other respects as well as choosing appropriate, becoming clothes. A psychiatric social worker, in addition to obtaining the family history, administers tests to grade adjustment and family cohesion. The scales in conjunction with the family history help to rate the adjustment of the family to the retarded member. Problem areas are uncovered and parents of trainees receive some counseling and guidance both individually and in groups.

REHABILITATION FOR INDEPENDENT LIVING

For years it has been recognized that there are many seriously handicapped mentally retarded adults who are not eligible for vocational rehabilitation services because they cannot hope to achieve a goal of complete self-support. Many of these seriously handicapped persons are confined in state institutions even though with proper training they could live in the community.

In view of the success of vocational rehabilitation services in helping more able retarded adults (mostly in the borderline and mild levels of subaverage general intellectual functioning) engage in gainful employment, proponents of rehabilitation of the more seriously mentally retarded believe that similar success would attend efforts to rehabilitate this group also. In order to be more realistic, however, for these handicapped persons rehabilitation goals should be to live more independently in the community, rather than vocational placement. Accordingly, legislation was proposed in Congress (but did not pass) in 1957, 1959, and 1961 to amend the Federal Vocational Rehabilitation Act of 1954 to provide seriously handicapped adults (including the mentally retarded) with appropriate rehabilitation services which would enable them to "achieve such ability of independent living as to eliminate or substantially reduce the burden of their care."[6] Although the proposed independent living rehabilitation legislation has not as yet been passed by Congress, it is likely that similar proposals will be advanced again and eventually passed.

Case of Sally Y.*

AGE 19   WAIS—Full Scale IQ 57

Socioeconomic status—Guardians (grandparents) owned business, presently retired; own their home, client residing with them.

After the death of this young lady's father, she was placed in a state training school until such time as the mother could make other arrangements. To make this placement, it was necessary to go through the probate court. After two years in the state school, the mother was able, once again, to bring her home and send her to a special class in public school.

This young lady lived with the mother a little over a year; then the mother died very suddenly. The grandparents, who are now over seventy-five years of age, took her to live with them. One year later this young adult was dropped from the school program. Her school report states she was not profiting from the school program; she was showing considerable interest in boys and, due to her childish judgment, she was vulnerable to anyone who would desire to take advantage of her. Her school evaluation recommended she be sent back to the state school.

On the recommendation of a diagnostic and treatment clinic, where she was known for a number of years, she was accepted into Project TRI-US. After six months of training in the program, she was able to ride the city bus into the project from home, and now, six months later, she is still riding the city bus and has given no real problem.

---

* Adapted from a case report provided by Bernice F. Vennert, R.N.

She does childish things periodically, for example, saying something had flown out the window, when actually, she had opened a window and thrown it out.

At this time she is getting along much better with young men and women and is able to do many things which she herself felt were impossible to do. Her guardians are trusting her a great deal more, and she is showing signs of better judgment.

She, too, is working with an instructor on a volunteer basis, making beds at a small hospital, ironing clothing for the children in the hospital. She enjoys cooking, sewing, and working outside; raking up leaves and brush.

She is enjoying the advantages of home life. Recreation is taken care of by the local recreation program, which provides companionship and fun—always under supervision. She realizes the work she is doing is useful and feels she is a contributing member of society.

FEW LONG-TERM WORKSHOPS

Existing long-term workshops barely scratch the surface in terms of the large numbers of less able retarded adults who urgently need such a program. In many communities where there is at present no long-term workshop, or perhaps only one,* there should be three, four, or five, in view of the need (see Table X). Furthermore, all predictions are that this situation is bound to become more aggravated with the advent of automation and the displacement of many handicapped workers now in competitive employment.

Why is it that more long-term workshops have not been established, even though there is a clearly demonstrated need for them? No public agency up to the present will continue indefinitely to pay for the cost of services for less able retarded adults in long-term workshops, and the cost to parents and to private resources is almost prohibitive. Those long-term workshops now in existence are struggling to survive, usually with few or no rehabilitative services.

Is there a solution? It hardly seems possible in this day of expanding services for the disabled that none has as yet been

---

* In 1965 it was estimated that there was a total of about one thousand workshops for the handicapped in the United States, many of which do not accept long-term clients.[7]

152 The Retarded Adult in the Community

found. One proposal would be to reinterpret the Federal vocational rehabilitation law to authorize funds to set up and operate long-term workshops. As the law is written, there is no direct prohibition against using funds for this purpose.[8]

Another proposal would be to more actively involve public agencies in financing part or all of these workshops. For example, many less able retarded adults are public welfare clients under the Aid to the Disabled (ATD) programs. Such clients are eligible for work rehabilitative services to help them become employable so that they need not rely entirely on public assistance or, in some cases, to keep them from deteriorating further. The cost of workshop services for ATD clients could be paid by the county welfare department. Another agency which might contribute support to the long-term workshops is the State Department of Mental Hygiene. It has a stake in insuring that retarded adult patients released from the state institutions are enabled to remain out of the institution. This can best be accomplished through community services such as are available in or through the workshop.

The fact that this problem of establishing and operating large numbers of needed long-term workshops remains unsolved to date points to the necessity for fresh thinking about finding adequate means for their financial support.

QUESTIONS FOR DISCUSSION

1. How do we evaluate the less able mentally retarded adult? Do you see any differences between evaluating the more able and the less able retarded adult?

2. A forty-eight-year-old mentally retarded woman is able to work a six-hour day in a long-term workshop at an hourly wage rate of twenty-five cents. What kind of program is most suited for her capabilities?

3. What benefits would a twenty-five-year-old mentally retarded man who can work most of the day in a long-term workshop gain from attending such a program?

4. How can the vocational rehabilitation counselor make the

best use of the long-term workshop in his community for his mentally retarded clients?

5. What is the significance of independent living rehabilitation services for less able retarded adults?

REFERENCES

1. Katz, Elias: *Independent Living Rehabilitation Program for Seriously Handicapped Mentally Retarded Adults.* (Final report for Vocational Rehabilitation Administration, Project No. RD-905.) San Francisco, Aid Retarded Children, 1965.
2. Tobias, Jack: *Training for Independent Living.* New York, Association for the Help of Retarded Children, 1963.
3. Katz: *op. cit.,* p. 16.
4. Katz: *op. cit.,* pp. 124-125.
5. Association for the Help of Retarded Children: *The Education of a "Non-educable."* New York, Association for the Help of Retarded Children, 1960.
6. U. S. House of Representatives: *H.R. 3756: The Rehabilitation Act of 1961* (not passed). 87th Congress, 1st Session, Feb. 2, 1961. Washington, U. S. Gov. Printing Office, 1961.
7. U. S. Dept. of HEW: Summary of 1965 provisions (of Vocational Rehabilitation Amendments of 1965). *Rehab Rec,* 6:6-14, 1965, p. 11.
8. U. S. Dept. of HEW: *Restoring Disabled People to Jobs and Useful Living.* Committee on Education and Labor, House of Representatives, 89th Congress, 1st Session. Washington, U. S. Gov. Printing Office, October 1965.

Chapter VIII

HOW ARE THE NEEDS OF THE LEAST ABLE RETARDED ADULT MET IN THE COMMUNITY?

T HE LEAST ABLE mentally retarded adults are those who are so severely retarded as not to be capable of engaging in productive work of any kind, or who are capable of doing only the simplest types of work for very short periods of time. They primarily need training in self-care, socialization, and recreational activities under supervision. If they are capable of doing so, they should engage in closely supervised work activities.

CHARACTERISTICS OF THE LEAST ABLE RETARDED ADULT

"The population of this group, like any other group, is composed of individuals who are unique in their differences. Therefore, the characteristics that are given as a general description of the population are rarely all seen in any individual but may appear in an individual singly or in clusters and in varying degrees. The day-to-day behavior of those individuals is 'immature' in that:

"1. Many of them are still occupied with playthings that are appropriate for younger children, such as dolls, toy guns and badges, fire and police caps, and children's coloring books.

"2. Their reactions to being denied their own way or to criticism usually are characteristic of younger children, such as crying, sucking, moodiness, and temper tantrums. They may belittle themselves in front of others or go crying to sympathetic persons with complaints.

"3. The motivation for much of their behavior is to seek attention and self-assurance. They frequently interrupt con-

154

versations of adults and inject irrelevant conversation, usually centered around their own personal needs.

"4. Some are hyperactive, distractible and constantly 'on the go.' Most of their day is spent walking to and fro and moving their hands about; for example, continuously fixing their belts or smoothing their dresses or repeatedly moving their hands from side to side. At this stage it is generally difficult to converse with these individuals for longer than a few minutes. Attempts to do so usually result in their walking away, fidgeting, or turning their heads.

"5. Some are very lethargic and sedentary. They prefer to sit all day (if allowed to do so). Their behavior with others is characterized by silliness, giggling, teasing and badgering, low level and unrelated communication. Some display repetitive finger and hand movements, rocking, teeth grinding, and drooling.

"6. They are deficient in some, if not most, areas of daily living activities (grooming, personal hygiene, communication, traveling) and are dependent upon others for their care and supervision.

"7. Some of them have poor coordination, motor difficulty, and awkward gait. This is readily seen in their posture, when stair climbing and in other activities.

"8. Many of the trainees have additional handicaps or disabilities such as cerebral palsy, epilepsy, cardiac, visual, auditory, or speech handicaps."[1]

LIVING ARRANGEMENTS

Until recent years it was thought that the least able retarded adults as here described would best be cared for in state institutions, or in private programs if the family could afford to pay the cost. Current thinking has shifted in the direction of keeping in the community those who can be cared for outside the institution. Living in the community is a normal way of life, while life in the large state institution for the retarded is likely to be regimented and restricted. In order to operate most efficiently, the large institution must organize, control, and direct the activities of the patients in a carefully scheduled manner.

Discipline must be maintained, and there is little room for individual initiative and freedom of movement. Recent studies of the populations of state institutions for the retarded have indicated that many of the least able patients do not need the institutional services provided. These retardates could be cared for in the community, whether in their own homes, in a twenty-four-hour nursing care facility, or in a family care home or foster home.[2]

Many parents of severely and profoundly retarded children have expressed a strong desire to keep them in the community, close to their homes and families.

The following is an excerpt from testimony before a state legislative inquiry into services for the retarded.[3] The testimony was based on a study of the families of 140 retarded children. Half of the families concerned had children on the waiting list seeking admission to a large state institution for the mentally retarded, and half had placed their children in the same institution during the previous five years. While this study was concerned with the families of retarded children, the same findings would probably be true for the families of retarded adults.

> . . . Of the seventy parents interviewed who had hospitalized their retarded child, fifty-six said they would prefer a community-centered residential facility. Of the other seventy parents interviewed who had their retarded child at home, forty stated that they would like a small twenty-four-hour facility closer to home than the present state hospital. It should be noted that the question was not worded, "Do you favor such and such?", but rather the question was "What additional services would *you* like to have?" The responses were spontaneous, and seemingly this item generated more force than many of the others.
>
> In summary, the need for *community* residential care was the need most frequently mentioned by the 140 parents interviewed . . .
>
> Listen to a few excerpts from the parents' statements:
>
> "It's so far to Porterville* . . . we can't go very often . . . and I feel so guilty . . . sometimes it's so long in between that S. doesn't even recognize me."
>
> "I'll tell you institutions are not the answer—as institutions are

---

* Porterville State Hospital for the mentally retarded, California.

now. If there were more and smaller, it would be different. We want S. to come home—but there's nothing for him here."

"We didn't want S. to go to Porterville, but we couldn't take the expense. We didn't always live this way; before this all happened, we had a good home and five rooms of furniture. Just one year cost us over $5,000; I finally had to take bankruptcy."

"I don't like huge institutions—you just feel you're letting someone else take care of your problems. Better to have smaller community facilities."

"Well, there's no hesitation for me on what I'd like to see— community twenty-four-hour care. We would like to see S. more often. The trip is really hard on us. We're older. Our car is older. There's so much traffic on Highway 99. If it were only forty or fifty miles, we could go for a Sunday or bring him home for a weekend."

I knew very little of the plight of the parents of severely retarded children when I began this study; I inadvertently stumbled on to their overwhelming need for community residential facilities such as your committee is proposing. Perhaps, as one parent expressed, this study will indicate to you in some small way, the desire of many parents for community residential care for the retarded.

With the steady growth of community programs to meet their needs, many of the least able retarded adults are being released from state institutions back into the community. Many others who previously would have had no choice but to be placed in a state institution are now remaining in the community, whether in their own home, in foster homes, boarding homes, or in small residential facilities.

PARENT COUNSELING

"The second need most often stated by the interviewed parents was that of counseling. The occurrence of mental retardation in a family is usually an event in which the parents have had no previous experience in adapting to the problem. The dilemmas produced by the incident do not end, but rather continue throughout the entire life of the retardate and his family members. Counseling only at the time of the diagnosis of the child seems to be insufficient. This was evidenced by the expressed need for counseling services by a significant number of the parents.

"It is believed that with available counseling services some parents would be able to cope with the presence of a retarded child without resorting to placement outside the home. Parents sometimes stated that they just didn't know what to do, so they institutionalized; occasionally they were influenced by neighbors or relatives to do this. Again some statements:

> There was just no one to talk to—we took her to Porterville because we didn't know what to do. In two weeks we brought her home again.
>
> You go down to the probation office . . . just fill out the forms . . . nothing is explained . . . you don't know if you're doing right or wrong. Even another parent would help . . . but they won't give out any names. So you're all alone.
>
> A lot of times I just wish I had someone to talk to . . . It really helps me, but there is no one . . . I'd like to ask about Porterville. Do they ever get to come home again? (Their child is one of those on the current waiting list.)
>
> People talk about you if you keep the child and they say you're sacrificing the other children. And then other people think you're awful if you put the child away, so you just don't know what to do.
>
> There's nothing more hopeless than to have no place to go. We need a place for authoritative advice."[4]

Although many parents of the least able retarded adult would like to keep their children in the community, anxieties are evoked when this is done. For example, fears expressed by parents when their severely retarded children begin to travel independently in the community have been reported by Tobias.[5]

1. Fear of sexual molestation.
2. Getting lost.
3. Physical defects that would be affected by crowds.
4. People would make fun of them.
5. Helplessness in any emergency situation.
6. Inability to learn because of illiteracy, inattentiveness.
7. Precarious health of mother would be affected by this added source of worry.

In some instances, parents may become so deeply disturbed over the *independence strivings* of their children that they are unable to handle the problem and may seek to institutionalize them. It is essential that professional counseling and guidance be available at such times. By providing them with appropriate guidance and necessary financial assistance, parents can be helped to keep their retarded children of all ages in the community. Regional diagnostic and counseling centers for the mentally retarded are being established in some states to provide these services. In such centers the parents (or guardians) are first counseled as to possible available alternatives to state institutionalization. If the parents decide to keep their child in the community, financial assistance is provided to make this possible. Such financial aid to parents is less costly to the state than the cost of institutionalization.

MEETING THEIR NEEDS IN THE HOME

Public Health Nursing Services

The public health nurse, whether assigned through the county or city public health department, or by the private Visiting Nurses Association, can help the least able retarded adult and his family on matters of feeding, dressing, bathing, and toilet training. She can help the family encourage greater independence in the retarded adult. She can make referrals to other available community resources. In many communities, the public health nurse is the one professional person who has initial and ongoing contact with the least able retarded adults because, for the most part, such severely handicapped persons are not likely to be involved in other community programs. The following case illustrates the role of the public health nurse in working with a severely retarded adult and his family.

Case of William P.*

Family
    Father   age: seventy-four
    Mother   age: seventy
    William   age: forty-one
Diagnosis
    Mental Retardation
Case Referred by
    The above family first became known to the agency when

---

* Adapted from a case reported by Mrs. Marie Rexroth, R.N., San Francisco Department of Public Health.

William's mother telephoned the health center asking for a list of foster homes for possible placement of William, age forty-one years. Mrs. P. felt that her age and that of her husband meant that a plan should be made for William in the event of either parent's death.

The public health nurse asked the mother if she could make a home visit to discuss this problem more in detail and the mother consented.

Findings

At the first home visit, mother gave the following background: William, now forty-one years old, attended public school classes for the trainable mentally retarded through the sixth grade. After that point he remained at home, with the mother giving him care. A family physician sees patient when he is physically ill. One older brother is a doctor and one an engineer. The father owns a factory.

William spends his days at home with his mother. He cannot complete dressing himself, cannot tie shoe laces, cannot shave himself. His mother cuts his meat, gives him his tub bath; the patient has no independent living patterns at all.

The mother feels she is aging and that she needed the nurse to help her find a good home for William, when necessary.

The nurse's first job was to attempt an assessment of the situation. There was no medical diagnosis available but, through talking with the mother, she was able to get the pattern of William's daily life. Observing William himself, the nurse felt it quite possible he could do much more than his mother allowed him to. It appeared Mrs. P. had given tender loving care and kept William as her baby, rather than understanding the need to develop his potential. The nurse, as she talked with the mother, became well aware that she would need to help William through the mother, that is, the mother's support and approval of teaching William to care for himself as much as possible. It was agreed among the three that the nurse would visit once a week for an hour and that she would work with William to teach him all the simple daily living activities that he could accomplish himself. These would include self-help in eating, dressing, bathing, going outdoors for a walk, and then on to other more complex activities if possible.

The beginning was made with eating. Using stale bread, William learned to cut with a knife and had a lesson in tying shoelaces the first day. Skill in cutting his food and feeding himself progressed rapidly and at the next visit the patient took his own bath with the nurse and mother at the door—then moved into cleaning his teeth. Within a few weeks William had accomplished the simple skills of eating, bathing, and dressing, but could not master the shoelaces.

At this point he seemed to become less motivated—did not seem to be practicing his skills daily. The mother began to reveal the need for constant reassurance that she was still needed and not becoming an outsider. A family discussion with the nurse produced the offer from the father to make a shoelacing board with nails on it. This was used for daily lacing practice. William now could lace his shoes but could not manage tying the bow, although several tie methods were tried. However, he became fiercely proud of his accomplishments, all of which the parent had been performing for him until the nurse had come into the home.

Next, such hand skills were taught as kneading dough, finger painting. William showed an attitude of revulsion to this, calling it messy and dirty. It was necessary to help him learn the difference between concepts of mess and dirt, and learning activity.

At this time he also learned to shave himself, and began to show pleasure in using his hands. He began to increase his reading. The nurse started William on thinking for himself, what he would like to learn, encouraging him to make choices. Outdoor walking was his selection. At this time the mother became very slow in accepting new areas of activity for the patient and grew increasingly protective. She assured the nurse that William always grew dizzy when walking outdoors alone, but within the week the mother and the nurse observed William walk a full block alone. At first, in street walking he gave attention to his feet, walking in silence and watching his feet constantly. However, several walks and he grew secure enough to participate in conversation with the mother and nurse. At this time there was an encounter with a dog which had to be learned and coped with. And the next point was to get his eyes off his feet so that he could cross a street in safety. Teaching safety points, use of crosswalks, judgment about distance of approaching cars were all mastered by this middle-aged retarded man, for the first time in his life. But still William could not master the shoelaces.

William was showing a great deal of zeal and pleasure in all his activities, and at this time, within nine weeks of the first teaching visit by the nurse, there was a family discussion of how to give William more independence. He was given a house key, money for car fare, and taught how to use a bus. Then he had to learn how to use a public telephone, since bus riding might result in his finding himself far away from home and with a problem! But here the nurse met Mrs. P.'s problem head on, for Mrs. P. had a crying spell and brought a paper to the nurse on which she had written, "Behind every deficient child there is a deficient mother." At this point the nurse was able to persuade the mother to accept the help of a psychiatric social worker in working through her problem of freeing her son for an independent life of his own. Mrs. P. accepted this. On her next home visit, the nurse learned, to her amusement, that William's great pleasure now was taking a walk and telephoning his mother every time he passed a phone booth. The public telephone became a valuable symbol of communication for William! At this time he suddenly accomplished the difficult task of tying his shoelaces. He was very happy at having a key and a purse, used public transportation, but had a great fear of crowds and felt that people stared at him.

Now Mrs. P. developed physical complaints and visited her doctor several times. During her absence from home William went to his father's factory on the bus and learned to put labels on the product. He appeared to want to do more and more things—yet he seemed to lack the ability to think them up and take initiative until a suggestion was made to him. His mother was very pessimistic about his use of public transportation, and she would cooperate only when his activities were *in the home* where she felt he was safe and she was in constant attendance. For him to go outside the home caused her severe anxiety. However, a medical authorization from the family doctor was given for William to travel on the bus lines, and it was necessary for the mother to see more and more of the psychiatric social worker for emotional support.

A month later the mother was hospitalized because her physical complaints had increased and she entered a hospital for a three-day series of tests and examination. A housekeeper was in the home at this time. The nurse decided to work on William's potential for intellectual activity. She discussed this with William, who decided himself to study arithmetic and spelling. He also did crossword puzzles. There were some old school books in the house, and William showed a true earnestness in his desire to learn. At this time the nurse noted that he had a good understanding of the breakdown of money and what it would purchase. He was using shopping lists to do the family shopping, and making progress with addition and subtraction. He talked with his mother on the phone while she was hospitalized, watched television, became an enthusiastic watcher of baseball and other sports, and attempted to help the housekeeper around the house.

The nurse felt the mother's period in the hospital was like a testing period, and when she returned home the mother told the nurse she was quite proud of William. A month later the nurse was visiting only every two weeks for an hour. William was reading aloud to her from a history book, showed good recall, and asked many appropriate questions about what he had read. He was now assuming more and more the responsibility of deciding what he would learn next. At this time the nurse went on a pregnancy leave, and when she brought the new nurse to the home the mother kissed the first nurse when she said goodbye. Nursing visits were reduced to once every two or three months, and William was launched on his new adult life!

Homemaker Services

Some parents and foster parents devote much time to the daily care of their severely retarded least able adult child at home, thus making it difficult for them to do regular household duties needed for home maintenance. Other parents are unable to perform household duties because they are temporarily or chronically physically or emotionally incapacitated. For all such parents, homemaker services are an invaluable assistance.

Homemakers may be privately employed by parents, may be supplied by a public or private agency, or may be volunteers. Homemakers help parents with cooking, cleaning, shopping, and other household chores. They may help the retarded adult to dress, to eat, to toilet, and to bathe. In many situations it is possible that some more able retarded adults and some more capable less able retarded adults could be trained to work as homemakers under supervision.

Baby-sitting

Baby-sitting services on behalf of the least able retarded adult are often needed in the same way as needed by young children, who cannot take care of themselves and need supervision when the parent is away. The retarded adult may be supervised for one or more hours at a time, regularly or intermittently, according to the needs of the family. Sometimes he is brought to the home of the baby-sitter who may supervise one, two, or more children or adults. It is regrettable that for the most part, there is no training for sitters for retarded adults, although encouraging efforts in training volunteer high school and college students to baby-sit with retarded children have been reported in a few communities.

MEETING THEIR NEEDS OUTSIDE THE HOME

Activity Centers (day facilities[6])

Activity centers are community programs where predominantly recreational and socialization activities are provided for least able retarded adults on a regular basis. Many of these activity centers serve persons with severe motor and physical handicaps who are not retarded, but who can also benefit from these experiences. The major emphasis includes music, drama, arts and crafts, dancing, trips, and day camping. The program stresses independence, self-care, motor skills, and improvement in communication skills. Emphasis is on achieving better social relationships with other persons in the program, with others in the home, and others in the community. Wherever possible, appropriate work experience may be provided. In some activity centers, social casework is available for parents and foster parents of the clients.

At the present time there are many activity centers for severely mentally retarded children usually below the age of fourteen years. These are known as *day care centers for the handicapped child*, or *developmental centers for the handicapped child*. They admit children with severe mental retardation who are too handicapped for existing public school classes for the trainable mentally retarded.

In these centers two important trends have been noted. First, the centers are being incorporated into the public school system, just as are day care centers and nursery school programs for normal children. This means general upgrading of staff, program, and facilities in line with professional education standards. Second, many centers have adopted the practice of parent participation. Parents serve as volunteers under staff supervision and attend regular weekly discussion meetings with other parents and the staff. This has provided these parents an opportunity to understand their own child's needs and problems, to carry over the center's training into the home, and to begin planning for the child's future.

As severely handicapped children now attending these activity centers grow older and continue to need an activity center program regardless of age, it is to be hoped that the upper age limit will be extended until there is no longer any age restriction. Following is an outline of socio-recreative activities[7] which can be adapted for activity centers for the least able retarded adult.

Games and sports activities:	bowling, table tennis, skating, billiards.
Outing activities:	picnicking, swimming, hiking, gardening, eating "out," attending a fair or concert, going to zoo.
Performing art activities:	dancing, dramatics, pantomime and puppetry, singing in a church choir.
Fine arts and crafts activities:	painting, drawing, woodwork, photography, handcraft.
Social activities:	visiting friends and relatives, attending parties, having a party at home, square dancing, social dancing.
Educational activities:	grooming, care of clothes, visiting library, visiting museums, reading.
Hobby activities:	collecting, cooking, growing plants, building models, playing games (bingo, checkers).
Spectator sports:	watching television, listening to radio, attending sporting events.*

* Many of these activities are adaptable for severely handicapped home-bound retarded adults and could be supervised by parents, friends, volunteers, or professional workers.

Table XII illustrates the scheduling of one day's activities for adults in a recreation center for the severely handicapped.[8] The program is open to physically and mentally handicapped persons. Efforts are made to set up activities in conjunction with non-handicapped persons.

TABLE XII
SCHEDULE OF ONE DAY'S ACTIVITIES IN A RECREATION
CENTER FOR THE SEVERELY HANDICAPPED*

FRIDAY
All-day program—Adults
Time and place: 10:00 a.m. to 3:30 p.m. Recreation Center
Enrollment: 35
Activities: Arts and crafts, cooking and meal planning, indoor gardening, music appreciation, hobby exploration, social activities, trips and outings
Evening program—Adults
Time and place: 3:30 to 9:30 p.m. Recreation Center
Enrollment: 50
Activities: Club groups, art and theater techniques, basic grammar, spelling, reading, creative writing, literature, cooking and meal planning, music appreciation, trips and outings, and social activities with nonhandicapped groups
* Reprinted with the permission of The Macmillan Company from *Recreation for the Physically Handicapped* by Janet Pomeroy. Copyright© Janet Pomeroy, 1964.

The activity center for the least able mentally retarded adult must be conceived as rehabilitative in its emphasis. No matter how severely handicapped the retarded adult or how slow his progress, he may have some potentials which can be developed through training. It has already been demonstrated that some clients of activity centers eventually develop to the stage where they become clients in a long-term workshop, and a few ultimately may become gainfully employed. In any case, activity centers for the least able retarded adults are an important service if these handicapped persons are to be kept in the community and out of institutions. The least able retarded adults who remain in the community must not be forced to stay at home and to vegetate for want of needed activity centers.

Respite Care

In *respite* care, a temporary foster home or hospital is made available to the least able retarded adult so that the family may obtain relief (respite) from the intensive twenty-four-hour care which may be required. Many parents and foster parents of severely handicapped retarded adults have accepted full responsibility for their care and are prepared to continue to do so. However, owing to emergencies such as family illness, the need to take a vacation, or to other factors beyond their control, they may be unable temporarily to carry on these duties, and must find some way to handle the situation. Such emergencies often result in the retarded adult's being housed in unsuitable temporary placements. In some instances it is necessary to resort to commitment to a state institution, although this is not the intention of the parents. Where respite care is available as a community service, it has been found that acute temporary emergencies can be relieved, and after the emergency has resolved itself, the situation can return to its previous basis.

QUESTIONS FOR DISCUSSION

1. A thirty-two-year-old man with Down's syndrome can work steadily at a simple packaging job for about an hour daily. The rest of the time he can keep busy only with play activities. What type of program should be provided for him, and where?

2. A twenty-one-year-old severely retarded man with an IQ of 30 has been able until now to play in a sandbox and to

do a little finger painting at home. He is being admitted to an activity center, and a recreational program is being planned for him. What should it consist of?

3. The mother of a twenty-five-year-old severely retarded woman needs to visit her husband who is hospitalized, and seeks a baby-sitter to look after her daughter for an hour or two each day during the next week. How should she go about obtaining the services of such a person?

4. A public health nurse visits a family whose severely retarded forty-five-year-old son lives with them. He needs help with toileting and dressing. How can she help him and his family?

5. A thirty-three-year-old severely retarded woman lives in the home of her older married sister, whose husband was seriously injured in an accident in a distant city. Her sister must leave immediately and plans to stay with her husband for the next few weeks. What arrangements can be made to deal with this emergency?

REFERENCES

1. Parents and Friends of the Mentally Retarded of Bridgeport: *A Project to Demonstrate New Directions in Community Programming for the Severely Retarded Adult.* Bridgeport, Conn., Parents and Friends of the Mentally Retarded of Bridgeport, 1963, p. 5.
2. State of California, Assembly Ways and Means Committee. Subcommittee on Mental Health Services: *A Re-definition of State Responsibility for California's Mentally Retarded.* Sacramento, Office of State Printing, 1965, pp. 48-50.
3. *Ibid.*, pp. 21-24. (Testimony by Dr. Carolyn Fowle.)
4. *Ibid.*, p. 23.
5. Tobias, Jack: *Training for Independent Living.* New York, Association for the Help of Retarded Children, 1963, p. 37.
6. U. S. Dept. of HEW: *Planning of Facilities for the Mentally Retarded.* Washington, U. S. Gov. Printing Office, November 1964, p. 9.
7. Avedon, Elliott M., and Arje, Frances B.: *Socio-recreative Programming for the Retarded.* New York, Bureau of Publications, Teachers College, Columbia, 1964, pp. 30-31.
8. Pomeroy, Janet: *Recreation for the Physically Handicapped.* New York, Macmillan, 1964, pp. 77-78.

Chapter IX

WHAT COUNSELING IS AVAILABLE TO PARENTS OF THE RETARDED ADULT IN THE COMMUNITY?

W HY IS THERE almost no information available on the subject of counseling parents of retarded adults? A striking evidence of this hiatus in published reports is the virtual absence of references to counseling parents of retarded adults in a recent review of the literature[1] and a recent extensive annotated bibliography on the subject.[2] Perhaps the answer lies in this being a child-centered society, and as a consequence, much more attention, sympathy, and help is given to the handicapped child and his parents than to the retarded adult and his family. For example, note the names of familiar agencies, Crippled *Children* Services, National Association for Retarded *Children,* Exceptional *Children's* Foundation. Does this mean that the problems which concern parents of the retarded disappear after childhood has ended? What about the problems which face the parents whose retarded children continue to live with them when they have become adults?

The problems faced by parents who become aware that their newborn or young child is mentally retarded have been described in many publications.[3] Initial questions—Is my child really retarded? Why did *we* have a retarded child? Whose fault is it? What can we do about it?—may or may not have been adequately answered. Even when the retarded person is an adult, parents may still be seeking answers to these questions.

PROBLEMS FACING THE PARENTS

When the retarded person leaves school, thereby supposedly

assuming an adult status, a new set of problems in addition to old ones may arise to disturb his parents. Following are some questions which have come up in counseling parents of retarded adults which are not likely to arise when the retardate is a child.

What happens to our adult retarded daughter when we are gone?

Our oldest son, who is twenty-two years old, has Down's syndrome. He rarely leaves the house. Our daughter who is now twelve years old finds that he interferes and wants to play with her friends when she brings them home. She cries and says that he embarrasses her so much that she will not bring them into the house again. How should we handle this problem?

Our son was OK when he was going to school. Now that he is graduated he stays at home all day, watching television or puttering around the house. Is there some way he can get a job and earn a living? Where can he go for recreation?

My retarded daughter, who is not married, has become pregnant. Should she be sterilized to prevent future pregnancies?

We have a retarded son married to a retarded girl. What program can help them make a better marital adjustment?

Should our severely retarded son who is now twenty-three years old be placed in the state institution?

Our son is out of school and has begun to hang around street corners with a group of young hoodlums who get him into trouble. What can we do to keep him away from this gang?

My son is very strong. When he has temper tantrums, I am afraid that he will do us physical harm. Where can we take him to get help?

Over the years many parents have received little or no help in dealing with the problems associated with their retarded child, and have come to think that no help is available for them. In those families where the siblings have grown up and left the home and the parents are left with the retarded adult child, family stability is often achieved and the status quo accepted. This state of balance in family relationships may persist for an extended period of time, as was noted in the case of William P. in Chapter VIII. When a crisis arises, the precarious balance of forces within the family may be thrown off, as when the retarded adult discovers that he is capable of being more independent, or when the parents find themselves physically or emotionally unable to continue to care for their child. It is at such points in the retardate's life that many parents need counseling (see Table XIII).

TABLE XIII

SOME NEEDS OF PARENTS OF RETARDED ADULTS WHICH
MAY BE MET BY COUNSELING

CATEGORY	GENERAL	SPECIFIC
Informational	To learn about community resources	Medical, recreation, vocational, educational, counseling
	To learn current scientific knowledge about mental retardation	Prevention, care, treatment, training
	To learn how best to care for the retarded adult in the home	Personal care, special training, work in the home, play, reading, intellectual stimulation, social activities, creative activities
Developing insights	To develop positive feelings about themselves as parents	Worth, self-confidence, elimination of guilt
	To develop awareness and acceptance of retarded adult	Independence strivings, sexual urges, limitations and capabilities
	To develop ability to understand and express own feelings associated with retarded adult	Grief, hostility, guilt, disappointment
Relieving anxiety	To gain reassurance about safety and health of retarded adult when not under parental supervision	Travel away from home, attending activity center or workshop, being left alone at home
	To be relieved of anxiety about the future of retarded adult after parents die or are disabled	Guardianship, foster care, institutionalization
	To meet with parents having similar problems	Parent organizations, classes
Developing positive attitudes in others	To encourage acceptance of retarded in family	Siblings, relatives, friends
	To encourage acceptance of retarded in community	Neighbors, shopkeepers, recreation and parks, movies

In helping parents who seek guidance in dealing with their retarded adult child, several considerations must be kept in mind.

The counselor must be aware of his own attitudes and biases towards the retarded person, and towards the retardate's parents. If the counselor or therapist entertains negative attitudes, this will inevitably adversely affect his work with such clients. There are many counselors and therapists who do not accept the retarded and their families as clients because of their negative viewpoint on therapy of the retarded. To overcome these negative attitudes in the professional counselor may require special training. Many professionals providing services for the retarded and their families have noted that they themselves had to work through their own disturbed feelings about retarded persons.

For example, in discussing the role of the nurse as a therapist in helping retarded individuals and their families, a nursing educator[4] has made this point: ". . . The nurse . . . must first face her own feelings about mental retardation. We have assimilated all too well the great value our culture places on brightness and high intellectual achievement. A proud mother often begins to describe her child by describing how bright he is. As nurses we have been action-oriented and trained toward cure. We also value physical beauty and attractiveness. So when we start working with individuals who are retarded and who often have other physical handicaps, it takes most of us a while to be of help to the child or adult behind the mask of mental retardation."

The relationship which is developed between the parents who are being counseled and the counselor should be one of mutual understanding and respect as to what each can contribute to help the retarded adult. It is true that in many instances the parents themselves may urgently need help in their own interpersonal relationships, or one or the other parent may be so emotionally disturbed as to require therapy. This should not divert the parents from the major goal in their counseling, which is to help them deal with the problems surrounding their retarded adult child. The counselor should provide the parents with a neutral and secure setting which makes it possible for them to express their feelings, including hostility and aggression, about their child and to reveal their disappointment and guilt feelings. As a result of understanding their own feelings, parents may be able to mobilize their efforts in a more constructive approach to their child's problems.

Those who counsel parents of the retarded adult should be aware of community resources and avenues of referral. Frequently parents arrive for counseling in a disturbed state with little awareness that other alternatives for action exist. They seek specific answers to pressing questions. In such instances the counselor's knowledge of what is available or not available may be reassuring and strengthening to the parents and may help in guiding them to the most acceptable solution.

Before proceeding with a few cases to illustrate the above ideas, two points must be made. First, the term *parents* has been used to refer to parents who seek help in dealing with the problems of their retarded adult child. It should be noted that in the present context, *parents* refers not only to the retardate's natural parents, but also to those persons in whose home the retarded person lives and who serve in place of parents. These may be older siblings, relatives, foster parents, or guardians when the natural parents are not in the picture. Although many retarded adults in the community do not live with their own parents, in the sense that the term is used here, they do have *parent figures* just the same.

Second, in many cases it is the family as a whole which is the client. Siblings of the retarded adult, and relatives living in the home may be as influential as the parents themselves on the retarded adult. To work only with the parents may therefore not resolve the problems. It is necessary to work with the family as a whole.[5] Wherever possible, family therapy should incorporate the retarded person himself as an integral part of the counseling process.

Institutional Placement

Case of Stanley J.

> *Should our son be institutionalized now? . . . If he is not to go to an institution, how can we keep him busy and happy?*

Mr. and Mrs. J. came to a family service agency for help in placing their retarded son, Stanley, in a state institution. Mrs. J.

had recently had a stroke from which she had recovered, with a mild residual left hemiplegia. She was fearful that she would not be able to continue to care for her son. Stanley was a moderately retarded twenty-eight-year-old man who had never been employed and had never been evaluated by the Vocational Rehabilitation Agency. Two older sisters and a younger brother were married and out of the home. Stanley had IQ scores in the 50's and had attended classes for the educable mentally retarded. In addition he had a severe case of astigmatism, requiring heavy corrective lenses, which had made him an obvious target of ridicule by his schoolmates. Mr. and Mrs. J. were also concerned because he did not want to leave home to enter an institution.

During the first interview the social worker learned that there was a long-standing conflict between the parents which had existed even before they had any children. Mr. J. had married after completing two years of college and was deeply resentful of his wife, who had discouraged him from further education. She had come from a poor socioeconomic background and did not believe that he needed better education to make a living for his family. All these years he had been employed in a large department store as a shoe salesman. The conflict between husband and wife had flared up on many occasions over the years. There were sharp differences about how to plan for Stanley's future, now that Mrs. J. was afraid that she could not care for him. Mr. J. felt that Stanley should be kept at home and be allowed to live whatever kind of existence he wished just as long as he did not hurt anyone. Mrs. J. felt that he should be placed in a state institution since, as she stated, "He will have to go there anyway when I can't take care of him." Over a period of time, Mr. J. gradually gave in to his wife, and it was at this point that they came to the agency for help in placing Stanley.

After the first session the social worker decided that to attempt to resolve the long-standing conflict between husband and wife would require treatment over a period of many months, perhaps years. During this time Stanley's problem would not be solved. Accordingly, whenever they brought up their personal conflicts, she helped them to concentrate on his problems.

Over a period of five weeks, the parents met weekly with the social worker. They learned that there were such resources as the vocational rehabilitation office to which Stanley could be referred for evaluation and possible training. There were some recreation programs for handicapped persons, but he would have to travel to the recreation center because there was no transportation provided. They found out about a parent organization for the mentally retarded. They learned that Stanley's ideas about what he would like to do should be considered since his future was involved. This prompted them to inquire whether he could be included in the counseling sessions.

During the next few weeks Stanley attended the counseling sessions with his parents. During this time he was interviewed by a vocational rehabilitation counselor who thought he might be placed in a long-term workshop, since he did not appear to be feasible for training for a full-time regular job. There was no immediate opening so he was placed on their waiting list.

As the family group met, changes in the parents' attitudes could be seen. They told the social worker that Stanley got a lot out of the counseling sessions. He was looking forward to starting in the long-term workshop. They observed that he enjoyed attending the recreation program and seemed interested in learning how to go there by himself, even though he had never before traveled alone. They had gone to a meeting of the parent association for the retarded, and had begun to realize that there were other parents who had equally serious problems in planning for their children. At one of the counseling sessions, Stanley began to talk about his fears about being "put away" in a state institution. He also was making clear how much he would rather remain at home. By the end of five months of counseling, after Stanley had proved he could do many things for himself, including traveling around the city, Mrs. J. admitted that he did not need as much care as she had previously thought. Once this conclusion was verbalized, she was ready to keep him at home. Mr. J. was relieved because he had always been reluctant to send his son to an institution against his will. The parents told the social worker they had been helped so much that they would like to think about going on with trying to work out their own problems with the worker's help.

Siblings of Retarded Adults

Case of Martin F.

Our oldest son has Down's syndrome. Our daughter is now dating, but she is ashamed to bring her boy friend into the home. What can we do about this situation?

The F.'s live in a comfortable home in a middle-class community in the suburbs of a midwestern city. In addition to the parents there are two children, Martin, a severely retarded (IQ about 30) man of twenty-two years with Down's syndrome, an odd-shaped head, and almost incomprehensible speech and Greta, a pretty seventeen-year-old girl, who is a senior in high school.

When Martin was young, the family lived in a small town in a rural area where there were no classes for trainable mentally retarded children. He was never a management problem. He played by himself in the back yard. His sister played with him before she started going to school, but after entering school she stopped doing so. She was not openly hostile to him, but she began to go to other children's homes to play and did not invite them to her home. Her parents continually urged her to play with her brother, but she found every excuse to avoid this.

When Martin was twelve, the family moved to their present home. The main reason for making this move was that the public schools in this community had classes for trainable mentally retarded children. Outside school, the pattern continued. His sister played with other children away from home, while he continued to play alone or with his dog in the back yard. Martin attended the class for trainable mentally retarded children. He made slow progress because of the long delay in getting him into a school and his lack of social development. At school he was a "loner," preferring to do most things by himself. One of the few activities he enjoyed doing with others was folk dancing, in which he managed quite well. He left school at eighteen. From then on he remained at home, doing little except watch television, clean his room, sweep the floors, and help his mother do household chores.

When Greta began to date, the parents noticed that she never brought any of her boy friends home. She would meet her boy friends outside but would not invite them in. At first her parents were not concerned, since she had never previously brought friends home. One day her mother asked her about this and was astounded at the reaction. Her daughter said that she was ashamed to have a defective brother. She did not want to bring her boy friends home, since she was sure she would lose them if they saw her brother. She also blurted out that she was afraid to get married because she was sure she would have a defective child like her brother. When her mother tried to reason with her, she was met with an outbrust of tears, followed by the girl's running off to her own room and locking the door.

When Mr. F. came home that evening, his wife told him about their daughter's reaction. They began to be aware that this was a serious problem of long duration to which they had shut their eyes. They tried talking with their daughter but could get nowhere because she was too emotional about the situation. That night Mr.

and Mrs. F. phoned their family doctor, who referred them to a psychiatrist.

They were seen by the psychiatrist two days later. At the first session they explained that they were deeply concerned about their daughter. They had always thought their retarded son got along well with his sister and they could not understand why she was "suddenly" so disturbed about his presence in the home. The psychiatrist indicated that this was not a simple problem and would require the participation of both the parents and their daughter. He told them that he had had some experience with similar cases and had seen some of the problems resolved. He asked them to bring their daughter with them for the next session.

The first few sessions revealed that Greta had never brought her friends home because she was ashamed of Martin. When she was younger, she had tried to explain this to her parents, but they had scolded her for not being kind to him. Over the years she had gotten the feeling that her parents favored her brother, although she was always told by them that both children were equally loved.

During the next few sessions, the parents came to realize that their own attitudes of excessive overprotectiveness towards their defective son had indeed colored their handling of their daughter. They had thought that their deep concern for his condition would be equally accepted by her, without realizing that she had interpreted this as favoritism toward him. She would rather have treated him as a playmate and a family member than as one set apart for special considerations. They began to realize that their own need to keep him infantile and dependent had caused a wide gap between their son and his sister. The basis for their own feelings towards Martin slowly emerged as they reviewed the period immediately after his birth when they first learned that he would always be mentally retarded. It was at that time that they had seriously considered placing him in a state institution. Their deep hurt and disappointment and their strong feelings of guilt over having a desire to get rid of their own child were discussed openly for the first time. Gradually they understood that it was these very feelings which had caused them to become oversolicitous of their son as a way of "atoning for the sin" of wishing to rid themselves of him.

Greta attended these sessions and soon began to understand that her own rejection of her brother was largely caused by her parents' early overindulgence of him. She realized that their overindulgence was related to their guilt feelings rather than to favoritism. She openly expressed some of her resentment towards Martin which she had always before repressed. The psychiatrist helped her see that her feelings about having a defective brother were not shared by many other people.

After a few sessions she began to arrange for some of her girl friends to come to her home. She discovered to her surprise that the psychiatrist was right—her friends did not seem disturbed by her brother's presence and her brother paid little attention to the company in the house.

Vocational Preparation

Case of Howard Z.

Our son likes to work around the house. Why shouldn't he be able to get a real job and make a living for himself? Can you tell me where I can get a job for him?

A report of a program especially developed to help moderately and severely retarded adults make a better community and vocational adjustment was printed in a local newspaper.

Mrs. Z., the mother of a moderately retarded adult, wrote a letter to the program director, Mr. P., asking for further information and help. She wrote that her retarded son, Howard, had been turned down by vocational rehabilitation, but she believed that the program as described in the newspaper would help her son develop so that he could get a job. She wrote, ". . . . it is regrettable that when these retarded children grow up and are adults, the community forgets that they still need help and training in order to get jobs."

Mr. P. contacted her and invited her to visit the program. She came with her husband and her son. Her husband was a mild-mannered man who agreed completely with everything his wife said and did. Her son was a tall, heavy-set, slow-moving man of thirty, who walked with a slight limp. His speech was hard to understand. He presented a neat appearance. Occasionally he giggled without any good reason. After her visit she told Mr. P. that she was much impressed with what she had seen, but she did not understand exactly what he was trying to do. Mr. P. gave her a pamphlet containing the following statement of the program's goals: ". . . Although most of the persons accepted for the program have been given up as hopelessly dependent upon others, the program is built around making them independent through performing relatively simple work tasks—sorting labels, folding notices, newsletters, and so on. These people usually have many social disabilities. It is not enough to train them to work and earn part or all of their support. They also, in many cases, need to learn how to cook, keep house, care for their clothing. They need to learn how to use their leisure time—in crafts, hobbies, and games—in a pleasurable way.

They need to learn how to meet and talk with others—to make friends."

After reading the pamphlet, she thanked Mr. P. and said that she felt that a vocational training program would be better suited to meet her son's needs. "Our son likes to work around the house. Why shouldn't he be able to get a real job and make a living for himself? Can you tell me where I can get a job for him?"

Mr. P. felt that Mrs. Z. was very unrealistic in her expectations about a regular job for Howard. From his brief observation of the family, coupled with the information that her son had already been found not feasible for vocational rehabilitation services, he thought that her son could profit from admission to his program. However, since Mrs. Z. did not wish to send him to this program and since she had asked Mr. P. for suggestions, he recommended that she go to the university's counseling center, which might help her work out a better solution for her son.

Mrs. Z. had never been to a counseling center, other than the Vocational Rehabilitation Agency. A counseling psychologist, after reviewing previous school and vocational rehabilitation records, which she had authorized him to request, also felt that Mrs. Z. had overestimated the vocational potentials of her son. He arranged for a series of interviews during which she could discuss with him in detail the different activities in which her son engaged, and her interpretation of these activities. He tried to help her see that there was a considerable difference between puttering around the house and earning a living by working full time on a job. When she spoke about her son's being able to sweep the floor at home, he pointed out that this was very different from meeting the demands of even the least competitive job in the janitorial trades. From her description it was apparent that her son had some good work habits, for example, doing his chores every day without being told to do so. This was a training potential which could be cultivated in the proper program.

After eight sessions, Mrs. Z. expressed the idea that perhaps Howard could benefit from Mr. P.'s program. She wondered whether this experience could be the stepping-stone to a full-time job. The psychologist said he did not believe that her son was likely to get a regular job. However, if he were admitted to that program, their staff would be able to evaluate not only his vocational potentials but also other aspects such as his socialization needs. She then mentioned that when she had observed Mr. P.'s program, she had felt that it was not the right place for her son. Now that she had had a chance to think about it and to discuss it with the psychologist, she thought she might have been mistaken. She wondered whether she had lost all chance of getting her son into the program because of her previous negative attitude. The psychologist suggested that if she really believed the program would help her son, she should apply again.

The next time they met, she told the psychologist that her son had been placed on the waiting list for Mr. P.'s program and that he would be admitted in about four months, when the next vacancy would occur.

Marriage of Retarded Adults

Case of Randy W. and Loretta S.

Should two mentally retarded young adults be allowed to get married? Could they take care of themselves? Do they know the real meaning of love? Will they have mentally retarded children?

The W. family lived in a pleasant suburb near a large city. Mr. W. commuted daily to the city where he operated a small business in wholesale automobile parts. Mrs. W. was a housewife, who had completed one year of college. Randy, the youngest of three sons, was mentally retarded, his IQ scores when he was in school averaging in the middle 60's. He had attended public school classes for educable mentally retarded children.

The three boys had worked in their father's business during summer vacations. Randy had learned to do some of the stock work, with much help from his brothers. While his older brothers went on to college, jobs, marriage, and family life, he continued working in his father's business. He knew the stock in this particular line, but it would have been very hard for him to handle a job as a stock boy in another business.

When he was twenty-three years old, he met Loretta S., a young retarded woman of twenty-two, who had been his classmate in classes for the retarded when they were in elementary school. He had not seen her for several years, since they had attended different high schools. After graduating from school, she had gotten a job as an assistant file clerk in a small office. She did not get along well with the other file clerks and was not happy on her job.

Randy and Loretta enjoyed one another's company. Initially there was some opposition from both sets of parents to the idea of the two seeing so much of each other, since the couple was considered too immature. However, the parents did not forbid them from dating occasionally. In a few months Randy asked Loretta to marry him. When Loretta told her mother about his proposing marriage, her mother became very concerned and contacted Randy's mother. Mrs. W. was upset, since she had not thought the affair would move so rapidly. Both mothers were concerned over whether Loretta was pregnant.

That evening the parents and Randy and Loretta got together for the first time to discuss the situation. The parents made it clear that they were opposed to the marriage. They demanded to know whether Loretta was pregnant. When Mrs. W. and Loretta's mother saw how upset the young people were and how sincere their affection was for each other, they suggested that they all talk with the W. family's minister and get his advice.

The next evening they met with the minister and presented him with the problems: Should Randy and Loretta be allowed to get married? Could they take care of themselves adequately? Did they know the real meaning of love? Would they have mentally retarded children? The minister was not prepared to give them answers to their questions. He had been in the community for the past fifteen years and knew that Randy and Loretta were retarded. Randy had attended church regularly and had not gotten into any trouble. The minister had not considered him to be a problem. After some discussion the minister said that he could counsel with them about some of these questions but that others, such as the probability of the couple's having retarded children, were beyond his present knowledge. In the more relaxed atmosphere of his study, Randy and Loretta did say that they had not had sexual relations and that she was not pregnant. Once this question had been answered, the parents were noticeably relieved. The minister said he wanted to meet separately with the couple and then he would like to meet with the parents again.

The following week the minister met for a lengthy session with the couple. They told him that they were in love with each other and they wanted to get married, to have their own home, and to raise a family. They felt their parents did not treat them like grownups, and they were resentful about this. The minister pointed out that it was natural for young people to be attracted to each other, but that their parents were concerned because of the realities of the situation, such as whether Randy would be able to earn enough to support a family and whether Loretta would be able to care for a family. He tried to show them that she had some problems in dealing with other persons and this might have been an indication to her parents that she could have problems in raising a family. Neither she nor Randy was convinced about this.

He urged them to postpone plans to get married for a few months while they worked out these questions with their parents. Meantime he phoned a physician for information about the inheritance of mental retardation. The physician did not know much about the subject and referred him to a pediatrician who was chairman of a committee on mental retardation in the local medical society. This doctor told him that there was not much known about the transmission of mental retardation on a hereditary basis. Since both were mentally retarded, there probably was a greater risk of their having a retarded child. He felt that under the circumstances he would recommend that they not have children. He also pointed out that in this state there was no legal way for the girl or the man to be sterilized simply because they were mentally retarded.

With this information, and after his meeting with the couple, the minister arranged several counseling sessions with the parents and the couple. Now when the parents raised questions, he was better prepared to answer. He explained what he had learned from the doctors about the lack of real knowledge as to the inheritance of retardation, especially in people like Randy and Loretta. The decision about marriage would have to be made by the couple and their parents. In pursuing the discussion of the economics of the future, he asked for more details about their income and expenses. Randy and Loretta indicated what their total income was. It turned out that this would be less than the cost of running their own home. After discussing this, the parents agreed that if Randy and Loretta decided to marry despite these problems, they would supplement their income so as to make it possible for them to have an apartment of their own.

Later on, the question came up about raising a family. The couple had done some thinking about this and now they "were afraid" that the raising of a family would be too hard for them. The minister said that if they should decide to marry and did not want children, they should see Loretta's physician who would explain how she could avoid pregnancy. However, he did not think they should approach the doctor until after they had made a decision to marry.

A few days before the wedding, Loretta went to see her doctor, who fitted her with an intrauterine device. The minister officiated at the wedding in the church, just as he had when Randy's two brothers were married before him.

The Emotionally Disturbed Retarded Adult

Case of Thomas R.

When Thomas was eighteen months old, his parents had no

inkling that he was mentally retarded. There had been no special problems during pregnancy and the delivery had been normal. He was showered with love and attention by both his father and mother. By the end of his first year, he was slightly delayed in development. At fifteen months he was not walking or saying even the easiest words, Mamma or Daddy. He was taken to the doctor, but his parents were told not to worry, as he probably was a slow developer. Mrs. R. became pregnant with her second child. Thomas' brother was born when Thomas was about two years of age. From the time the new baby was born, she shifted her attention to him.

When Thomas was two and one-half years of age, it was more obvious that he was slow in many respects. He had just begun to walk and say a few words. When the doctor was questioned, he reluctantly reported to the parents that he might be mentally retarded and would bear watching. From this point on, his mother's attitude rapidly changed. Because of her disappointment in Thomas, she lavished even more attention on his brother, who was a bright, lovable baby. The only way Thomas could get his mother to give him attention was to yell and bang his head on the floor. Whenever he did this, she left the baby and went to him.

During this period Thomas' father, who had been a light drinker became a heavy drinker. When he was sober he played with Thomas and gave him much love. When he was drunk, he neglected him. During the next few years he came home less and less. When Thomas was seven years old, the father deserted. The family was able to manage adequately financially because Mrs. R. had an independent income.

After her husband left, Mrs. R. turned more and more to her younger son for consolation. Thomas felt left out. He missed his father, who had paid attention to him. Although he played with his brother, he showed his hostility by hurting him or breaking his toys. He did not play with other children.

When he was five years old, his mother placed him in kindergarten. After a few days the teacher told the principal that he was not ready for school, owing to his temper tantrums and his problems with the other children. He was referred to the school psychologist, who tested him and interviewed his mother. He was found to have an IQ of 68, moderate mental retardation. After learning about her many problems and difficulties in handling Thomas, the psychologist recommended that both Thomas and his mother get psychiatric treatment immediately. The principal told Mrs. R. that Thomas would be admitted to a class for educable mentally retarded children when he became eight years of age, since that was the age when such retarded children were admitted to school in that district. He would also have to be able to get along with the other children.

Mrs. R. was very angry with the school people for thinking that her son was mentally retarded, and that she and her son needed psychiatric treatment. She refused to consider treatment, since she said she did not need it. She then decided to enroll him in a private school. At the end of three weeks the school's director informed her that Thomas' problems were emotional disturbance and mental retardation and he could not be kept because he did not belong in his school.

During the next few years she made several attempts to place him in different schools. At one time she tried to enter him in a military academy. After several weeks, the headmaster demanded that he be withdrawn because of his temper, his constant fights with classmates, his defiance in taking orders, and his inability to do the regular school work. Other attempts met similar failure.

When Thomas was eleven years old, his mother finally entered him in a public school class for educable mentally retarded children. He was unpopular with his classmates because of his fighting and constant demands for attention. Several times he was almost expelled but was kept in school only because his mother wept and pleaded with the principal to give him another chance. At home he was very jealous of his brother, who was a bright student. His mother insisted that he study in order to be like his smart brother. Thomas did everything he could to annoy his brother, such as tearing up his papers, a sure way of getting his mother's attention.

In high school he developed into a physically well-built, tall, good-looking youth. He had a temper which would erupt at little provocation. When he was sixteen years old, after being punished for infraction of school rules, he went on a rampage and broke much of the school's science equipment. He was expelled, and his mother's pleading could not get him reinstated. During the next few years he wandered around the neighborhood, getting into minor difficulties from which his mother managed to extricate him.

On the night his brother was graduated from high school with honors, he slashed the tires of his brother's car and broke three windows in a neighbor's home. He was picked up by the county police, who already knew his reputation.

He was assigned to a probation officer, who made a thorough study of the whole situation. He recommended to the court that

Thomas be placed on three years' probation on condition that both he and his mother receive psychiatric treatment. He emphasized that unless Thomas' mother also received therapy, Thomas should be placed in a state correctional facility. The probation officer's report was approved by the judge.

Mrs. R. was stunned by the judge's decision. She said she could not understand why she needed therapy, since it was her son who was in trouble. She was willing, however, to do anything to keep him out of jail.

It was arranged that Mrs. R. and Thomas should be treated by different therapists in the nearby community mental health center. Periodic reports were to be submitted to the probation officer.

The major approach of Mrs. R.'s psychiatrist was to help her realize how much of Thomas' difficulties stemmed from her rejection of him and from her unrealistic expectations. He retraced with her, step by step, her early feelings towards Thomas. They discussed the changes in her attitude after her second child was born and after she was told that Thomas was mentally retarded. She had not accepted this diagnosis, and had believed that he would grow out of it. She was always urging him to be like his brighter younger brother and thought he could be if he tried hard enough. She admitted that she often scolded Thomas in front of his brother and strangers. She also talked about her husband's failure as a husband and how much Thomas missed his father. She recalled how Thomas demanded her attention, which she had not always given him.

As they continued their sessions, she was able to see more clearly that Thomas' behavior was an expression of his feelings of resentment and hostility towards her because of her rejection of him and because of his inadequacy in living up to her expectations. As a child he had developed temper tantrums and destructive actions as his way of getting his mother's attention. Since he had found that this method worked, he had continued using it even though it often had bad results for him. Mrs. R. admitted that she lived in fear that he might cause physical harm to his brother or to her in one of his fits of temper.

In the process of working through some of these complex feelings, she gradually came to the conclusion that Thomas' brother might be happier in a college away from the disturbances at home. There he would lead a more normal life, and she would not have to worry about Thomas harming his brother in a jealous rage.

She decided that she must give undivided attention to Thomas and try to help him create a future for himself.

QUESTIONS FOR DISCUSSION

1. What are some of the difficulties which an adult retardate might cause his parents, which are not likely to be present when he is a child? How should they deal with these problems?

2. The parents of a severely retarded adult man with Down's syndrome, living at home, learn that their other children will not bring their friends home because of him. They turn to their minister for counseling. What guidance could he offer them?

3. A vocational rehabilitation counselor strongly believes that one of his clients, a borderline retarded young man, can be placed in a job as a janitor. He learns that the parents of his client have little faith that their son can hold any type of job and have been discouraging him at home. What counseling would he provide for these parents?

4. A normal young man and a mildly retarded young woman who have known each other for some time decide to get married. When they tell their parents about their plans, the parents become very upset and seek help from a psychiatrist. What counseling could he offer in this situation?

5. A retarded twenty-five-year-old man with a long history of minor hostile behavior towards members of his family and close friends (slapping, tripping, pulling away chairs as they sit down) causes an accident in which his favorite younger sister is injured. His parents consult a social worker who is familiar with his case. What counseling approaches could she use in helping them with this problem?

REFERENCES

1. Milligan, Glenn E.: Counseling parents of the mentally retarded. *Ment Retard Abstr,* 2:259-264, 1965.
2. Snodgrass, Joel S.: Counseling parents of the mentally retarded (an annotated bibliography). *Ment Retard Abstr,* 2:265-270, 1965.
3. Milligan, *loc. cit.*
4. Adams, Martha: Professional education of nurses to care for children who are retarded. *Intl J Nurs Stud,* 3:181-190, 1966.
5. Segal, Arthur: Social work with mentally retarded adults in a rehabilitation setting. *Soc Casework,* 55:599-604, 1964.

Chapter X

WHAT IS THE MOST EFFECTIVE PROGRAM FOR THE RETARDED ADULT IN THE COMMUNITY?

To be most effective a program for the retarded adult in the community must be founded on basic principles. These principles derive from faith in the dignity of man, and belief in society's responsibilities to enable all men to enjoy inalienable rights of security and freedom.

The following principles generally reflect current thinking in program development of services for the retarded adult in the community. Most have been enunciated in one form or another in many documents and proposals.[1, 2]

TEN BASIC PRINCIPLES UNDERLYING A PROGRAM FOR THE RETARDED ADULT IN THE COMMUNITY

1. *Every retarded person cared for in the community, not in a large state institution for the mentally retarded*

The author is in agreement with the California Study Commission on Mental Retardation[3] in their statement, ". . . no retarded person should enter an institution who can be cared for in the community, and no one should remain in an institution who can adjust outside." However, this principle goes farther. A place in the community should be found or created for *every* retarded person. Even the most profoundly and severely retarded persons should be placed in community facilities, if they cannot be cared for in their own homes.

2. *Every retarded person integrated into community life as much as possible*

Wherever possible, the retarded should be permitted, trained, and encouraged to participate in normal community life, including recreation, training, rehabilitation, and social activities. The general public should be educated to accept the retarded as an integral part of the community.

3. *A fixed point of referral and information in the community for the mentally retarded and his family*

The President's Panel on Mental Retardation[4] has stressed the importance of a "life-time consultation and referral service," to which every retarded person and his family could turn for guidance and help as needed.

4. *A comprehensive array of services*

Every service needed by the retardate and his family should be available. Each service must be comprehensive both in coverage of all age levels and of all levels of mental retardation.

5. *A continuum of services*

There should be a continuum of services from childhood through adolescence through adulthood.

6. *Coordination among public and private agencies and individuals providing services, with special reference to services for the retarded and his family*

When services are coordinated, those who are providing the services are aware of what every other service is doing. Coordination reduces duplication of services and reduces cost and effort. Coordination clarifies the gaps in services needed by the retarded person and his family.

7. *All sectors of the community involved in planning the program*

This should include civic leaders, representatives from all professional groups, public and private agencies, labor, management, the general public, parents of the retarded, and wherever possible, the mentally retarded person himself.

8. *The highest quality of service to be provided*

Essential to the program is the most adequate professional leadership drawn from the fields of psychology, medicine, education, social work, psychiatry, rehabilitation counseling, nursing, using the best facilities and equipment.

9. *Services easily accessible to the retardate*

The retardate and his family should be able to readily avail themselves of service, since excessive distance, inaccessibility, or poor transportation may make it impossible to use a service which is available.

10. *Ongoing program evaluation*

From the start, the program should have built in a research process for evaluating the program's effectiveness in accomplishing its goals. This requires good record keeping in agencies serving the client, as well as high standards of reporting.

Table XIV lists the direct services which should be available in a coordinated, comprehensive community program for the mentally retarded adult and his family, as well as supportive aspects necessary for the program.

TABLE XIV

DIRECT SERVICES AND SUPPORTIVE ASPECTS OF A COMPREHENSIVE
COORDINATED COMMUNITY PROGRAM FOR RETARDED
ADULTS AND THEIR FAMILIES

Direct Services

CATEGORY	TYPES OF SERVICES
Centralized information and referral service	Information Referral Counseling (for referral purposes)
Comprehensive evaluation	Psychological, social, medical and dental, psychiatric, vocational, educational
Financial assistance	Public Aid to the permanently and totally disabled (ATD), other aid from Welfare Department Social Security benefits, other governmental pension benefits Division of Vocational Rehabilitation (DVR) Private Family Private agencies Pension benefits
Residential arrangements	Living independently Living with own family Foster home, family care home Halfway house Boarding home Private institution (residential school, convalescent home)
Clinical services	Medical Psychiatric Dental Physical restoration, prosthetic appliances, orthotics Occupational therapy, physical therapy Public health nursing Home training Psychotherapy, case work, social group work, personal counseling, family counseling Speech therapy
Vocational services	Vocational evaluation Vocational rehabilitation counseling Work training, on-the-job training, short-term workshop Job placement (by DVR counselor or State Employment

Service)
Job follow-up
Independent living rehabilitation services
Long-term workshop

Socio-recreative — Activity center
programming — Camping
Sporting events (spectator and participating)
Trips
Parties, dances
Creative activities

Religious — Church going
activities — Religious classes
Social activities

Education and — Adult education in schools (public and private)
training — Junior college
Tutoring
Adult education in workshops

Transportation — Private agencies
Public agencies
Coordinated system

Respite and — Emergency
day care — Short-term
(outside home)

Assistance to — Homemaker service
parents at home — Visiting nurse
Baby-sitting

Legal aid — Guardianship
Legal assistance

Supportive Aspects

Financial support — Public
for programs — Federal agencies
State agencies
City, county agencies
Private
Foundations
Agencies
Organizations, clubs
Individuals

Public education — Lectures, classes
TV, radio, movies
Newspapers, magazines, pamphlets, books
Billboards, posters

Professional — Undergraduate
training — Postgraduate
In-service training, institutes

Coordination — Public
Federal agencies
State agencies
City, county agencies
Private
Coordinating councils
Central registry
United community funds (social planning)

Research — Development of new programs
Evaluation of existing programs
Studies of effects of methods and programs on individuals
and groups

DIRECT SERVICES

Information and Referral Service for the Mentally Retarded

The major purpose of an Information and Referral Service for the Mentally Retarded (IRS) is to inform professionals, public and private agencies, the general public, and especially the mentally retarded and their families about available services, and to refer the inquirer to appropriate resources or services to meet his needs.[5] The IRS takes different forms in different communities. Most IRS provide a widely circulated directory of community resources for the retarded which is periodically brought up to date. Those persons who seek information may do so through phone inquiries, letter, or personal interview. The referral may be made after a brief telephone call or it may require one or more interviews with the retardate and his family before the best referral can be made. The IRS is usually staffed by social workers.

Comprehensive Evaluation of Needs and Potentials

By comprehensive evaluation is meant a complete study of the retarded adult's medical, personal, social, and vocational needs and potentials. Such an evaluation requires the services of several professionals, including social workers, physicians, psychologists, educational and vocational evaluators, and, where needed, psychiatrists. Comprehensive evaluations may demand extended periods of observation and interpretation to gain a clearer understanding of the individual. Wherever possible, parents and siblings should be involved in contributing to the evaluation.

There is little question that at present the major emphasis in comprehensive evaluation of the mentally retarded is on the infant, the preschooler, and the school-age child. Comprehensive evaluation of the retarded adult has not been widely available. A few retarded adults are being evaluated in medically oriented rehabilitation facilities, while others are being evaluated in vocationally oriented workshop settings.

As the dimensions of his problems become sharper, more precise short-term and long-term goals for treatment and training are formulated. Ongoing evaluation makes it possible to modify the goals as each individual retardate's capacities and limitations make themselves evident.

Financial Assistance

All retarded adults who cannot support themselves out of their earnings or from independent income need financial assistance. This takes a variety of forms. Many retarded adults live at home and are either partially or fully supported by their families. Many retarded adults are eligible for social security benefits as "dependent children." Grants-in-aid are made to eligible retarded adults under the ATD program of the county welfare department. State vocational rehabilitation counselors "purchase" services for retarded clients from workshops or rehabilitation centers. Some retarded adults receive financial help from private agencies.

Residential Arrangements

The living arrangements of a retarded adult should be closely related to his capabilities to function independently in the community. Some retarded adults need to live in a protected setting, whether in their parents' homes or in foster homes. A halfway house may be helpful to patients being released from a state institution as a step between institutional living and independent life in the community. In a substantial number of cases, the mildly retarded adult can manage to live in his own home with spouse and children, provided that help is available when needed.

Clinical Services

Medical Care

It is the opinion of many medical authorities that the retarded as a group are more prone than those of normal intelligence to physical illness such as respiratory diseases, and to conditions associated with birth injuries and congenital defects. At the present time there are pediatricians and physicians in child development clinics who specialize in diagnosis, care, and treatment of retarded children. This is in sharp contrast to an almost complete absence of physicians or medical clinics specializing in the treatment of retarded adults.

Dental Care

There is general agreement that the retarded have more

dental problems than normals. In most communities there are few dentists who are willing to accept severely retarded adults as patients, especially those who are immature and present difficult dental problems. Such patients often remain untreated.

Psychiatric Care

There is little question that at present only a few psychiatrists are willing to treat the mentally retarded, despite the fact that retarded persons are equally prone, or more so than the non-retarded, to suffer from serious emotional disturbances and could benefit from psychotherapy. Most psychiatrists believe retarded persons to be lacking in the ability to develop insight into their problems and to work them through to a satisfactory resolution.

Physical Rehabilitation Services

The physical rehabilitative services include orthopedic surgery, physical restoration (prosthetic devices), occupational therapy, and physical therapy. In the past many physicians did not provide the services to mentally retarded children because they believed these children would not benefit sufficiently from such procedures. As a consequence there are many retarded adults whose untreated orthopedic problems become more severe as they grow older. In addition many retarded adults develop new conditions requiring physical rehabilitative services. Although there are no statistics on handicapped retarded adults who need physical rehabilitation, the number who can benefit from such services must be large.

Public Health Nursing

Most of the focus of modern public health nursing in relation to mental retardation is on prevention, early case finding, follow-up care of young retarded children, and assistance to parents in coping with the problems associated with these children.[6] The public health nurse has much to offer in home training of severely retarded adults, as was so clearly demonstrated in Chapter VIII. Public health nurses are becoming increasingly aware of the existence of retarded adults in their case loads and of the training and counseling necessary for the retardate and his family.

Personal Counseling

Since a retarded adult meets many disturbing situations at various critical periods in his life, his needs for counseling may be extensive and ongoing. For the more able, insecurity often develops in the late adolescent and young adult periods when he is faced with the problem of finding a vocation. He may be conflicted because his sexual desires run counter to family or community attitudes which frown on his becoming sexually involved. He is usually discouraged from following a course leading to marriage which may well be fraught with grave financial and social uncertainties. As an employed adult he may have trouble handling his job or he may be disturbed by hostile attitudes of co-workers. It is well known that the major reason retarded individuals have trouble holding jobs is poor social adjustment, rather than poor work skills.

Less able retarded adults who are more dependent on their families face similar problems at a somewhat different level. Their often-delayed strivings for independence may lead to bizarre and unacceptable behavior. Some may withdraw into lethargic and dependent states far below their capabilities.

These varied emotional disturbances can be helped by counseling, psychotherapy, case work, group work, and other therapeutic approaches. A consistent finding of all studies of needed services for the retarded adult in the community is the shortage of ongoing counseling and therapy.

Family Counseling

Those with whom the retarded adult lives, his parents, siblings, relatives, are often faced with emotional problems arising out of their relationship with the retarded person. There are many situations in which a retarded adult is frustrated or depressed because his parents and siblings are unable to cope with his needs. This difficulty may arise where the retardate has trouble communicating with parents and other family members. It may develop during periods when he may be experiencing a desire to act like other adults but does not have the skills or opportunities to do so. Parents may need guidance to enable them to help their adult child cope with such emotional problems.

If parents of retarded persons are already emotionally disturbed, the retarded person in their lives may intensify the disturbances. There are many parents of the retarded who live with intense feelings of depression and inferiority over bringing a handicapped person into the world. Often they withdraw from normal social life with their neighbors and old friends in order to avoid reinforcement of the hurt they feel. Some find it hard to adjust to their feelings of grief and guilt. Others develop distorted attitudes towards other children in the family who suffer in their turn. Such families need the help of a counselor.

When the retarded adult lives in a boarding home or foster home, the foster parents may need counseling to help them cope with the problems presented by the retarded adult, as well as in dealing with troublesome interactions between the retarded adult and others in the home and in the neighborhood.

Vocational Services

Vocational Rehabilitation Services

All more able retarded adults in the community are eligible for, and should be provided with, vocational rehabilitation services. These include case finding, evaluation, physical restoration, vocational counseling, vocational training, work adjustment, on-the-job training, job placement, job follow-up. Some of these services such as counseling and job placement may be performed by vocational rehabilitation counselors, but other services are usually purchased on a fee basis from professionals or agencies, e.g., physical restoration may be purchased from a medical rehabilitation facility. Funds to pay for these services are available to each vocational counselor in the form of a case services budget which the counselor uses for his clients. The amount and variety of service which can be purchased for each client is in direct ratio to the available budget.

Because of limited state and Federal appropriations, vocational rehabilitation services are usually provided to those among the more able who show the greatest promise of becoming economically independent and self-supporting following the conclusion of their rehabilitation plan. This effectively excludes many more able and less able retarded adults who could and should profit from these services.

Selective Placement in Competitive Employment

The State Employment Service (SES) is charged with the responsibility of referring job applicants to employers needing workers. After applicants file information about themselves, are interviewed by employment counselors, are tested when necessary, they are referred to job vacancies. In most district offices there is at least one *selective placement counselor* who is specially trained to work with handicapped applicants. Until recently these specialists handled mostly physically handicapped clients. However, there is now an increased interest in placing the retarded in competitive employment. Published reports on selective placement of the retarded by state employment counselors have stressed that the best results are obtained through a coordinated effort involving close cooperation with employers, unions, public schools, and vocational rehabilitation agencies.

Special Placement in Civil Service

In most civil service systems, there are unskilled and semi-skilled jobs which can be performed by retarded persons. They have been excluded in the past because they could not pass the required written examinations. Since 1964 a program has been in operation in the Federal civil service and in some state civil service systems which has opened this source of gainful employment. Jobs which can be performed by retarded persons are identified. Clients who are certified by their vocational rehabilitation counselors as being capable of performing the work are appointed without a written examination. So far, these placements have been highly successful.

Workshops for the Handicapped

The general role of the workshop lies in the opportunities it offers for evaluation of capabilities and limitations, for vocational training leading to job placement, and for providing long-term employment for disabled people. Jacobs, Weingold, and Dubrow[7] have suggested that the following groups of retarded adults could be served in a workshop for the handicapped:

1. Those who may be placed in industry after a short period of training in a sheltered workshop.

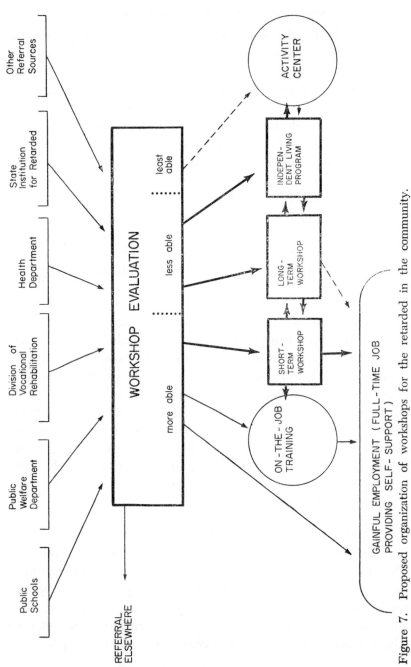

Figure 7. Proposed organization of workshops for the retarded in the community.

2. Those who may be placed in industry but will probably need a more or less prolonged training period.

3. Those who will probably be able to work in the sheltered workshop environment only, and be able to achieve self-support.

4. Those who will probably be able to work in the sheltered workshop environment only, but on a marginally productive basis.

Chapter VI has indicated some ways in which the more able retarded adult can be helped by evaluation and training in a short-term workshop, while Chapter VII suggests how the less able retarded adult can be helped through finding sheltered employment in a long-term workshop.

Figure 7 illustrates how workshop services could be organized for retarded adults in the community. Activity centers, although not workshops, are included in this plan because it is possible that over a period of time and with appropriate rehabilitative services, some of the least able retarded clients may develop into long-term workshop clients. In some communities more able and less able retarded adults attend the same workshop, but for different purposes. The major point is that these workshops must have a rehabilitation orientation, with evaluation, training, counseling, and work opportunities directed toward enabling each retarded client to move as far as possible along the path of realizing his full potentials. The value of workshops is attested by the support for establishing new workshops and for improving existing ones made possible by the Vocational Rehabilitation Amendments of 1965.[8]

Independent Living Rehabilitation Services

There are many retarded adults in the community for whom the training goal must be self-care and independent living rather than economic self-sufficiency. The term *independent living rehabilitation services* was coined to differentiate this rehabilitation goal from *vocational rehabilitation services,* which are oriented towards placement of the retarded adult in gainful employment.[9] These services involve training in self-care, homemaking, leisure-time activities, and limited vocational preparation. There is widespread agreement that training for independent living is necessary if the less able retarded adult is to make a better adjustment to normal community living.

A few experimental programs have already demonstrated that the rehabilitation goal of independent living is realistic and achievable.[10, 11] It is lack of financial support that so far has hindered widespread development of independent living rehabilitation services as an integral part of a comprehensive, coordinated program for retarded adults.

Activity Centers

An activity center is a program providing severely mentally handicapped adults with opportunities for socialization, recreation, habit training, and self-development, as well as whatever minimal amount of productive work they can perform. Many retarded adults in activity centers have associated physical handicaps. There are very few activity centers serving the least able retarded adult, since in the past it was felt that such persons might best be cared for in a state institution for the retarded.

Respite Care

Respite care is a service for parents and foster parents who need some relief from the ongoing daily task of supervising their severely retarded adult children. Many of these parents have devoted years to close supervision and are willing to continue with this task. Occasionally they may have to leave their children for a few days, because of family emergencies, illness, or simply taking a vacation. Having access to professionally staffed respite care reduces the possibility that retarded adults will be inappropriately placed at such times. Despite its obvious value to the retardate, his family, and the community, there are only a few programs which provide this care.

Homemaker Services and Baby-sitter Services

Parents of a retarded adult who need regular help in the home to carry on their household chores or to assist them in caring for the retarded adult may be provided with the services of a *homemaker* or *home helper*. These services can be supplied by a public agency, such as a county welfare department, or the parents may be financially able to employ a homemaker full time or part time. A baby-sitter for the severely retarded adult would also relieve the parent, but usually a sitter is not expected to perform household chores. Baby-sitting is rarely a full-time assignment. In some situations, the retarded adult is brought to the baby-sitter's home.

Socio-recreative Programming

The goal of *socio-recreative programming*[12] for retarded adults is to insure social and recreational opportunities for them, with due recognition of their varied needs. There are many retarded adults who display excellent coordination and athletic skills and who can find their place in normal recreation activities. For the most part, however, the retarded adult's poor motor coordination, limited comprehension of rules and techniques in sports, poor speech, and feelings of inadequacy militate against his being accepted as an integral part of recreation programs.

Special recreation and socialization programs for retarded adults, as for most other handicapped groups, have come into existence recently and have been established in only a few communities. Where they do exist, they are usually sponsored by publicly supported recreation services, associations of parents of the retarded, and service organizations. Parties and dances, bus trips, quiet games, museum visits, outdoor camping, swimming, and bowling have been increasingly popular, but these activities are still far too few to meet the need. With the enthusiastic support of the Joseph P. Kennedy, Jr., Foundation, the National Recreation Association, and the National Association for Retarded Children, a broad approach to recreation and physical fitness for the mentally retarded is being sponsored. This reaches into community centers and group-work programs where normal and handicapped persons are being offered recreational experiences. It also reaches into colleges and training programs where professionals are being offered special courses in recreation for the handicapped.

Religious Activity

Little is known of the churchgoing habits of retarded adults except as reported by a few specific churches. From the scattered information available, some religious denominations are making a determined effort to involve retarded adults in churchgoing. The President's Panel on Mental Retardation,[13] recognizing the potential values of religion for the retarded, stated, ". . . It is the obligation of religious leaders in all faiths to provide whatever special opportunities for religious instruction and worship are needed for retarded persons living in the community."

Adult Education

Adult education should be available for all adults, including any retarded adult who can profit from such training. Adult education encompasses teaching of the basic tool subjects of reading, writing, and numbers, as well as more advanced educational subjects, practical arts, and training in vocational skills.

In practice, there are sharp limitations on what adult education programs offer for retarded adults. In some smaller communities, there is no adult education program for anyone or only a token program with limited offerings. Where there is a program, the academic course offerings are geared for those with the equivalent of a high school education or at least the literacy level of the upper elementary grades. This effectively excludes most retarded adults. The adult education teaching staff is drawn from professions, business, and trades, and is not trained in teaching the retarded. There is little recognition among adult education administrators that it is necessary to teach the adult retarded in small classes, a fact which is not only recognized but allowed for in the elementary schools and high schools.

This is not to say that mentally retarded adults are nowhere being included under adult education. In some communities adult education programs have provided effective vocational training in workshops for the handicapped, special remedial and tutoring services for individuals and small groups, and training for the less able retarded adult to help him make a better community adjustment.

Guardianship

Those retarded adults who are incompetent to manage their own affairs need legal guardians who will assume responsibility for their safety and welfare. The establishment of legal guardianship may be simple, as in those cases where the normal parent so declares in a court of law after the retarded person passes his twenty-first year of life. However, guardianship may be extremely complicated where the retarded adult has no parents, where the parents may be themselves inadequate or incompetent, where the parents may wish to give up their parental responsibilities, or where substantial financial estates are involved. It is sometimes forgotten in the complex legalistic procedures surrounding the establishment of guardianship that the general goals of legal guardianship are to assist the retarded adult in enjoying the liberties and opportunities of a democratic society.

Currently proposals are emerging to deputize a "guardian of the person to exercise the right and responsibility to make choices on behalf of the disabled one."[14] As community services for the retarded adult increasingly provide alternatives to institutional living, guardianship which includes continuity of concern for those who need lifetime supervision in the community becomes increasingly important. The various forms of public guardianship are still being actively explored. It is to be hoped that where public guardianship for the retarded adult does become available, it will be exercised not by some impersonal faceless governmental agency, but by individuals who serve a limited number of specific wards and maintain a continuing personal responsibility for them.

Transportation

An important limitation on the use of available services by all handicapped persons is the difficulty in getting to and from these services. Even in cities where there is an excellent public transportation system, the problems of transportation for the mentally and the physically handicapped may be very serious. As a consequence, plans are being developed in many communities to establish a coordinated transportation service for the handicapped. In one city a private carrier which has had successful experience in transporting severely handicapped individuals is arranging with a group of public and private agencies to transport handicapped people at a nominal cost.[15]

SUPPORTIVE ASPECTS

In addition to direct services to retarded adults and their families there are other elements in a comprehensive coordinated community program which are essential to make direct services possible. These have been designated as *supportive aspects*.[16]

Financial Support for the Program

The cost of programs serving the retarded adult is higher than the cost of similar programs for normal adults. For example, it usually takes much longer to train a retarded adult in clerical work than it takes to train a person of normal intelligence. In addition specially trained teachers may be required. In the long run, however, there is a considerable net gain both to the individual and to the community. The retarded adult who, after training, is gainfully employed as a clerical worker is not only able to take care of his financial needs but also to contribute his share of taxes.

It may cost a great deal to establish and operate a community-wide transportation system for retarded adults and other physically handicapped persons so that they will be able to attend workshops, activity centers, and recreation programs. For some it may make the difference between being a welfare recipient or a self-supporting citizen. The community is well repaid by the productivity and self-fulfillment of the retardate himself and the satisfaction of his family. Furthermore a transportation system for the handicapped may pay for itself through better utilization of existing facilities and through greater flexibility and economy in developing new facilities.

The financial support for a comprehensive coordinated program for retarded adults would come from a variety of sources, including Federal agencies, state agencies, county and municipal agencies, service clubs, parent associations, philanthropic foundations, special events, united community funds, and individual contributors and bequests.

Education and Participation of the Public

A successful community program for retarded adults must be

grounded in favorable attitudes towards the retarded. To achieve this it is necessary to inform the public on a wide and varied front about the retardates' assets and capabilities without creating false impressions about their true limitations. The public in this context includes not only the man-on-the-street, who often has little or only distorted knowledge of the mentally retarded, but also those in leadership positions in government, business, labor, and the professions.

All media of public information must be used, including newspaper stories, radio and television programs, and magazine articles. Displays of work done by adult retardates, when shown at conferences and at large public meetings, in theater lobbies, and shop windows, are highly effective.

Many employers are prejudiced against employing retarded persons because they think customers and other employees will be alienated. Employers who have worked through their prejudices and have had success with retarded employees are in the best position to inform other employers about the capabilities of the retarded.

An important public information process is that of visits by interested persons to programs such as workshops, halfway houses, and activity centers. Such direct observation clarifies the productive work and activities of the retarded adults in the program.

A well-known radio personality, while conducting his regular question-and-answer program, received a phone call stating that the caller knew of a workshop for retarded adults which was exploiting its handicapped workers by paying them substandard wages. The announcer expressed his anger and disappointment and bitterly criticized the workshop management and staff. A member of the workshop staff contacted him and invited him to visit the workshop.

A few days later he made an unscheduled visit to the workshop. The operation of the program was explained to him, and he was shown anything he wanted to see. He was impressed by the severity of the clients' handicaps and their productivity despite their handicaps. He was also impressed by their pride in the work. Many of the clients had never worked before coming to the program. He learned that all workers were being paid according to their actual productivity, except those who were being paid at a higher

level for therapeutic reasons. He gained some idea of the difficulties
the workshop was experiencing in obtaining the necessary contract
work suited to the capabilities of the clients. In fact, the workshop
was operating at a deficit, which was being made up by private
contributors. He was deeply moved by the earnestness and dedica-
tion of the staff.

Before he left he asked some clients what he could do for them.
One client asked for table tennis equipment for the use of clients
during the coffee break. The next night on his program he apologized
to the workshop staff. He asked the listening audience if there was
someone who could contribute a table tennis set. The following week
the retarded client visited the studio and the announcer made the
presentation of the equipment as part of his regular program.

Trained Staff

Working with retarded adults demands well-trained and
dedicated staff. Training of professionals in medicine, education,
vocational rehabilitation, social work, and public health fields,
with specialization in mental retardation, is being introduced in
many centers of higher education.[17] The U. S. Department of
Health, Education, and Welfare provides support to more than
thirty universities to develop multidisciplinary training programs
in mental retardation and underwrites large numbers of mental
retardation traineeships on the undergraduate and postgraduate
levels. An increasing effort is also being directed to in-service
training for improving the skills of those now working with
retarded adults.

The earlier that young people are exposed to the problems of
mental retardation, the more likely they will become interested
in this field. In some communities high school and college
students are encouraged to work with the mentally retarded under
professional supervision. Their activity not only directly helps
the client but also provides an opportunity to explore their own
feelings about pursuing work with retarded adults as a future
career.

In view of the present and anticipated shortages of trained
personnel in all health fields it will be increasingly necessary to
provide training on the subprofessional level. For example, after
a comparatively short training period, persons can become *case*

aides. They are employed to help social workers or rehabilitation counselors by performing routine tasks such as taking retarded clients to appointments or teaching clients to make phone calls and use public transportation. This leaves the professionally trained worker to deal with the more serious problems such as those requiring evaluation and counseling.

Training of foster parents who care for retarded adults has been long neglected. Foster parents are faced with serious problems of helping the retardate adjust within the home and in the community. Unless they are prepared to understand the retardate's problems and are trained in the use of community resources, they may fail as "parents." The retardate would then have to be removed from the foster home and in some cases placed in an institution.

Coordination Among Community Agencies and Individuals Serving the Retarded Adult

In each community there are government and private agencies, groups, and professionals serving retarded adults in one way or another. In many communities several agencies may be providing services to an individual retarded adult and his family. There is often little or no communication among these agencies, leading to fragmentation and to duplication of services. In many instances the retarded adult "falls between the cracks" since his needs do not fit into any agency's prevailing admission requirements.

In some communities there is a coordinating group to serve the retarded, whether this is a governmental body or a parent association. Opportunities exist to share concerns, to discuss agency goals and limitations, and to use community resources not only to resolve procedural problems but also to help each adult retardate and his family work out solutions.

Since the problems presented by mentally retarded adults frequently cut across many professions, the importance of inter-professional communication and coordination of services cannot be too strongly emphasized. This applies to direct services for adult retardates in evaluation and treatment and to the more extended planning and development of community programs which demand advance planning and discussion well before actual service can be initiated for a given individual.

Central Registry of the Retarded

A central registry of all retarded persons in an area (city, county, group of counties, state) has been proposed as a means of centralizing all information about all the mentally retarded in the area covered.[18, 19] A central registry of all the retarded would make readily available for each retarded person a complete social, medical, psychological, educational, and vocational file. This information would be helpful in planning for and providing services for retarded persons as they need help, as well as for follow-up to learn how they are getting along. It would also serve as a basis for the planning of programs for the retarded in the community.

While there are undeniable values to a central registry of the retarded, many ethical, legal, and administrative problems have made it difficult to establish such registries. First, there is a reluctance on the part of many social agencies to turn confidential records of individual cases over to a central registry, regardless of how safeguarded the information is to be. Second, there is resistance among parents of the retarded to being compelled to register their children as mentally retarded, both because doing so breaches essential freedom of choice, and because there is a widely held aversion to being stigmatized as the parent of a retarded person. Third, the registry must be comprehensive in its coverage of the *total* retarded population or else it will fail in its purpose. Fourth, there are many cases where an early diagnosis of mental retardation has been found to be in error, and irreparable harm may have been done to the child. Fifth, there are many definitions of mental retardation,[20] and a person might be diagnosed and registered as mentally retarded according to the definition in one community, while in another community, he would not be classified as mentally retarded.

As a result of these difficulties, few central registries of the retarded have been established, although some of the values of such registries may be realized by other means. Community agencies should be encouraged to maintain records in a more uniform manner so that information can be more readily available to other agencies or professional workers as the need arises. Information about the retarded population leading to development of needed services might be undertaken by the more impersonal census survey procedures. A census study, using either the sampling or complete coverage approach, can be undertaken in the community. The cooperation of large numbers of persons can be obtained more easily if it is made clear that individuals will not be identified, and that the information obtained will be used only for purposes of general planning.

Case Finding

As has been noted in many investigations, large numbers of retarded adults in the community need help, but for one reason or another are not receiving it. For some retarded adults and their families there are no services available. Others have little awareness of available community services and resources or of the way to use them. Some parents are ashamed to identify their adult child as mentally retarded. Still other families, especially those living in low socioeconomic neighborhoods, have learned to accept the same hopeless and negative attitudes of those who surround them and no longer seek help to improve their condition.

In the absence of a central registry for the mentally retarded, case finding by a typical social agency serving the retarded adult and his family may rely on either or both of two approaches. In one approach the problem becomes known to the agency when the retardate and his family seek help. At this time they usually are in a state of emergency or crisis. When this point is reached, it may be very difficult and costly to all concerned to deal with the problem. The family's call for help triggers the process in which the agency either makes services available or refers the client elsewhere. In the second approach, aggressive case-finding techniques attempt to reach the retarded adult and his family *before* they seek help to deal with an emergency. This preventive approach is far more satisfactory and less costly to the family, to the agency, and to the community. However, despite obvious advantages, aggressive case-finding techniques in identifying and serving the retarded adult and his family before the development of inevitable crises (such as the death of parents) are not generally employed.

Research on Retarded Adults

The importance of research has been emphasized by all workers in mental retardation. The President's Panel on Mental Retardation[21] placed at the head of its list of recommendations: "1. *Research* in the causes of retardation and in methods of care, rehabilitation, and learning." Major responsibility for research in mental retardation on the national level has been placed in Federal agencies under the U. S. Department of Health, Education, and Welfare with strong support from many national organizations, state agencies, private foundations, and local sources.

In recent years research findings in the biological sciences have contributed heavily to better understanding of the causes of mental retardation, with the possibility of eventually preventing this condition. A vast program of educational research has yielded significant findings which will greatly improve the education of mentally retarded children of school age. Although about half of the mentally retarded are in the postschool adult group, smaller allocations are made for research on this group, with emphasis on vocational rehabilitative aspects.

Goldstein[22] has summarized research on social and occupational adjustment of the mentally retarded. Some of his findings were optimistic, since so many retarded persons have been found making a good community adjustment. Others of his findings were gloomy, especially in relation to the dwindling vocational opportunities for the retarded in an increasingly automated society. His appraisal of previous research suggests that not only is more research essential in social and vocational adjustment, but also that much of what is already known is not put to use in the field.

An important research goal is improvement in understanding of the retardate's personal, social, and vocational potentials. Since many available evaluation procedures are not applicable to the retarded adult, it becomes necessary either to adapt existing approaches or to develop new ones; for example, one group of researchers[23] is developing a standardized procedure for measuring adaptive behavior among the retarded, while another[24] is investigating vocational interests of the retarded using a new pictorial-interest inventory technique. There is a need for studies of learning, motivation, self-image, and performance under differing environmental and stress conditions, as part of the never-ending search for meaningful knowledge about this group.

Urgently needed is a census-type national survey of the retarded adult population. This would provide base-line information about all retarded adults. It would make possible comparison of retarded and nonretarded adults on many physical, health, social, and economic variables. It could furnish basic information necessary for long-range planning of programs and services, so greatly needed at the present stage of development of services.

Much effort should be devoted not only to the planning and carrying on of original research, but also to the dissemination and field testing of available research findings. It is unfortunate that much research of direct relevance to services for retarded adults and their families does not reach practitioners in the field setting who could make use of the results to excellent advantage.

It is often apparent to observers such as parents, staff members, volunteers, and visitors that many retarded adults are significantly improved by being involved in programs like summer camping, workshop, or personal counseling. Little research has been reported which defines those aspects of operating programs which have contributed most to bringing about these changes. Program-evaluation research calls for systematic analysis of program objectives and operating procedures and careful evaluation of changes in clients. Generally speaking, the practitioner does not have the opportunity, the time, or the research skills to analyze program effectiveness. However, unless such research is conducted, it is virtually impossible to rely on anything but personal opinion and subjective impressions in evaluating the significance of programs. Furthermore there may be no meaningful basis on which to make decisions about modifying program to achieve greater effectiveness. In the absence of appropriate program evaluation there is little question that many procedures are being continued which have little meaning for those retarded adults they are intended to help, while procedures which could be of benefit are not being used.

There are wide gaps in present knowledge about the retarded adult in the community which systematic research is beginning to eradicate. "In the past decade there has been an almost incredible awakening of the public conscience concerning mental retardation. With this resurgence of concern, research has increased manyfold during this period. With the increased interest in mental retardation on the part of Federal and state governments, as well as numerous private foundations, the future for increased knowledge concerning mental retardation through research is insured."[25]

QUESTIONS FOR DISCUSSION

1. What advantages do you see to developing a comprehensive, coordinated program for the mentally retarded adult in your community?

2. What problems would you expect to encounter in developing such a program?

3. What goals did the President's Panel on Mental Retardation consider appropriate for a comprehensive, coordinated program for the mentally retarded adult?

4. How does the program for mentally retarded adults in the President's Panel on Mental Retardation compare with the program presented in the AAMD Manual on Program Development in Mental Retardation?

5. What kind of training program would you develop for training vocational rehabilitation counselors who are assigned a case load of mentally retarded adults?

6. Your community is in the process of developing a comprehensive, coordinated program for mentally retarded adults. How would you evaluate the program's effectiveness?

REFERENCES

1. President's Panel on Mental Retardation: *A Proposed Program for*

National Action to Combat Mental Retardation. Washington, U. S. Gov. Printing Office, 1962.

2. Gardner, William I., and Nisonger, Herschel W.: *A Manual on Program Development in Mental Retardation.* Monogr. Suppl., *Amer J. Ment Defic, 66*(4): 1962.

3. State of California, Study Commission on Mental Retardation: *The Undeveloped Resource: A Plan for the Mentally Retarded of California.* Sacramento, Study Commission on Mental Retardation, Jan. 1965, pp. 1-2.

4. President's Panel on Mental Retardation: *op. cit.,* pp. 92-95.

5. Information and Referral Service for the Mentally Retarded: *Services for the Mentally Retarded in San Francisco.* San Francisco, Information and Referral Service for the Mentally Retarded, Apr. 1966.

6. Adams, Martha: Professional education of nurses to care for children who are retarded. *Intl J Nurs Stud, 3:*182, 1966.

7. Jacobs, Abraham; Weingold, Joseph T., and Dubrow, Max: *The Sheltered Workshop: A Community Rehabilitation Resource for the Mentally Retarded.* 2nd ed. New York, New York State Association for the Help of Retarded Children, 1962.

8. U. S. Dept. of HEW: *Restoring Disabled People to Jobs and Useful Living.* Committee on Education and Labor, House of Representatives, 89th Congress, 1st Session. Washington, U. S. Gov. Printing Office, October 1965, pp. 27-30.

9. Whitten, E. B.: *Statement to Special Education Subcommittee of the House Committee on Education and Labor, Considering H. R. 3465, the Rehabilitation Act of 1959.* Washington, National Rehabilitation Association, 1959.

10. Katz, Elias: *Independent Living Rehabilitation Program for Seriously Handicapped Mentally Retarded Adults.* (Final report for Vocational Rehabilitation Administration, Project No. RD-905.) San Francisco, Aid Retarded Children, 1965.

11. Tobias, Jack: *Training for Independent Living.* New York, Association for the Help of Retarded Children, 1963.

12. Avedon, Elliott M., and Arje, Frances B.: *Socio-recreative Programming for the Retarded.* New York, Bureau of Publications, Teachers College, Columbia, 1964.

13, President's Panel on Mental Retardation: *op cit.,* p. 97.

14. Boggs, Elizabeth M.: Legal aspects of mental retardation. In Philips, Irving (Ed.): *Prevention and Treatment of Mental Retardation.* New York, Basic Books, 1966, p. 426.

15. San Francisco Coordinating Council on Mental Retardation: *Community*

Organization Action Plan for the Mentally Retarded. (Project progress report for Vocational Rehabilitation Administration, August 1965 to July 1966.) San Francisco, San Francisco Coordinating Council on Mental Retardation, 1966, p. 9.

16. Gardner, and Nisonger: *op cit.*, p. 40.
17. U. S. Dept of HEW: *Financial Assistance Programs in Mental Retardation of the U. S. Dept. of Health, Education, and Welfare.* Washington, U. S. Gov. Printing Office, January 1966, pp. 10-14.
18. Glogower, Jules, and Kaplan, Milton M.: *A Central Registry Study: Vocational and Employment Needs of Mentally Retarded Persons and Implications for Program Planning.* Pittsburgh, United Mental Health Services of Allegheny County, Sept. 1965.
19. Galazan, Michael M.: *A Structured Community Approach to Complete Services for the Retarded.* (Progress report to Vocational Rehabilitation Administration, July 1, 1964, to October 1, 1965.) Milwaukee, Jewish Vocational Service, 1965, pp. 3-5.
20. Gelof, Malvin: Comparison of systems of classification relating degree of retardation to measured intelligence. *Amer J Ment Defic, 68:*297-317, 1963.
21. President's Panel on Mental Retardation: *op cit.*, p. 14.
22. Goldstein, Herbert: Social and occupational adjustment. In Stevens, Harvey A., and Heber, Rick (Eds.): *Mental Retardation: A Review of Research.* Chicago, U. of Chicago, 1964, pp. 214-258.
23. Leland, Henry; Nihira, Kazuo; Foster, Ray; Shellhaas, Max, and Kagin, Edwin: *Conference on Measurement of Adaptive Behavior.* Parsons, Kans., Parsons State Hospital and Training Center, 1966. (NIMH Grant No. S-R11 MHO1862-02.)
24. Parnicky, Joseph J.; Kahn, Harris, and Burdette, Arthur: Preliminary efforts at determining the significance of retardates' vocational interests. *Amer J Ment Defic, 70:*393-398, 1965.
25. Nisonger, Herschel W. (Foreword): In Stevens, Harvey A., and Heber, Rick (Eds.): *Mental Retardation: A Review of Research.* Chicago, U. of Chicago, 1964, p. vii.

Chapter XI

WHAT ARE SOME APPROACHES TO PROGRAM PLANNING FOR THE RETARDED ADULT IN THE COMMUNITY?

M ANY COMMUNITIES IN the United States are on the move in the direction of developing a comprehensive, coordinated program for the mentally retarded. Spurred on by the Report of the President's Panel on Mental Retardation, the American Association on Mental Deficiency, the National Association for Retarded Children, the U. S. Department of Health, Education, and Welfare, and many other national, state and local groups and agencies, community planning and implementation of programs are taking on momentum. Wherever such plans are being developed, services for retarded adults are incorporated into the total program.

At what stage of development are these programs at the present time? *The simple fact is that there is no community in the United States which adequately serves more than a fraction of its retarded adults.*

Table XV* paints a grim picture of the widespread shortage and inadequacy of direct services for retarded adults and their families in five communities: San Francisco,[1] Bridgeport,[2] Milwaukee,[3] Los Angeles,[4] and Cleveland,[5] during the period 1963 to 1965. These communities were chosen for this book because each was awarded a five-year project grant by Vocational Rehabilitation Administration, U. S. Department of Health, Education, and Welfare, during the period 1963 to 1965, to develop and to

---

* Table XV should not be viewed as accurate and complete. From the writer's personal knowledge, more services were available in some of these communities than reported in the published summaries on which Table XV is based.

213

TABLE XV

DIRECT SERVICES* FOR RETARDED ADULTS AND THEIR FAMILIES IN FIVE COMMUNITIES (CIRCA 1963-1965)

COMMUNITY	CITY AND COUNTY OF SAN FRANCISCO	GREATER BRIDGEPORT AREA	GREATER MILWAUKEE AREA	LOS ANGELES COUNTY	GREATER CLEVELAND METROPOLITAN AREA
POPULATION SERVED	750,000	150,000	1,000,000	6,000,000	2,000,000
Information and referral service for mentally retarded	Available	Available	Available	Not available	Not available; "Urgently needed"
Evaluation services	Available but limited by financial eligibility; much duplication of evaluation services	Available	Available through VRA Project	Little for adult	——†
Financial assistance	Available from County Dept. of Social Services; Social Security benefits	——†	——†	Available from County Bureau of Public Assistance; Social Security benefits	Available from County Welfare Dept.; Social Security benefits; many supported by their families
Living arrangements	Many living with family; 91 patients on leave from state hospital; 10 men in private boarding home	Many living with family; 10 men in private boarding home	Shortage of foster homes	Shortage of foster homes; family care homes available only to patients on leave from state hospitals; shortage of boarding homes	"Urgently needed"; no group homes or dormitory residences for retardates receiving vocational rehabilitation services"
Clinical services medical care physical restoration public health nursing, counseling, psychotherapy individual far l	Medical care available; shortage of psychiatric care; public health nursing available from county health dept.;	Medical care available; physical restoration services; counselor available; speech therapist available; family	Counseling services "inadequate or not available"; family counseling available	Shortage of medical care; "almost none" available; no public health nursing services for adults; counseling "very	Medical care available; further study of counseling needed

Vocational services vocational rehabilitation counseling selective placement long-term and short-term workshops "Independent living" services	104 DVR clients; 15 clients in Independent Living Rehabilitation Program; 5 clients in short-term workshop; 61 clients in two long-term workshops	DVR services; short-term workshop and long-term workshop available	DVR services; short-term workshop and long-term workshop available	DVR services; selective placement in state employment services; almost no short-term workshops; almost no long-term workshops	DVR serves 15 and normal, 44 slow learners, 54 of unknown classification"; "75 dull normal and slow learner retardates in two United Appeal workshops serving predominantly persons with other handicaps"; "107 retardates in four long-term workshops"
Recreational services socialization	50-75 adults attend monthly social dances sponsored by SF Aid Retarded Children	Available playground; summer camping	—†	County Park and Recreation Dept. and State Dept. of Mental Hygiene provide some programs for "semi-independent" retardates; "extremely limited" camping	"Demonstration program needed to meet recreational needs of retarded adults"
Activity center	A few in Recreation Center for the Handicapped	Available	Goodwill Industries and United Association for the Retarded Workshop	None	Workshop available offering "an activity program, with emphasis on occupational therapy"
Respite and day care	No respite program; some day care in Recreation Center for the Handicapped	No respite program; day care available	—†	Not available	Not available—"needed"
Homemaker services	—†	—†	—†	Available only for Bureau of Public Assistance clients	—†

Religious activities	——†	——†	Available	——†	——†	——†
Adult classes	——†	——†	"Craft classes" for adult retardates and their fathers	Little available—"planning stage only"; "Work-Study program in workshop"	Not available	——†
Transportation	——†	Coordinated transportation plan for retarded and other handicapped in "planning stages"	"None needed"	"Planning stage"	Special funds available for Bureau of Public Assistance clients only	——†
Guardianship and legal aid	——†	——†	——†	——†	Guardianship of property only; no free legal aid	Need for protective services for the adult retardate under public auspices

* As reported in the following publications:

San Francisco Coordinating Council on Mental Retardation: *Service Needs of the Mentally Retarded in San Francisco: A Pilot Study* (San Francisco, San Francisco Coordinating Council on Mental Retardation), November, 1965. Parents and Friends of the Mentally Retarded of Bridgeport: *A Project to Demonstrate New Directions in Community Programming for the Severely Retarded Adult* (Bridgeport, Conn., Parents and Friends of the Mentally Retarded of Bridgeport), 1963. Also, *Implementing Adult Services: Initial considerations* (Nov., 1963), and *Summary of Grant Proposal to the Vocational Rehabilitation Administration* (Nov., 1963). Michael M. Galazan: *A Structured Community Approach to Complete Services for the Retarded*, Progress report to Vocational Rehabilitation Administration, July 1, 1964, to October 1, 1965 (Milwaukee, Jewish Vocational Service), 1965. Mental Retardation Joint Agencies Project: *Summary: The Mental Retardation Survey of Los Angeles County* (Los Angeles, Welfare Planning Council), 1965. Greater Cleveland Mental Retardation Planning Project: *Mental Retardation: Blueprint for Action* (Cleveland, The Welfare Federation), 1965.

† This table is based solely on material in the above publications. It is likely that some services for adults were available in these communities but were not mentioned in the publications; for example, from the author's personal knowledge, certain services were available in San Francisco but were not reported in the publication by the San Francisco Coordinating Council on Mental Retardation. —— means *"not reported as being available."*

demonstrate a comprehensive, coordinated program for all mentally retarded in their communities. If these communities— which probably represent some of the most advanced progress in this field—present so bleak a report, what must the picture be in the rest of the country?

The programs in these communities have much in common. First, their goals are almost identical: to develop comprehensive, coordinated programs to meet the needs of all retarded persons and their families in the community. Second, they have been organized in such a way as to involve the greatest amount of participation among all interested segments of the community. Third, their emphasis is on laying the groundwork for a program of services which will continue as part of the fabric of health, education, and welfare services in the community long after the *project* aspect has terminated. Fourth, their findings are intended to be helpful to other communities developing similar programs.

Despite these similarities, variations have developed largely due to such factors as the size of the population to be served, the area covered, the history of local programming for the retarded, the impact of personalities and strongly held viewpoints of individuals and small groups.

To better understand the approaches in these communities, some background material is briefly presented. Readers may find features of these programs helpful in planning and developing services for the retarded adult in their own communities.

THE SAN FRANCISCO COORDINATING COUNCIL ON MENTAL RETARDATION*

The SFCCMR was founded in 1961. Between 1963 and 1966, its basic operation was subsidized by National Mental Health Act funds through the State Department of Mental Hygiene. The membership is "made up entirely of professionals: social workers, psychologists, physicians, vocational rehabilitation counselors, nurses, educators, working in one capacity or another

---

* The operation of the San Francisco Coordinating Council on Mental Retardation (SFCCMR) has been presented in somewhat greater detail since the author was a founding member and still is a member of its board of directors (1967).

in the field of mental retardation. Members of the council do not officially represent the agencies where they are employed, but through their participation in the council, they bring into a common pool information about the program, plans, and problems of their respective agencies and in turn feed back to their own agencies from this pooled information any new thinking that may result from joint efforts at community problem solving. The lay-citizen support necessary to the accomplishment of community goals is introduced through action committees set up to carry out specific objectives set up by the council. These are *ad hoc* committees, combining professional and lay membership, responsible to the council's board of directors but reaching into the community."[6]

The SFCCMR does not offer any direct services. Community action is brought about by the "voluntary approach, employing traditional community organization methods, education, joint discussion and decision-making in relation to the problems at hand, and the steps toward their solution."[7]

Since its founding, the SFCCMR has been active on a variety of fronts. It laid the groundwork for the establishment of the San Francisco Information and Referral Service for the Mentally Retarded, which has been funded since 1964 by the National Institute of Mental Health as a demonstration project. It sponsored training institutes for social workers, clergymen, physicians, public health nurses. It developed plans for a multipurpose center for the mentally retarded in San Francisco. In 1966 these plans resulted in an expansion of community-based professional services for the mentally retarded under the San Francisco Department of Public Health. It participated in planning and implementing the Development Center for Handicapped Minors, a new program under the San Francisco Unified School District (1965). It assisted in bringing to San Francisco one of the first state Regional Diagnostic and Counseling Centers for the Mentally Retarded, serving five San Francisco Bay Area counties. Its action committees have been addressing themselves to extending day care activities for the severely retarded, to developing a coordinated transportation system for the handicapped, to expanding workshop and vocational services, and to strengthening professional education.

In 1963, the SFCCMR conducted a "study of the patterns of service for the mentally retarded and their families in San Francisco as a basis for mapping priority needs and setting up the strategy for a community action program."[8] Some of the findings of this study* are reported in Table XV. After completion of this study, the SFCCMR received a demonstration grant to develop a comprehensive, coordinated program for the mentally retarded in San Francisco.

The following case illustrates procedures used in San Francisco.

Case of Richard G.†

Richard G. is a twenty-year-old mentally retarded man. His mother is widowed and works as a secretary.

The mother read about our services in the paper and called, stating that Richard was at a residential training school where he had been for the last three years. He now had to leave because he was approaching the age of twenty-one and there were no longer funds available to keep him in school.

When the mother was seen, she advised us of having had Richard at five clinics and developmental centers where they had tried to determine his particular problem. He has also attended eight or nine schools during his life time. The final diagnosis appeared to be borderline intelligence, with slight handicap in the use of his hands presumably due to cerebral palsy. In addition, he was diagnosed as having emotional problems, particularly in regard to his relationship with an overprotective, but rejecting, mother.

The mother was advised by our worker to apply for vocational rehabilitation services prior to his release from school so that some preparatory work could be started. She was also advised that Richard was eligible for social security benefits as a dependent retarded child, and for Aid to the Disabled (ATD) support. Instructions for applying were given to her.

The mother was helped in several interviews to think through

---

* Funded by Vocational Rehabilitation Administration, U. S. Department of Health, Education, and Welfare.

† Adapted from a case report of the San Francisco Information and Referral Service for the Mentally Retarded.

what plans she would like to make for her son. She decided to have him living in San Francisco in a family care home, where she could see him occasionally but where they would not be so close together that their difficulties in relating would prevent a satisfactory adjustment.

At Information and Referral Service a list of fifteen to twenty possible homes for Richard was reviewed. His mother was taken on visits to several where there were vacancies and where it seemed he might fit in. It took several visits and many hours of counseling with the social worker before the mother could accept the reality of the kinds of homes that were available. She had some very unrealistic ideas about the sort of people and the situation she wanted, but finally she was able to find a home that satisfied her and where it was felt that Richard's needs would be met.

When Richard was released from school he was started on vocational rehabilitation and the vocational rehabilitation counselor placed him in a workshop for evaluation. Meanwhile, he was placed in the home that we had helped the mother select. Regular visits by our caseworker to the caretaker were necessary to insure the success of the placement. Richard and his mother were also seen on a regular basis to clarify the visiting procedures—such as telephoning—which tended to create difficulties for the caretaker and threatened the placement.

Meanwhile, arrangements had been made to refer Richard for social contacts to a Saturday group which was under the auspices of Aid Retarded Children.

After he started in the workshop, he appeared to have difficulties in relating to other men. A social-work student was assigned to help him adjust to the demands of the work and to the social situation in the workshop.

The mother obtained social security benefits for her son and also was helped to apply for ATD. In both of these instances there were confusions about the amount of the grant that he would be eligible for, and the Information and Referral worker was able to help clarify this. Richard is now receiving regular financial help.

In addition, Richard's mother appeared to be in need of a good deal of counseling. She had given up her job when he first came home. She seemed to need supportive help in planning for her future, now that he seemed to be fairly well settled. Counseling has attempted to involve her in an ongoing referral to family agencies, but she has resisted this. The Information and Referral Service continues to maintain regular contact in the hope that eventually the mother will be helped to use counseling elsewhere.

Our agency will also maintain some contact with Richard, with the family caretaker, with the workshop until the evaluation period is over, and with vocational rehabilitation until he is established in an ongoing situation.

It is unknown whether Richard will be able to make the adjustment in view of his multiple problems or whether at some time a referral for psychiatric or counseling help will be needed in addition to the supportive help he has had so far.

THE BRIDGEPORT STORY

The Bridgeport, Connecticut, project was initiated in November, 1963. The purpose of the project was "to develop a model or plan of comprehensive services based upon the resources of the community and to show that the development of such comprehensive community-based services is the logical and most effective way of achieving a 'spectrum of opportunity' for the retarded individual,"[9] The proposal grew out of the experience of the Parents and Friends of the Mentally Retarded of Bridgeport. Starting in 1951, this organization developed a broad program of services for the retarded in the Bridgeport area. At great effort the group established a community center for the mentally retarded, the Kennedy Center, which included training classes for the severely retarded, a preschool program, recreational and social programs, a community diagnostic clinic, and a sheltered workshop (See Table XV). In 1964 Faust Hall, a small residential boarding home for young men "on the way to independence,"[10] was established. Even before the formal initiation of the project, the Kennedy Center was a center for professional training and for demonstration of services for the retarded and their families.

A key concept underlying the grant proposal was that the basic demonstration of services would be conducted at the Kennedy Center. These services would be known as *core* programs. Later, with the success of core programs, *branch* programs would be established in neighboring areas.

So far as mentally retarded adults were concerned, two programs were planned. One program would be vocationally oriented for more able retarded adults and would be centered around a workshop and work-training programs. This core program at the Kennedy Center for more able retarded adults would be staffed by a workshop manager, vocational rehabilitation counselor, and work supervisors.[11] In addition, recreation and special education would be available as needed. The second core program would be for severely retarded less able and least able adults, and would stress "suitable and productive training opportunities,"[12] supportive counseling, and continuing family counseling services. Special focus would be placed on helping move patients from the state hospitals back into the community.

Following is a case of a client who was served in the Bridgeport program for severely retarded adults.

*Case of Michelle R.**

DOB: 9-18-43   Stanford-Binet M.A.: 6-0
Age: 23 years   IQ: 40
Socioeconomic status: Moderate means, parents own home, both parents working

This young woman was referred by Division of Vocational Rehabilitation to the Kennedy Center Diagnostic and Treatment Clinic. The reason stated for referral: "To determine level of intellectual functioning and to evaluate assets and potential for vocational planning. Due to her hyperactivity and restlessness, she was unable to function in the workshop program."

Our records state that she was dropped from public school at the age of sixteen. This female counts only to eight and reasons like a six-year-old.

The Kennedy Center Diagnostic and Treatment Clinic recommended Project TRI-US (for severely mentally retarded adults) for work training and evaluation. She was accepted into Project TRI-US.

On coming into the program her hair never looked combed; she did not join in with the group; she was withdrawn and muttered to herself. Her speech was very poor and difficult to understand. She seemed fearful and lacked the ability to listen when someone was talking to her. She would repeat the last two words and then say, "Yes, I know, I know," but was unable to do what she had been told to do.

A month after admission this young woman rode her bicycle into a neighboring town, approximately twelve miles from her home.

---

* Adapted from a case report of the Kennedy Center, Parents and Friends of the Mentally Retarded of Bridgeport, Connecticut.

Late in the afternoon the family was called and told their daughter was in jail. She had been caught stealing. At the time this happened her father was in the hospital seriously ill, and the mother's spare time was used in visiting with the father. It would appear this was her way of saying, "I'm helpless, please help me." Her speech is extremely poor, and my feeling is this young woman wanted someone to realize her helplessness and need for her mother.

The law states that if this young woman really doesn't understand the seriousness of the crime, she must be committed to an institution.

Through the efforts of Kennedy Center, this young woman was allowed another chance. She was given the same opportunity that any individual would expect (consideration of the total situation). The judge gave her a five-day suspended sentence and then put her on a two-year probation period. She is to meet with the probation officer every two months. This episode was the only time that this young woman got into difficulty.

The neighbors in her community all reported that this female had always conducted herself well around her own neighborhood. She is doing very well in Project TRI-US, and we feel certain that with further training she will be a useful, contributing member of society. She can work well, but someone will have to help her make decisions. Recreation at the Kennedy Center will give her an outlet when she is not working. She will enjoy the benefits of living at home with her family, and at the same time feel she is a contributing member of society through the work she is doing in Project TRI-US.

It is one less responsibility for the institution and the taxpayer.

STRUCTURED COMMUNITY APPROACH: MILWAUKEE

The purpose of the Milwaukee project is to "establish and evaluate the effectiveness of a comprehensive network of co-ordinated community services to retardates and their families."[13] The project's goal is to be achieved "through a demonstration study of the seventeen to twenty-one year old population of identified mentally retarded in the Milwaukee community."[14] In the course of the project, as gaps in services to this age group are identified, "new services are to be created and implemented and their effectiveness and feasibility evaluated. If the new services established in connection with the demonstration program prove adequate in meeting the needs of this group of mentally retarded, the project will attempt to implement the model on a community-wide basis, taking into consideration the needs for services of all age groups of retardates."[15]

Since May 1964, a *central registry* of about 10,000 mentally retarded persons known to eighty-six Milwaukee community agencies has been in operation. The central registry was used to identify and to provide information on "approximately 1,500 mentally retarded between the ages of seventeen and twenty-one who are in the demonstration program."[16] Although the central registry of the mentally retarded has definite values for program development, major problems have been encountered, involving "legal considerations with respect to the distribution of confidential data concerning clients. . . . Considerable attention has been given to seeking a mechanism through which this resource can be made available to community agencies and yet not violate the rights of individual families to privacy."[17] From these available reports it is not clear as to whether the central registry is able to fulfill its possible uses.

Among the accomplishments of the structured community approach as reported in October 1965 (see Table XV) were the following:[18]

Establishment of a "Retardation Consulting Center," providing "mentally retarded persons and their families with a central point of contact for exchange of information and consultation and for referral to appropriate agencies within the community for specifically needed services."[19]

Comprehensive directory of services for the retarded in the Milwaukee area.

Setting up of comprehensive "medical, social and behavioral evaluation" of each seventeen to twenty-one-year-old identified mentally retarded person. This evaluation conducted at the Central Wisconsin Colony in Madison, the Milwaukee Curative Workshop, and the Milwaukee Sheltered Workshop of the United Association for Retarded Children.

Expansion of existing social services in agencies to

include previously unserved retardates and their families.

Major gaps in services were found to be 1) continuing counseling to the retarded client and his family, 2) continuing formal adult education classes, 3) leisure-time activities, 4) independent living arrangements.

A cooperative program to expand day-care services was arranged by Goodwill Industries and United Association for Retarded Children.

A half-day academic and a half-day work experience in school was developed.

Division of Vocational Rehabilitation agreed to be more flexible in reopening closed cases of retarded persons who might profit from their services.

Following is a case report which illustrates the type of *summary evaluation* (based on extensive study) being conducted on *all* seventeen to twenty-one-year-old retardates in the Milwaukee project.

Case of John O.*

Summary of Assessment Findings

John O.   November 1, 1965
Age: 21 years.

The client lives at home with his mother, father, and two younger brothers. Family income is above average. He attended special classes for the retarded starting with the fifth grade and continuing through high school. He has been employed for the past one and one-half years as kitchen helper and dishwasher, earning $1.10 per hour. Family would like to get him into a civil service job so that he can be self-supporting. Both parents strongly feel that he should not get married.

Social Assessment Summary

This family has actively sought and used community services to assist this client. The family unit accepts his handicap and focusses on his strengths, rather than his weaknesses. As John has matured, the effects of the handicap have diminished somewhat, particularly in the area of coordination.

In considering new assignments for this client, it will be helpful

---

* Adapted from a case report from Structured Community Services for the Retarded, Milwaukee, Wisconsin.

to remember 1) that he has done best in the past when he is given specific directions and is asked to learn only one assignment at a time; 2) that excitement contributes to his problems in coordination. While it is anticipated that this family will request services when they need them, it would be well for the project to contact the parents every three to four months to determine the client's progress and review the need for services.

Psychological Summary Statement

John is a young man who is able to function at the borderline level of mental efficiency. His *verbal* ability appears to be much better than his performance ability and may be termed low normal. His learning of new tasks may be accomplished with a certain amount of extended effort on his part and with cooperation of the teacher. In the use of basic tools of learning, John is able to handle arithmetic problem-solving at the ninth-grade level (his best subject), and his reading is that of the average fifth grade student.

Considering his ability to put to use his limited capacity into new learning situations, he is deemed to be a favorable subject for vocational training in some area of interest to him. He may take longer than the average subject to master certain aspects of a new task, but with effort and encouragement he should be able to handle semiskilled tasks fairly well.

Medical Summary

Diagnosis: This young man has steady employment in a non-skilled job and is happy. There are absolutely no problems of adjustment within the community. I feel he is performing up to potential. Physical examination and family history give no clue to etiology of retardation. Possible chromosomal abnormality.

GREATER CLEVELAND MENTAL RETARDATION PLANNING PROJECT

The Welfare Federation of Cleveland, Ohio, has been active in working with the retarded for many years. "Acting on 1962 recommendations from its children's council, the Federation intensified these activities, starting in March, 1963. Central to this development was appointment of a mental retardation committee which has been vigorously engaged in a number of efforts, of which the launching of this planning project is particularly important. The mental retardation committee is the sponsor, within the Welfare Federation, for this Greater Cleveland Mental Retardation Planning Project."[20]

"A Project Committee has been set up in which the members will share responsibility for fact gathering, exchanging information, preparing written material. Some members will have individual assignments, i.e., within the legal, financing, and public relations fields. Others will serve on one of the following sub-committees: 1) medical: prevention, diagnosis, treatment, 2) education, 3) recreation and day care, 4) vocational rehabilitation, and 5) residential care and lifetime planning.

"In addition, each member will belong to his county delegation. This is important since there are different local problems in each county. Its two-way method of organization, therefore, will insure adequate attention by the project both to the overall needs of the retarded and to the unique situations within each of the three counties.

"Membership on the project committee is drawn as widely as possible from many groups: public officials, professionals, concerned citizens . . . The project will make every effort within the time available to solicit information and suggestions from every concerned source. The Agency Forum, organized last year by the mental retardation committee, is one such channel for direct discussion. The committee set up this organization to help the many local agencies and organizations exchange information and suggestions based on their work with the retarded and to provide a channel for feedback of information to the committee from the groups most closely associated with the retarded."[21]

Of some interest is the scope of the project. Uniquely among these five VRA projects, Cleveland's ". . . is concerned with individuals having an IQ of 90 or below. Although terminology and associated IQ scores vary, the following listing suggests the four broad groupings to which separate attention must be given:

Ohio Terminology	*IQ Score*	*USA Terminology*
Dull Normal	76-90	Slow Learner
Slow Learner	50-75	Educable
Trainable	30-49	Trainable
Severely Retarded	Under 30	Severely Retarded

"The varying needs of people in these different categories must be identified. Moreover, certain flexibility in defining the upper level of retardation is considered necessary in view of the changing demands of our society, especially in the employment market. People who formerly would not have been thought of as retarded may now be handicapped, at least vocationally, because of these changing conditions. Obviously it is of great importance that each retarded adult be enabled to earn as much from employment as his talents permit."[22]

While the goals of this project stress vocational rehabilitation of the mentally retarded, there is little question that the whole range of programming for retarded children and adults is involved. This is reflected in *Blueprint for Action,* which developed sixty-two recommendations for action in relation to the age groups—early life, school age, adolescence and young adulthood, and adulthood—as well as in the areas of prevention, rehabilitation, and residential care (see Table XV).

To summarize, "the *Mental Retardation: Blueprint for Action* is the plan or blueprint to guide Greater Cleveland in accomplishing the rapid, orderly, and economical further development of measures in the community to care for the retarded and to help them achieve their fullest potentials."[23]

THE JOINT AGENCIES AGREEMENT: LOS ANGELES COUNTY

In Los Angeles County, a well-populated and large geographical area, there are many state, county, city, and voluntary agencies offering services to the mentally retarded and their families. Until 1963, when the Mental Retardation Joint Agencies Project was established, there was "nothing inherent in the pattern of such programs to assure the provision of the broad array of services needed in a master plan for the retarded."[24] The project (initially funded by a grant from the State Department of Mental Hygiene, using National Mental Health Act funds) set out "to create an effective instrumentality for improved planning, development, and coordination of services needed by the mentally retarded."[25]

The project conducted a survey, "using an interview schedule and a questionnaire designed to gather factual and descriptive data about the nature and quantity of agencies' programs for the retarded. Of the 334 public and private agencies contacted by the staff, 92 per cent of the agencies completed interview schedules or questionnaires and an additional 6.5 per cent of the agencies presented partial information. The survey data were then compared with a model comprehensive program to identify the major gaps, duplications, and problems in the provision of the following services: 1) social welfare, 2) educational, 3) clinical, 4) recreational, 5) vocational habilitation and employment, and 6) legal"[26] (see Table XV).

"To implement the project survey's findings and recommendations, a Mental Retardation Services Board will be formed by the county's public agencies under the legal authority of the Joint Exercise of Powers Section of the California Government Code. The board will consist of the signators to the Joint Powers Agreement, who will be representatives of public agencies serving the mentally retarded, and who will be responsible for the cooperative development and implementation of the master plan [of services for the mentally retarded]."[27]

From this brief summary it appears that the essence of the Los Angeles County approach is to develop a legal and binding covenant among the multitudinous public agencies in the geographical area. This agreement commits those who participate as members of the Mental Retardation Services Board to work cooperatively in implementing a comprehensive, coordinated program for the mentally retarded in the community. Through active participation in the Mental Retardation Services Board's planning and decision-making activities, public and private agencies are in a better position to coordinate their efforts, to allocate funds more meaningfully, and to work towards filling gaps in needed services. The Joint Agencies Agreement approach can literally move mountains (as is done when state, county, and Federal agencies jointly undertake freeway planning, construction, and maintenance). It represents an important approach in comprehensive community planning for the retarded.

Following is a case which illustrates how various agencies in Los Angeles County coordinate services to help a retarded adult client.

The Case of George O.*

George O., a twenty-three-year-old male, was first referred to the Division of Vocational Rehabilitation [DVR] in the fall of 1961. After several months' evaluation, DVR closed his case, judging him vocationally not feasible because of a low IQ of 64 and a psychiatric diagnosis of hebephrenic schizophrenia. An earlier psychiatric evaluation reported that he expressed ideas of reference and had experienced some auditory hallucinations. In that same month, he was referred to the Exceptional Children's Foundation [ECF] for workshop services. He was enrolled in December, 1961.

George lived with his father, his mother having died in 1959 after a long chronic illness. For three months after his mother's death, he would not eat. Three years later, he still visited his mother's grave every Sunday by himself. The father soon remarried. Although George had a congenial relationship with his stepmother before the marriage, afterwards the stepmother became quite antagonistic towards George. As a result, he began living part time away from home. In fact, hospitalization was considered for him. However, later he moved completely out of the home into a home-care situation.

In 1963 a second psychiatric evaluation indicated that his mental retardation was accompanied by a borderline psychotic state defended against by good compulsive defenses. Also in 1963, he was re-referred to DVR and subsequently received services from four different DVR counselors. He also began receiving BPA [Bureau of Public Assistance] benefits. In January of 1964, the workshop staff reported considerable immature behavior. George tended to avoid jobs he did not like, occasionally not coming to work because there was a movie he wanted to see. Also, he occasionally faked illness to get out of disliked work. The workshop psychologist predicted at that time that it would take a year longer for him to become a reliable worker. Two months later he was placed on the WTC† program. A year later he was reported to be one of the high producers in the workshop. He was able to handle complex tasks, work reasonably independently, and make adequate decisions. However, emotional immaturity remained his greatest problem, functioning emotionally

---

* Adapted from a case from the Exceptional Children's Foundation, Los Angeles, through the courtesy of the Mental Retardation Services Board. This client was helped during the period prior to the ratification of the Joint Powers Agreement in 1965.

† See p. 137.

at the ten or eleven-year-old level. He was referred to an industrial workshop for placement but deliberately failed on his job assignments in order to return to the ECF workshop. Counseling helped him to realize that his judgment had been poor. He thus was motivated toward another chance to prove himself in industry. A need for follow-up counseling in future job placements was emphasized by the workshop psychologist.

The DVR counselor next placed him in a food packaging firm where he performed well until there was a reduction in personnel. Next he was placed in a cafeteria for on-the-job training. The cafeteria supervisor found George a willing and conscientious worker. He stated that he was anxious to learn and was very quick to learn new routines. After this training the counselor secured a job for him in the VA [Veterans Administration] Hospital as a janitor. At this time he was receiving $143 per month from ATD for room and board and special allowances. The workshop was being paid $50 a month tuition. Three months later his ATD grant was completely suspended. George remains still somewhat immature but responded well to continued follow-up counseling. His employer expressed satisfaction with his work. In July of 1966 his wage increased from $2.08 per hour to $2.19 per hour. His DVR counselor closed him as successfully placed in April of 1966.

This history illustrates how a case initially considered not feasible because of multiple disabilities and emotional social problems developed work ability over several years of intensive counseling and workshop services. The introduction of ATD and WTC benefits allowed him to maintain himself outside an unhealthy family situation while continuing to receive workshop services.

THE AREA CENTER FOR THE MENTALLY RETARDED

It should not be supposed that the preceding programs represent the only approaches to developing comprehensive, coordinated community programs for the retarded. The President's Panel on Mental Retardation pointed out the desirability of *area centers* for serving the retarded in a geographical area. "Among the services which may be offered in an area center are referral, diagnosis, day care, special medical care, recreation, short-term residential care with flexible admission procedures, halfway and self-government houses for the more able retarded youth, and workshops and adult activities in which both day

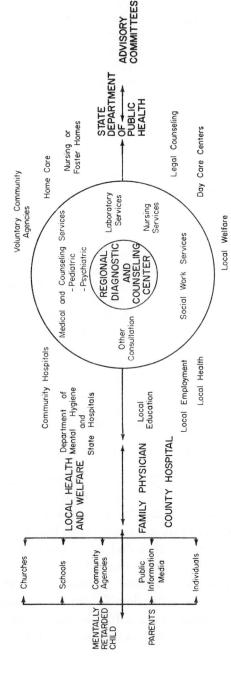

Figure 8.   Organization of a Regional Diagnostic and Counseling Center for the Mentally Retarded (California). From *The Undeveloped Resource: A Plan for the Mentally Retarded in California*, January, 1965, p. 49. Courtesy of Mental Retardation Program and Standards Board, Sacramento, California.

and resident clients participate. Some facilities for long-term care may be included, depending on the place of the area center in the overall state plan."[28]

It is of interest that of the demonstration projects just described, only one, the Bridgeport Kennedy Center, has been moving towards becoming an area center for the retarded in the sense the President's Panel on Mental Retardation uses the term, which is to *provide direct services* to the retarded and their families. The other programs are more focussed on *coordination of services.*

An interesting variation on the area-center concept is the network of Regional Diagnostic and Counseling Centers in California.*[29] In these centers *only* diagnostic and counseling services will be offered to the mentally retarded and their families. No other treatment, training, rehabilitative, recreational, or residential services will be provided by the center staff. The assignment of the center staff is to counsel with the retarded and their families to help them select and use appropriate community facilities and services. If retardates and their families can effectively use existing programs in the community, the center will pay the cost of these services. Where a service is needed and does not as yet exist, the center will offer to pay the cost of these services, thereby stimulating the creation of needed services. In view of the shortage of many services and facilities in the community, this approach should significantly increase the quantity and quality of services. Figure 8 indicates how these regional centers would operate and what relationships they would maintain with other public and private agencies.[30]

QUESTIONS FOR DISCUSSION

1. What are some of the similarities and differences among the approaches to program planning for the retarded adult in San Francisco, Bridgeport, Milwaukee, Los Angeles, and Cleveland?

---

* Regional Diagnostic and Counseling Centers in California are operated by *sponsors,* through a contract with the State Department of Public Health. The first two centers were established in 1966 in San Francisco and in Los Angeles.

2. Which approach do you consider the best? Why?

3. Which approach do you consider will work the best in your community? Why?

4. In what ways do the California Regional Diagnostic and Counseling Centers for the Mentally Retarded differ from the *area center* concept in the Report of the President's Panel on Mental Retardation?

REFERENCES

1. San Francisco Coordinating Council on Mental Retardation: *Community Organization Action Plan for the Mentally Retarded.* (Project progress report for Vocational Rehabilitation Administration, August 1965 to July 1966.) San Francisco, San Francisco Coordinating Council on Mental Retardation, 1966.

2. Parents and Friends of the Mentally Retarded of Bridgeport: *A Project to Demonstrate New Directions in Community Programming for the Severely Retarded Adult.* Bridgeport, Conn., Parents and Friends of the Mentally Retarded of Bridgeport, 1963.

3. Galazan, Michael M.: *A Structured Community Approach to Complete Services for the Retarded.* (Progress report to Vocational Rehabilitation Administration, July 1, 1964, to October 1, 1965.) Milwaukee, Jewish Vocational Service, 1965.

4. Mental Retardation Joint Agencies Project: *Summary: The Mental Retardation Survey of Los Angeles County.* Los Angeles, Welfare Planning Council, 1965.

5. Greater Cleveland Mental Retardation Planning Project: *Mental Retardation: Blueprint for Action.* Cleveland, The Welfare Federation, 1965.

6. San Francisco Coordinating Council on Mental Retardation: *op. cit.*, p. 3.

7. *Ibid.*

8. San Francisco Coordinating Council: *Service Needs of the Mentally Retarded in San Francisco: A Pilot Study.* San Francisco, San Francisco Coordinating Council on Mental Retardation, November 1965.

9. Parents and Friends of the Mentally Retarded of Bridgeport: *Summary of Grant Proposal to the Vocational Rehabilitation Administration.* Bridgeport, Conn., Parents and Friends of the Mentally Retarded of Bridgeport, Nov. 1963.

10. Parents and Friends of the Mentally Retarded of Bridgeport: *Faust Hall* (circular). Bridgeport, Conn., Parents and Friends of the

Mentally Retarded of Bridgeport, 1966, p. 1.

11. Parents and Friends of the Mentally Retarded of Bridgeport: *Implementing Adult Services: Initial Considerations.* Bridgeport, Conn., Parents and Friends of the Mentally Retarded of Bridgeport, Nov. 1963.

12. Parents and Friends. . . . *A project to demonstrate* . . ., p. 6.

13. Galazan: *op cit.*, p. 1.

14 *Ibid.*, p. 5.

15. *Ibid.*, p. 1.

16. *Ibid.*, p. 3.

17. *Ibid.*, p. 3.

18. *Ibid.*, pp. 3-12.

19. *Ibid.*, p. 3.

20. Greater Cleveland . . . Project: *op. cit.*, App. A., p. 1..

21. *Ibid.*, App. A, p. 3.

22. *Ibid.*, App. A, pp. 1-2.

23. *Ibid.*, p. 1.

24. Mental Retardation . . . Project: *op cit.*, p. v.

25. *Ibid.*

26. *Ibid.*, pp. v-vi.

27. *Ibid.*, p. vi.

28. President's Panel on Mental Retardation: *A Proposed Program for National Action to Combat Mental Retardation.* Washington, U. S. Gov. Printing Office, 1962, p. 169.

29. State of California, Study Commission on Mental Retardation: *The Undeveloped Resource: A Plan for the Mentally Retarded of California.* Sacramento, Study Commission on Mental Retardation, January, 1965, pp. 47-50.

30. *Ibid.*, p. 49.

Chapter XII

CURRENT TRENDS AND IDEAS

T O MEET THE needs of the retarded adult in the community, existing approaches, methods, and facilities must be strengthened and new ideas developed. In this chapter are presented a few suggestions, for the most part based on themes previously discussed. The topic, "Current Trends and Ideas," should be viewed by the reader as a challenge addressed both to himself and to the leaders in the field: What is now being done to help the retarded adult remain in the community? What should be done to help the retarded adult in the community fulfill his potentials? The answers to these questions will determine whether a substantial segment of the population becomes a part of the main stream of society or continues to remain a relatively useless and unproductive appendage in institutions, in the home, or in the community.

NATIONAL ACTION

"We must undertake a comprehensive and coordinated attack on the problem of mental retardation. The large number of people involved, the great cost to the nation, the striking need, the vast area of the unknown that beckons us to increased research efforts—all demand attention. It is for that reason that I am calling together a panel of outstanding physicians, scientists, educators, lawyers, psychologists, social scientists, and leaders in this field to prescribe the program of action. I am sure that the talent which has led to progress in other fields of medicine and the physical sciences can enlarge the frontiers of this largely ignored area."[1]

RESEARCH AND DEVELOPMENT CENTER

A research and development center should be established to mobilize human and financial resources over an extended period of time in order to make significant contributions toward understanding and improvement of services for retarded adults and their families in the community. Such a center would conduct basic and applied research studies in laboratory and in field settings. It would systematically translate research findings into usable materials or procedures and field test the methods and products developed. It would demonstrate new programs and approaches growing out of the research and development efforts. Information would be distributed, including preparation of films, tapes, displays, publications, as well as presentation of lectures, symposia, and conferences.

In order to achieve its goals, the center should be based in a comprehensive research program in mental retardation. Close contact would be maintained with institutions of higher education, government agencies, private organizations, parent groups, and professional workers in the field. Such a center could make great progress in improving the present and future status of several millions of mentally handicapped adults, whose unresolved problems cost the nation billions of dollars annually.

NATIONAL SURVEY

In Chapter I, retarded adults in the community are defined as those who are of subaverage general intellectual functioning, are impaired in adaptive behavior, and need special help from their families or social agencies. There are only general notions as to the number and distribution of retarded adults, what their needs are, and what services are available to meet their needs. Urgently needed is a national survey of the retarded adult in the community. Such a national survey should be undertaken by the National Health Survey, which was established by Congress in 1956 and charged with "laying the factual foundation for new thinking about national health problems and the level and extent of medical care."[2]

Information from this survey would confirm or deny many assumptions which prevail in thinking about the retarded adult and his family. The findings would indicate where they live, their physical, mental, social, economic, and vocational characteristics, and what services are being provided for them. Until such data are available on a national scale, as well as on the community level, those responsible for developing community programs for the retarded adult must continue to depend on very personal and often inaccurate or distorted information.

NEIGHBORHOOD CENTERS IN POVERTY AREAS

Although no national survey has been made showing where retarded adults live, there is a widespread belief based on many studies, that large numbers of retarded persons live in deprived economic circumstances in the *poverty areas,* urban, suburban, or rural. The President's Panel on Mental Retardation called for both a broad effort "to correct the fundamental social, economic, and cultural conditions with which mental retardation is closely associated,"[3] and, specific measures to meet the needs of individual retarded persons "that will offset or alleviate the adverse factors in their environment."[4]

There are many problems in meeting the needs of the retarded in poverty areas. One approach is to establish a center serving the retarded and their families in the heart of each poverty area. Such a center must be organized with the cooperation and participation of those who live and work in the poverty area, including parents of the retarded and, wherever possible, the retarded adults themselves.

VISTA (Volunteers In Service To America) could be assigned to serve in such centers. The center should be staffed by professionally trained workers, aided by indigenous aides recruited from the local neighborhood.

COMPREHENSIVE COORDINATED PROGRAMMING

The major hope for the improvement of services for the retarded adult in the community lies in the development and strengthening of comprehensive, coordinated community programming for *all* mentally retarded. This approach makes it possible efficiently and effectively to mobilize existing services, to identify needed services, and to institute new services for the benefit of the retarded adult and his family.

COMPREHENSIVE EVALUATION

Comprehensive evaluation is an extensive evaluation covering personal, social, medical, psychological, and vocational aspects. This evaluation must be conducted by a well-trained and experienced evaluation team. Despite general agreement that comprehensive evaluation is essential, there are few facilities in the United States which are set up to carry on such evaluations.

The Vocational Rehabilitation Amendments of 1965 provide both authorization and funds for comprehensive evaluation of the retarded adult to determine his vocational potential.[5] Despite their liberality, these provisions are not all-inclusive, since they are concerned only with vocational potential. Comprehensive evaluation should be made available when necessary to *all* retarded adults in the community *regardless of vocational potential*. High priority should be given to development of such comprehensive evaluation services.

PARTICIPATION IN PROGRAM PLANNING

Can the retarded adult participate in program planning for himself and other retarded adults? There are many retarded adults in the community who are capable of participating in program planning.

Reports of family group therapy with retarded adults and their families have indicated that some retarded adults can participate actively and effectively in developing meaningful programs and activities for themselves.[6]

An interesting example is provided by a mentally retarded adult who served as a member of a task force on residential care, which participated in preparing the Master Plan for Mental Retardation in Hawaii. He was a former patient of the state institution for the mentally retarded, who had made a very good adjustment in the community. He attended the task force meetings faithfully, and shared with his fellow committee members in making final decisions and recommendations. It was reported that ". . . the value that John [the retarded adult] served was that it must have been a revelation for some of the other committee members who had never worked with retardates before this experience."[7]

EXTENDED FOLLOW-UP

Many vocational rehabilitation counselors have noted that retarded clients have serious problems in social and vocational adjustment even after they have been placed on a job and their cases closed. One solution that is being considered is to maintain the case in an *extended follow-up* status. This involves periodic contacts with the retarded client for many months after the client is placed on the job. It also requires that the client be maintained in a continuing counseling relationship, directed toward his achieving total independence. To maintain such contact takes additional counselor time and demands a lower case load. The principle of extended follow-up of retarded clients has been adopted in only a few communities. It is likely that there would be a smaller incidence of failure in vocational adjustment of retarded clients if extended follow-up were available.

LONG-TERM WORKSHOPS FOR THE LESS ABLE

Long-term workshops are most urgently needed by large numbers of less able retarded adults. As more patients are moved out of state institutions for the retarded, this need will become greater. These workshops are virtually the only opportunities open for them to work at their own pace under supervision. Here they can earn salaries based on their productivity. In these workshops opportunities for recreation, socialization, and education should be provided. Since there is little anticipation of marked improvement, these workshops place no limits on the length of time clients remain in the program. In addition to the less able retarded adult, there are many other disabled persons, such as those with physical, emotional, or neurological conditions, who could be included in long-term workshops.

Under the provisions of the Vocational Rehabilitation Amendments of 1965, Federal funds are available to help construct and initially staff workshops with a view to vastly increasing the number of new workshops, at the same time improving existing ones. However, there is no provision for funds to finance the services for long-term clients in workshops after construction and initial staffing of the workshop. No Federal agency sees itself as assuming this ongoing fiscal responsibility. Under existing legislation it is therefore almost impossible to adequately finance long-term workshops for the large number of handicapped persons who can profit from this type of productive activity. Legislation is urgently needed to correct this situation. It is to be hoped that if tax-support funds are made available for long-term workshops, provision will be made for a rehabilitative emphasis in these workshops.

SUPERVISED TEAMS

Reports have appeared indicating that groups of retarded adults, organized as a team and working under supervision, have been trained to carry out many jobs. In one suburban community, the team is hired by home owners to mow lawns, rake leaves, and do general yard work, including simple gardening. In one city, a team cleans up freshly painted apartments after the painters finish, and before the new tenants move in. In another community, the team works in a small institution for the chronically ill, members of the group making beds, carrying linens and supplies, operating vacuum cleaner and floor polisher.

The idea of teams of retarded adults working under supervision can be extended to many different areas in the community; for example, a retail store making and selling doughnuts could be operated by a group of retarded adults under supervision; in rural and mountainous areas, a team could be trained to build and repair fences, or to work as farmhands under supervision; a team could be used to work under supervision in one section of a factory, carrying out one portion of the process.

The team approach has several advantages:

A less able retarded adult who could only master the simple task of sweeping the floor can be employed as a member of a house-cleaning team whose other members can do more complicated tasks.

A supervisor usually can work with six or eight retarded persons on the job, providing almost individual attention to each team member.

Most teams gain a high degree of efficiency through constant repetition of their work. They are able to do more work more rapidly, thereby increasing their earning power.

Team work provides a wholesome social experience to the participating members, since they must learn to work together in harmony.

Through the team approach, some team members can develop their work skills to the point where they become employable in regular jobs.

The team approach must be carefully safeguarded against exploitation in terms of low salaries and poor working and living conditions. The supervisor of the team must be a responsible, mature, trained individual who understands and can work with the handicapped adult and who is appropriately supervised by state and Federal regulations.

JUNIOR COLLEGE AND ADULT EDUCATION

It is well recognized by teachers of the mentally retarded that many of their students could profit from continued training after they are graduated from high school. Why should these retarded young adults not be provided with junior college courses or adult education at a time in their lives when they may be most ready for such training?

In those junior colleges where possession of a high school diploma is the only requirement for admission, retarded adults meeting this requirement are being admitted. These students should be counseled (whether by the regular counselors or special counselors for the retarded) to take only college courses in which they can be successful with little competition from other students. Courses in woodworking, physical education, music, and art fall into this category. However, when no special counseling provisions are made for them, they usually take courses which are too difficult, and most flunk out very soon. The emotional trauma associated with repeated failures is reinforced in retarded persons subjected to this experience.

Those who remain probably get little out of their college education, since most courses are not designed for them. Junior colleges should add special courses to their curricular offerings designed to further train the retarded student after he is graduated from high school. Courses with vocational implications should be based on the work-experience model, in which the student attends classes and has concomitant work experience on the job.[8]

In adult education programs, the same set of factors operate as in junior colleges. Retarded adults should be counseled to take special adult education classes adapted to their needs or regular classes in which they can be successful.

There is little question that the retarded adult and the community will gain much from this type of training in junior colleges and adult education classes.

THE GENERALIST

Comprehensive community programming for the retarded adult inevitably calls for a generalist whose skills and experience cross the borders of traditional professional disciplines. Postgraduate training should be available for physicians, educators, psychologists, social workers, rehabilitation counselors, public health nurses, and professionals in other disciplines in order to train them as generalists in dealing with the myriad problems of the retarded adult and his family. Such training should include close collaboration with other disciplines and direct contact with mentally retarded clients and their families. From the ranks of the specially trained will emerge the leaders in service for the mentally retarded adult and his family.

THE LARGE STATE INSTITUTION FOR THE RETARDED—AN ANACHRONISM

For the past few years we have seen such statements as "no retarded person should enter an institution who can be cared for in the community, and no one should remain in an institution who can adjust outside."[9]

". . . As an infant and as a child he [the mentally retarded person] is best served in a small family setting which assures him the necessary psychological stimulation and a consistent interpersonal relationship with a limited number of warm, loving, and permissive adults. As an adolescent he deserves the usual opportunities of his age group in the community, and as an adult he ought to be afforded a chance to contribute, within his limitations, to his own and to his community's welfare. Basically, therefore, his place is not in an institution."[10]

". . . The 13,000 retarded persons in the 'hospitals' include children who attend school, able-bodied adults who work in the wards and on the grounds, and elderly people virtually indistinguishable in disability from the senile patients in mental hospitals. Many are there because, years ago, their own homes were not able to care for them, or neighbors would not stand for their 'different' behavior. Clearly, such people do not require hospital care merely because of their retardation, yet they are in state hospitals because there is no alternative service to meet their needs . . . They are receiving inappropriate services for their needs."[11]

Among the least able retarded adults are a small number of severely and profoundly retarded, some of whom are so handicapped as to require constant nursing care. It has been widely assumed that these severely handicapped individuals inevitably must be cared for in a large state institution for the retarded. However, institutional placement is *not* inevitable even for these persons.

First, many severely and profoundly retarded persons are *not* in state institutions at the present time, but are cared for in the community by their parents. These parents feel that placement in a large state institution would not provide *tender loving care* which their children have received at home. Second, such patients now in institutions could be cared for in nursing homes or convalescent-type facilities in the community. Unfortunately there is a shortage of appropriate nursing homes and not enough funds to pay for such nursing care. If these shortages could be alleviated, there is evidence to indicate that severely and profoundly retarded persons could be cared for at home or in community facilities as adequately as they could be in a state institution, and probably at less cost. There is essentially no reason existing large state institutions should be maintained for these patients.

The author's position is that all resident patients of state institutions for the mentally retarded can and should be cared for in the community. These persons may need medical supervision, nursing care, convalescent-type care, foster-home care, vocational opportunities, and recreation. These needs can be met in the community at a lower cost than present state institutional expenses, and with far greater personal attention to each retardate.

This position does not intend to give the impression that the author advocates immediate and wholesale evacuation of all state institutions for the retarded. It is obvious that such action is neither possible nor advisable.

The state institutions for the mentally retarded should be phased out of existence in several steps. First, those on waiting lists for admission to the institution should be placed in community programs to meet their needs. Where such community programs are not presently available, they should be established immediately with public and private funding.

Second, all patients now in state institutions for the retarded should be classified into two categories:

1. Those who can readily be absorbed into the community. For this group, *existing* community programs and services should be expanded, so that they can be moved out of the institution as soon as possible.

2. Those who will have to be delayed until *new* facilities are constructed or *new* services established in the community to meet their needs. Immediate steps should be taken to build these facilities and to establish these services so that this group can be moved into the community in the near future.

CONCLUSION

This nation is dedicated to the principle of preventing dependency and helping each person overcome his handicaps. Until recent years, however, most retarded adults were rejected, isolated, and deprived of adequate understanding, appropriate care, and suitable educational opportunities for full development of their skills and competencies. Their families have received little help in dealing with the serious problems associated with their presence in the home and in the community.

When potentially capable retarded adults are not helped to achieve their maximum levels of self-care and self-support, it becomes necessary to expend vast sums for their financial support and to devote extensive professional services, volunteer assistance, and family energies to their care.

Today there is an increasing realization that most retarded adults are capable of achieving progressively more adequate personal, social, and vocational adjustments in the community. Acceptance of the concept that they must be included in all services generally available for the entire population is becoming more widespread.

The mentally retarded adult is entitled to the rights, privileges, and protection provided to all citizens in a democratic society.

QUESTION FOR DISCUSSION

What are your ideas for meeting the needs of retarded adults and their families in the community?

REFERENCES

1. President's Panel on Mental Retardation: *A Proposed Program for National Action to Combat Mental Retardation.* Washington, U. S. Gov. Printing Office, 1962, p. 201.
2. Linder, Forrest E.: The health of the American people. *Sci Amer,* *214*:21-29, 1966, p. 22.
3. President's Panel on Mental Retardation: *op. cit.,* p. 63.
4. *Ibid.*
5. U. S. Dept. of HEW: Summary of 1965 provisions (of Vocational Rehabilitation Amendments of 1965). *Rehab Rec,* *6*:6-14, 1965.
6. Segal, Arthur: Social work with mentally retarded adults in a rehabilitation setting. *Soc Casework,* *55*:599-604, 1964.
7. Letter of Dr. Saturo Izutsu to Dr. Harold E. Dent.

8. State of California, Dept. of Education: *Handbook on Work Experience Education: A Guide to the Organization and Operation of Work Experience Education Programs.* Preliminary edition. Sacramento, Office of State Printing, 1959.

9. State of California, Study Commission on Mental Retardation: *The Undeveloped Resource: A Plan for the Mentally Retarded of California.* Sacramento, Study Commission on Mental Retardation, Jan. 1965, pp. 1-2.

10. Tarjan, George: The role of residential care—past, present and future. *Ment Retard,* 4:4-8, 1966, p. 5.

11. State of California, Assembly Ways and Means Committee. Subcommittee on Mental Health Services: *A Re-definition of State Responsibility for California's Mentally Retarded.* Sacramento, Office of State Printing, 1965.

APPENDIX A

ARRAY OF DIRECT SERVICES FOR THE RETARDED*

Components of special need

Physical, mental health–Shelter nurture protection–Intellectual development–
Social development–Recreation–Work–Economic security

Infant
Specialized medical follow-up
Special diets, drugs or surgery — Residential nursery — Sensory stimulation — Home training
Home nursing — Child welfare services — Environmental enrichment

Toddler
Correction of physical defects — Foster care — Nursery school
Physical therapy — Trained baby-sitter — Playground programs

Child
Psychiatric care — Classes for slow learners
Homemaker service — Special classes—educable
Special classes—trainable
Dental care — Day care — Religious education

Youth
Short stay home — Work-school programs — Day camps — Scouting — Swimming
Boarding school — Residential camps
Psychotherapy — Occupational training — Speech training — Social clubs — Youth groups

Young adult
Halfway house — Vocational counseling–Personal adjustment training — Selective job placement — Health insurance — Disabled child's benefits
Facilities for retarded in conflict — Guardianship of person — Marriage counseling — Sheltered employment — Total disability assistance
Long-term residential care — Sheltered workshops

Adult
Group homes — Evening school — Bowling — Guardianship of property — Social supervision
Life annuity or trust — Evening recreation

Older adult
Boarding homes — Old age assistance
Medical attention to chronic conditions — OASI benefits

249

* Not included are diagnostic and evaluation services, or services to the family; the array is set forth in an irregular pattern in order to represent the overlapping of areas of need and the interdigitation of services. Duration of services along the life span has not been indicated here.

Array of direct services for the retarded. From *A Proposed Program for National Action to Combat Mental Retardation*, 1962, p. 76. Courtesy of President's Committee on Mental Retardation, Washington, D. C.

APPENDIX B

INSTITUTE OF INDUSTRIAL LAUNDERERS NATIONAL
MDTA-ON-THE-JOB TRAINING PROJECT FOR
THE MENTALLY RETARDED
In Cooperation with
The Bureau of Apprenticeship Training
U. S. Department of Labor
[1965]
Project Office Address
Institute of Industrial Launderers
National MDTA-OJT Project
1726 M Street, N.W.
Washington, D. C. 20036
Project Director
Bernard H. Ehrlich
Project Field Director
Harry Fauber

Synopsis

Purpose

To establish on-the-job training for 1,000 mental retardates
in industrial laundry occupations on a nation-wide basis.

Method

By establishing training subcontracts with member com-
panies of the Institute of Industrial Launderers under the
authority of the Institute's prime MDTA-OJT contract with the
Bureau of Apprenticeship Training, U. S. Department of Labor.
The project will reimburse subcontractors on a flat rate basis of
$25 per week per trainee.

Eligibility

Any mentally or functionally retarded male or female, eighteen years of age or older, without severe secondary physical

251

or emotional disabilities, who can be certified by a State VR agency as being feasible for training and employment in the industrial laundry occupations listed.

Type of Training

Training will be done on-the-job in approved industrial laundries in one or more of the following basic occupations: presser, preventative maintenance, alterations, folding and counting shop towels, mender, shirt presser, folder (pressed work), sorter, shake out, tumbler operator, janitorial duties, loader and puller, extractor operator, and/or other industrial laundry occupations that may be considered feasible for the retarded.

Length of Training

Each approved trainee will be assigned to a participating industrial laundry for a training period of 10 weeks; total OJT hours, 400 (40-hour week).

Cost Reimbursement

Only training costs can be paid by the project. The project does not provide funds for such other expenses as maintenance and transportation.

Trainee Wages

All trainees assigned to OJT will be paid the minimum-wage rate established for the position for which he or she is being trained. Each trainee will be covered by workmen's compensation at the same rate as other plant employees and in conformance with applicable state laws. Wherever possible, successful trainees will be retained in the plant where trained.

Source of Trainees

Trainees from all sources, public and private, will be considered for the project.

Referral

All trainees, regardless of initial referral source, must be referred to the program by the local office of vocational rehabilitation. Thus, all prospective trainees must first be referred to

DVR, who will make application to the project. Standard referral forms will be furnished by the project. These must be completed by the DVR counselor assigned to the case and forwarded to the project field director (name and address on cover sheet).

DVR Certification

All prospective trainees must be certified as work-ready by the DVR counselor or supervisor by signing the statement on the referral form that the trainee is considered capable of performing satisfactorily the requirements of the job for which training is to be given. However, once certified by the state vocational rehabilitation agency, the trainee may begin training without waiting for final approval by the project field director. This will obviate any delay in initiating the training.

Other Agencies Participating In or Supporting the Project

The Bureau of Apprenticeship and Training, U. S. Department of Labor

The Vocational Rehabilitation Administration

The President's Committee on Employment of the Handicapped

The National Association for Retarded Children

The major labor unions representing industrial laundry workers

Selection Criteria

To help insure success and continuation of the objectives of the project, certain selection criteria have been recommended by the participating agencies.

All candidates for the program will be accepted on the basis of his or her ability to do as indicated by past performance in workshops, training programs or other job experience which required similar physical dexterity and mental ability, or other demonstrated ability to successfully complete the program.

Candidates must be at least eighteen years old, capable of self-maintenance and independent travel, and must demonstrate an acceptable degree of personal-social adjustment.

DVR Counselor Role

It is hoped that each counselor referring clients to the project will support the client with job or social problem counseling, assist the client in arranging for transportation, proper dress for the job, and necessary pre-OJT preparation. The project is only to develop on-the-job training opportunities for the retarded and should in no way interfere with the counselor-client relationship. Without active DVR counselor support, many trainees may not succeed.

A standard data form and narrative summary must be furnished with each candidate. Psychological and medical data shall be less than one year old.

Social background should include a brief family background: economic status, size, education of parents and attitudes toward child's disability, such as overprotection, encouragement, and cooperation.

Once a local subcontract has been established, the counselor may schedule starting dates for trainees with the industrial laundry up to the maximum number of trainees established and within the time limits set forth in the subcontract. Counselors will be kept fully informed as to contract content, et cetera. In all cases, referral forms and placement schedules must be sent in advance to the project field director so that proper reporting and billing forms can be sent to the industrial laundry and supplements to the subcontract can be sent to the Bureau of Apprenticeship and Training.

Secondary Objectives

Secondary objectives are to develop the interest and support of trade associations and labor unions in OJT for the retarded, to carry out a study during the term of this contract to determine the effectiveness of the program and to ascertain the safety, productivity, and absenteeism of the mentally retarded so as to evaluate the employability of the mentally retarded in jobs in competitive industry, and to establish methods, techniques, and guidelines for use in developing similar programs in other trades.

Probable Training Locations

Since training must be done in areas where there are industrial laundries, the states and cities wherein plants are located are listed below. Tentative allocation of trainees by state has been set as a guide for the distribution of trainees on the basis of OJT funds available for that state and the number of plants located in that state. The allocation is subject to change as necessary by availability of area funds, trainees, and participating plants.

State	No. of Trainees	Cities in which plants are located. Number in ( ) indicates number of plants in city
Alabama	10	Birmingham, Decatur, Mobile
Arizona	20	Phoenix (3), Tucson, Yuma
California	125	Anaheim, Bakersfield (2), Chula Vista, Compton, El Centro, Fresno (2), Lompoc, Long Beach, Los Angeles (9), Oakland (4), Redding, Riverside, Sacramento (2), San Diego (4), San Jose (2), South San Francisco (2), Union City, Van Nuys, Ventura, Walnut Creek, Watsonville
Colorado	10	Denver, Grand Junction, Greeley
Connecticut	42	Bridgeport (2), East Hartford, Hartford (2), New Haven (3), New London, Stamford, Waterbury, Woodbridge
District of Columbia	10	Washington, D. C. (3)
Florida	20	Dania, Jacksonville (2), Miami, North Miami, St. Petersburg, West Palm Beach
Georgia	12	Atlanta (3), Thomasville
Idaho	10	Blackfoot, Boise
Illinois	75	Carbondale, Chicago (8), Decatur, Evanston, Moline (2), Niles, Peoria, Rockford (3), Springfield, South Holland
Indiana	20	Evansville, Fort Wayne, Gary, Indianapolis (2), Muncie, South Bend
Iowa	10	Cedar Rapids, Des Moines
Kansas	10	Kansas City, Topeka
Kentucky	10	Lexington, Louisville (2)
Louisiana	10	Alexandria, Baton Rouge, New Orleans
Maine	4	South Portland
Maryland	30	Baltimore (5), Brentwood, Colmar Manor, Laurel
Massachusetts	40	Boston (2), East Taunton, Indian Orchard, Malden, New Bedford, Somerville, Springfield (2), Worcester (2)
Michigan	30	Detroit (6), Flint, Grand Rapids
Minnesota	10	Duluth, Hibbing, Minneapolis (2), St. Paul
Mississippi	4	Hattiesburg
Missouri	20	Kansas City, St. Joseph, St. Louis (4), Springfield
Nebraska	10	Omaha (3)
Nevada	6	Las Vegas, Reno
New Hampshire	4	Manchester
New Jersey	30	Camden, Elizabeth (2), Garfield, Irvington, Linden, Newark (2)
New Mexico	10	Albuquerque, Las Cruces, Roswell

New York	70	Bronx, Brooklyn (4), Buffalo (3), Kingston, Long Island City, Mamaroneck, New York (4), Richmond Hill, Rochester (2), Schenectady, Syracuse, Utica
North Carolina	10	Charlotte, Goldsboro, Greensboro, Rocky Mount
Ohio	60	Akron (2), Bellefontaine, Cincinnati (3), Cleveland (4), Columbus (3), Dayton (2), Sidney, Toledo, Youngstown
Oklahoma	10	Oklahoma City (2), Tulsa (2)
Oregon	10	Portland (3)
Pennsylvania	70	Altoona, Easton, Erie, Harrisburg, Philadelphia (9), Pittsburgh (4), Reading, Scranton, York (3)
South Carolina	4	Columbia
Tennessee	10	Chattanooga, Memphis, Nashville (2)
Texas	70	Austin, Beaumont, Brownsville, Corpus Christi (2), Dallas (2), Fort Worth (2), Harlingen, Houston (5), Lubbock (2), Odessa, San Antonio, Victoria
Utah	10	Ogden, Salt Lake City (2)
Virginia	20	Arlington, Norfolk, Petersburg, Richmond (2) Roanoke
Washington	10	Seattle, Spokane, Tacoma
West Virginia	20	Charleston, Clarksburg, Huntington, Parkersburg, Wheeling
Wisconsin	20	Appleton, LaCrosse, Madison, Milwaukee (2)

INDEX

A

AAMD, *see* American Association on Mental Deficiency
Abilities, Inc., 131-132
Activity center, 80, 164-166, 198
  in communities, 215
Adams, Martha, 185, 211
Adaptive behavior, 5, 7-9, 47
Adult education, 80, 104-105, 200, 216, 242-243
Adulthood, 16-19
Adult Psychiatry Clinic, 95
Aid to the Needy Disabled Program, *see* ATD Program
Aid to the Permanently and Totally Disabled Program, *see* ATD Program
American Association on Mental Deficiency (AAMD), 94, 213
  definition of mental retardation, 5, 7, 8
  nomenclature, 46
American Medical Association (AMA), 41, 72, 92, 114
Antisocial behavior, 25-26, 30, 32-34, 37, 131, 181-184, 223
Area center, 231-233
Arje, Frances B., 167, 211
Association for the Help of Retarded Children, 147, 153
ATD Program, 19-20, 26, 31, 93, 137, 152, 219, 220, 231
Avedon, Elliott M., 167, 211

B

Baby-sitter services, 80, 163, 198-199
Barden-LaFollette Act of 1943, 117
Bass, Medora S., 15, 27
Billy, Joel J., 114, 115

Birch, Jack, 8, 27
Boggs, Elizabeth M., 42, 211
Bridgeport, Conn., 221-223
  community programs, 213-216
Brown, S., 37, 42
Buck, Pearl, 30, 41
Burdette, Arthur, 72, 212
Burgemeister, Bessie, 71

C

Cain, Leo F., 27, 47, 72
California Arithmetic Test, 66
California Reading Test, 66
California State Psychological Association, 100
California Test of Mental Maturity, 33
Camping, 107-109
Case finding, 207-208, 224
Central registry, 206-207, 224
Central Wisconsin Colony, 224
Chicago Public Schools, 128
Civil service, 124-125
Cleveland, 213-216
  community programs, 226-228
Clinical services, 191-194
  community programs, 214
  see counseling and therapy
  dental, 90, 191-192
  home training, 158-163
  medical, 32, 51-55, 91-93, 118, 120, 191, 226
  physical rehabilitation services, 118, 192
  see psychiatric services
  see psychological services
  public health nursing, 159-163, 171, 192
  see social services
  speech training, 159-163, 188

257

Cohen, Peter, 51
Columbia Mental Maturity Scale, 44
Community, 21-23
Community adjustment of former patients of state institutions, 13-14, 36-38, 83-86, 90-91, 100-102
Community programs, 39-40, 188-189, 213-233
  Bridgeport, 213-216, 221-223
  case finding, 207-208
  central registry, 206-207, 224
  chart, 213-216
  Cleveland, 213-216, 226-228
  coordinated, 205-208, 238-239
  direct services, 188-201, Appendix A
  effect of, 37-38
  financial support for, 34-35, 151-152, 194, 202, 241
  Los Angeles County, 213-216, 228-229
  Milwaukee, 213-216, 223-226
  need for, 75-81, 112-113
  principles, 186-187, 188
  public education, 202-204
  see recreation
  residential facilities, 156, 157
  San Francisco, 213-216, 217-221
  staff, 112, 130, 171, 204-205, 243
  see supportive aspects
  see workshops
Comprehensive evaluation, 65-71, 80-81, 120-122, 190, 225-226, 239
Conard House, 86
Costa, Frances, 145
Counseling and therapy
  family, 140-141, 157-163, 168-185, 193-194
  group, 24-25, 60-62, 97-100
  marriage, 90-91, 179-181
  minister, 179-181
  needs for, 93-100, 112, 157-159
  parents, 140-141, 151-163, 168-184, 193-194
  personal, 93-104, 193
  psychiatrist, 24-25, 26, 93-94, 174-177, 181-184, 192
  psychologist, 94, 177-179

public health nurse, 159-163, 171
  in regional centers, 232-233
  social worker, 80, 90-91, 97-100, 140-141, 172-174, 219-221
  vocational rehabilitation counselor, 60-62, 125-126
  work as therapy, 100-104
Creative activities, 109
Crippled Children Services, 168
Current trends and ideas, 236-246

D

Daughters of Israel Day Nursery, 148
Davies, Stanley P., 33, 41
Day facilities, 164-166, 198, 215
  see recreation
  see workshop
Delinquency, 25-26, 30, 32-34, 37, 131, 181-184, 223
Demonstration and research projects, 117-118, 138
Dent, Harold E., 246
Dental care, 90, 191-192
Development center for handicapped minors, 164, 218
Devereux Schools, 86
Diagnostic and counseling centers, 159, 221, 232-233
Diagnostic team approach, 57-59, 65-71, 121-122, 190, 225-226, 239
Differences among mentally retarded adults, 9-11, 154-155
DiMichael, Salvatore D., 87, 88, 114
Direct services, 188-201, Appendix A
  see clinical services
  education and training, 80, 104-105, 200, 216, 242-243
  see evaluation services
  financial assistance, 159, 191, 214, *see also* ATD Program
  guardianship and legal aid, 38-39, 113, 200-201, 216
  information and referral service, 76-78, 190, 211, 214, 218-221
  see parents
  see recreation
  religious, 110-112, 199-200, 216

residential, 82-86, 155-157, 191, 214, 221

transportation, 113, 118, 201, 216

see vocational services

Doll, Edgar A., 7, 8, 26, 72, 81

Down's syndrome (mongolism), 22, 90, 148, 169, 174

Dubrow, Max, 195, 211

E

East Bay Association for Retarded Children (EBARC), 145

Educable mentally retarded (EMR), 18, 34

Education and training, 80, 104-105, 200, 216, 242-243

Educational needs, 104-105, 242-243

Ehrlich, Bernard H., Appendix B

Emotionally disturbed, 11, 23-26, 93-97, 101-103, 140-143, 181-184

Employer attitudes, 22-24, 86, 102, 123, 138, 203

Employment Aptitude Survey, 60

Employment counselor, 122, 195

Etiologic factors, 32, 56, 181, 208

Eugenic sterilization, 73-74

Evaluation services

comprehensive, 65, 118, 120-122, 138-143, 190, 225-226, 239

medical, 51-55, 120, 226

psychiatric, 55-59, 137, 230

psychological, 6, 14, 43-47, 66, 120, 182, 226

social, 47-51, 121, 149, 225-226

vocational, 4, 59-71, 116-118, 121, 141-142

workshop, 4, 62-71, 90, 121, 141-142

Exceptional Children's Foundation (ECF), 123, 136, 137, 168, 230, 231

Expressed needs, 75-81

Extended follow-up, 126, 240

F

Family

see parents

see siblings

Family care, foster care, 22-23, 83-84, 156, 205

Family counseling, 140-141, 157-163, 168-185, 193-194

Family service agency, 172

Farber, Bernard, 30, 41

Fauber, Harry, Appendix B

Faust Hall, 221

Fears of parents, 58, 137, 158-163, 173, 184

Federal-state program for vocational rehabilitation, 12-13, 59, 117-120

Federal Vocational Rehabilitation Agency

see Vocational Rehabilitation Administration

Feeley, Mary, 41

Financial assistance, 80, 159, 191, 214

see also ATD Program

Financial support of programs, 34-35, 151-152, 194, 202, 233, 241

First Christian Church of Oakland, 110

Follow-up, 13, 35-38, 118, 126, 240

Fooshee, D. K., 72

Former patients of state institutions, community adjustment of, 13-14, 36-38, 83-86, 90-91, 100-102

Foster care, family care, 22-23, 83-84, 156, 205

Foster, Ray, 27, 212

Fowle, Carolyn, 167

Fraenkel, William A., 133

French, Edward L., 114

G

Gainful employment, 116

Galazan, Michael M., 212, 216, 234, 235

Gardner, William I., 211, 212

GATB (General Aptitude Test Battery), 46-47

Gellman, William, 134

Gelof, Malvin, 212

General Aptitude Test Battery

(GATB), 46-47
Generalist, 243
Ginglend, David, 115
Glogower, Jules, 212
Goldstein, Herbert, 27, 42, 208, 212
Goodwill Industries, 15, 26, 60, 128, 225
Gould, Kay, 115
Greater Cleveland Mental Retardation Planning Project, 213-216, 226-228, 234, 235
Group for the Advancement of Psychiatry (GAP), 30, 41, 55, 56, 72, 93-94, 114
Group home facilities, 21, 84-86, 150, 222-223
Group therapy, 24-25, 60-62, 97-100
Guardianship and legal aid, 38-39, 113, 200-201, 216
Gumrukcu, Patricia, 114
Guyer, Michael F., 81

H

Halfway house, 84-86, 150-151, 222-223
Health and medical, 20, 32, 51-55, 91-93, 118, 120, 191, 226
Heber, Rick, 6, 8, 26, 27, 42, 114, 212
Hegge, Thorlief G., 15, 27, 35, 42
Homemaker services, 163, 198-199
in communities, 215
Home training, 159-163
Hot Springs Rehabilitation Center, 66
Human Resources, 134

I

Illinois Division of Vocational Rehabilitation, 129
Illinois Test of Psycholinguistic Abilities, 47
Impairment in adaptive behavior, 5, 7-9, 47
Independence strivings, 45, 74-75, 90-91, 99-100, 129, 180

Independent Living Rehabilitation Program, 38, 100-104, 138-143, 177-178
Independent living rehabilitation services, 149-151, 197-198
Industrial Launderers Project, Appendix B
Information and referral service, 76-78, 190, 211, 218-221
in communities, 214
Intelligence, 5, 6, 94
Izutsu, Saturo, 246

J

Jacobs, Abraham, 114, 195, 211
Jastak, Joseph F., 15, 27, 88, 89, 114
Jenne, W. C., 41
Job follow-up, 4, 118, 126, 240
Job placement, 4, 13, 14, 61, 118, 122-125, 131
civil service, 124-125
employment counselor, 122, 195
Industrial Launderers Project, Appendix B
more able, 122-125
supervised teams, 148, 241-242
Johnstone, E. R., Training and Research Center, 47
Jones, E. M., 133
Junior college, 242-243
Junkers, Karin Stensland, 30, 41

K

Kagin, Edwin, 27, 212
Kahn, Harris, 72, 212
Katz, Elias, 10, 27, 38, 42, 115, 133, 153, 211
Kelley, Douglas, 71
Kennedy Center, 221, 222, 223, 233
Kennedy, Joseph P. Jr., Foundation, 199
Kent EGY, 66
Kirk, Samuel A., 72
Klopfer, Bruno, 71

Kukoda, Louis J., 114

L

Langley Porter Neuropsychiatric Institute, 57
Lannestock, Gustaf, 41
Large state institutions for the mentally retarded, 14, 21, 155-156, 186, 243-245
Least able, 154-167
  activity center, 164-166, 198
  baby-sitting, 80, 163, 198-199
  see counseling and therapy
  definition, 88, 154-155
  evaluation, 51-53
  fears of parents, 158
  homemaker services, 163
  home training, 159-163
  living arrangements, 155-157
  needs, 112-113
  public health nursing, 159-163
  recreation, 164-166, 198
  residential facilities, 156-157
  respite care, 80, 166
  vocational, 164, 166
Lee, John J., 15, 27, 35, 42
Legal aid and guardianship, 38-39, 113, 200-201, 216
Lehman, Harvey C., 115
Leland, Henry, 27, 212
Less able, 135-153
  definition, 86-87, 117, 135
  evaluation, 138-143
  needs, 112-113
  rehabilitation for independent living, 149-151
  workshops, 143-152
Levine, Samuel, 27, 47, 72
Linder, Forrest E., 246
Living arrangements
  see residential arrangements
Long-term workshop
  see workshop, long-term
Lorge, Irving, 71
Los Angeles County
  Bureau of Public Assistance, 230

community programs, 213-216
Joint Agencies Project, 228-229
Mental Retardation Services Board, 136

M

MacPhee, Halsey M., 27, 88, 89, 114
Manpower and Development Training Administration (MDTA), 132, Appendix B
Marriage, 14-16, 88-91, 179-181
Maslow, Abraham H., 75, 81
Mattei, Rita, 107
McCarthy, J. J., 72
Mary McDowell Settlement House, 86
Medical and health, 20, 32, 51-55, 91-93, 118, 120, 191, 226
Mental illness
  differences from mental retardation, 23-25
  psychiatric evaluation, 57-59
  schizophrenic reaction, 102-103
  therapy, 24-25, 93-94, 95-97, 181-184
Mental retardation, 3-26
  definition, 5, 7, 8, 206, 227
  differences between mental retardation and mental illness, 23-25
  differences among mentally retarded, 9-11, 154-155
  effect on family, 30-31
  poverty, 31-32, 238
  prevention, 32
  size of problem, 7, 28-30, 33-34, 236
  variations within mentally retarded, 10, 11
Mental Retardation Joint Agencies Project, 216, 234, 235
Mental Retardation Services Board of Los Angeles County, 136
Merrill, Maud, 26
Mikels, Elaine, 114
Miller, Dorothy, 36-37, 42
Milligan, Glenn E., 185
Milwaukee
  community programs, 213-216, 223-226

Curative Workshop, 224
Sheltered Workshop, 224
Minister as counselor, 179-181
Mongolism (Down's syndrome), 22,
    90, 148, 169, 174
More able, 116-133
    definition, 86, 116
    Federal-state program for vocational
        rehabilitation, 12-13, 59, 117-
        120
    needs, 112-113, 116-134
    vocational rehabilitation services,
        120-127
    workshops, 127-132
Moss, John, 27
Murray, Henry A., 72, 81

N

National action to combat mental re-
    tardation, 237
National Association for Retarded
    Children (NARC), 31, 41, 107,
    110, 123, 124, 168, 199, 213
National Association of Sheltered
    Workshops and Homebound
    Programs (NASWHP), 63, 72
National Health Survey, 237-238
National Institute of Mental Health,
    218
National Mental Health Act, 217
National Policy and Performance
    Council, 130
National Recreation Association, 199
National survey of retarded adults,
    209, 237-238
Needs
    community programs, 75-81, 112-113
    counseling and therapy, 93-100
    educational, 104-105
    hierarchy, 75
    of parents, 157-159, 170
    physiological, 73-75
    psychosocial, 74-75
    recreational, 48-51, 105-110
    see vocational needs
    workshop, 151-152, 240-241

Neighborhood centers in poverty
    areas, 238
Nihira, Kazuo, 27, 212
Nisonger, Herschel W., 211, 212
Nomenclature, 6, 8, 46, 227
Nurse as therapist, 159-163, 171

O

Occupation Day Training Center,
    138, 147-149
Ogg, Elizabeth, 133
Olshansky Simon, 30, 41
On-the-job training, 4, 121-122, 131,
    Appendix B
Otis Employment Test, 66
Overage from contract work, 136

P

Pacific State Hospital, 37
Parents
    baby-sitting, 163, 198-199
    counseling, 140-141, 157-163, 168-
        184, 193-194
    definition, 172
    effect on, 30-31
    family care, foster care, 83-84,
        156, 205
    fears, 58, 137, 158-163, 173, 184
    financial assistance, 159, *see also*
        ATD Program
    homemaker service, 163, 198-199,
        215
    problems, 30, 156-158, 169
    public health nurse, 159-163, 192
    respite and day care, 164-166,
        198, 215
    visiting nurse, 159
Parents and Friends of the Mentally
    Retarded of Bridgeport, 167,
    216, 221, 222, 234, 235
Parnicky, Joseph J., 72, 212
Peck, J. R., 47, 72
Personal counseling, 93-104, 193
Personnel, 34, 47, 85, 112, 130, 171,
    204-205, 243

Peterson, R. O., 133
Philips, Irving, 41, 42, 211
Physical Ability Rating Form, 54-55
Physical examination, 51-55, 118, 120
Physical handicap, 9-11, 13, 23, 95,
 110, 135-136, 165, 198, 219
Physical rehabilitation services, 118,
 192
Physical therapy, 192
Physiological needs, 73-74, 75
Pomeroy, Janet, 165, 167
Porterville State Hospital, 156, 158
Potentials, 12-16, 39-40
Poverty, 31-32, 92, 238
President's Committee on Mental
 Retardation, 250
President's Committee to Employ the
 Handicapped, 124
President's Panel on Mental Retarda-
 tion, 32, 39, 41, 42, 92-93, 114,
 187, 208, 210, 211, 212, 213,
 231, 233, 235, 246, 250
Probation, 83, 131, 158, 183-184, 223
Professional training, 112, 130, 171,
 199, 204-205, 243
Project TRI-US, 150-151, 222-223
Psychiatric services, 192
 evaluation, 55-59, 137, 230
 therapy, 24-25, 26, 93-94, 95-97,
 174-177, 181-184
Psychological services
 counseling and therapy, 94, 177-179
 evaluation, 6, 14, 43-47, 66, 120,
 182, 226
 research, 47, 208-210
Psychometric Data Report, 66
Psychosocial needs, 74-75
Psychotherapy
 see counseling and therapy
Public education, public information,
 202-204
Public health nursing, 159-163, 171,
 192

R

Raven, J. C., 71

Raven's Progressive Matrices, 44, 60
Records and reports, 126-127
Recreation, 48-51, 105-110, 199
 in activity centers, 80, 164-166, 198,
 215
 camping, 107-109
 in community programs, 215
 definition, 105
 in long-term workshop, 144-146
Red Cross, 111, 146
Regional Diagnostic and Counseling
 Center, 232-233
Rehabilitation for independent living,
 149-151, 197-198
Rehabilitation workshop
 see workshop
Religious activity, 110-112, 199-200
 in communities, 216
Research, 9, 36-38, 47, 90, 94, 117-118,
 138, 156-158, 208-210, 217, 219,
 221, 223, 227, 228-229,
 237-238
Residential arrangements, 21, 82-86,
 90-91, 150-151, 155-157, 221
 in communities, 214
Respite and day care, 164-166, 198,
 215
Revised Beta Examination, 66
Rexroth, Marie, 159
Richman, Sol, 133
Rockefeller, Nelson A., 124
Rorschach Ink-Blot Test, 44, 45
Rothstein, Jerome, 41

S

San Francisco
 Aid Retarded Children, 105, 107,
 220
 community programs, 213-216
 Community Rehabilitation Workshop, 63
 Coordinating Council on Mental
 Retardation, 211, 216, 217-
 221, 234
 Department of Public Health,
 159, 218

Information and Referral Service, 78, 218, 219, 220

Unified Schools
  Adult Education Division, 105
  Development Center for Handicapped Minors, 218

Schapps, Myra, 97, 115

Scheerenberger, Richard C., 41

Schizophrenic reaction, 102-103, 230

Schreiber, Meyer, 41

Segal, Arthur, 140, 185, 246

Selective placement, 13, 122, 137-138, 195

Self-help, 91, 142-143, 239-240

Self-image, 18, 91, 96-97, 99, 103, 140-142, 151

Service clubs, 107

Severely mentally retarded (SMR), 34

Sex, 14, 16, 37, 58, 73, 88-91, 150, 158, 169, 179-181

Shellhaas, Max, 27, 212

Sheltered workshop
  see workshop

Shortage of trained personnel, 47, 85, 163, 204-205
  generalist, 243
  postgraduate training, 243
  teachers, 34, 105, 200

Short-term workshop, 118, 127-132

Siblings, 30-31, 174-177, 181-184

Size of the problem, 7, 28-30, 33-34, 213-216, 236

Sloan, William, 8, 27

Small, Katharine T., 123

Snodgrass, Joel S., 185

Socialization
  see recreation

Social services, 149, 190
  counseling and therapy, 80, 90-91, 97-100, 140-141, 172-174, 219-221
  social evaluation, 47-51, 121, 225-226

Socio-recreative programming
  see recreation

Special education, 12, 18, 34-36

Spectator sports, 109-110

Speech training, 131, 159-163

Staff, 34, 47, 85, 112, 130, 171, 190, 204-205, 243

Standard deviation, 6, 8

Stanford-Binet Intelligence Scale, 3, 6, 52, 102, 140

State Employment Service, 195

State of California
  Assembly Ways and Means Committee, 167, 247
  Department of Education, 246
  Department of Mental Hygiene, 133, 217, 228
  Department of Rehabilitation, 60, 63, 133
  Department of Social Welfare, 27, 41, 114
  Department of Youth Authority, 33
  Mental Retardation Program and Standards Board, 232
  Regional Diagnostic and Counseling Centers for the Mentally Retarded, 232-233
  Study Commission on Mental Retardation, 33, 41, 186, 211, 235, 247

State of Hawaii
  Master Plan for Mental Retardation, 239-240

State of New York
  Department of Mental Hygiene, 125, 133
  Division of Vocational Rehabilitation, 124, 125
  Governor's Committee on Employ the Handicapped, 125
  Governor's Council on Rehabilitation, 125
  Interdepartmental Health and Hospital Council Committee on Mental Retardation, 124, 125

Stephens, W. B., 72

Sterilization, 73-74, 91

Stevens, Harvey A., 27, 42, 114, 212

Stewart, E., 37, 42

Structured Community Services for the Retarded, 48, 225

Subaverage general intellectual functioning, 5, 6

and counseling and therapy, 94
Supervised teams of retarded workers, 148, 241-242
Supportive aspects, 202-210
case finding, 207-208
central registry, 206-207, 224
coordination of services, 205-208, 238-239
financial support of program, 202
public education, public information, 202-204
research, 9, 47, 117-118, 208-210, 237
staff, 112, 130, 171, 204-205, 243
Survey of Degree of Physical Handicap, 10

T

Tarjan, George, 247
Technical Assistance Projects, 130
Terman, Lewis, 26
Tests and rating forms
California Arithmetic Test, 66
California Reading Test, 66
California Test of Mental Maturity, 33
Columbia Mental Maturity Scale, 44
Employment Aptitude Survey, 60
General Aptitude Test Battery, 46-47
Illinois Test of Psycholinguistic Abilities, 47
Kent EGY, 66
Otis Employment Test, 66
Physical Ability Rating Form, 54-55
Raven's Progressive Matrices, 44, 60
Revised Beta Examination, 66
Rorschach Ink-Blot Test, 44-45
Stanford-Binet Intelligence Scale, 3, 6, 52, 102, 140
Survey of Degree of Physical Handcap, 10
Texas Screening Battery for Mental Subnormals, 47
Thematic Apperception Test, 44, 45
Vineland Social Maturity Scale, 7, 8, 9, 44

Wechsler-Bellevue Intelligence Scale, 6, 43, 44, 46, 60, 63, 64, 66, 98, 131, 150
Wide Range Achievement Test, 66
Texas Screening Battery for Mental Subnormals, 47
Thematic Apperception Test, 44, 45
Therapy
see counseling and therapy
Tobias, Jack, 153, 158, 167, 211
Trainable mentally retarded (TMR) 34
Training, 80, 87, 118
in workshops, 130
least able, 159-163
less able, 143-151
more able, 122, 123-124, 127-132, Appendix B
on-the-job training, 4, 122, 123-124, 127, 132, Appendix B
professional, 112, 130, 171, 199, 204-205, 243
Training Service Projects, 130
Transitional workshop, 118, 127-132
Transportation, 113, 118, 201, 216
Tucker, Thomas A., 123

U

United Association for Retarded Children, 225
United Community Fund, 136
U. S. Department of Health, Education, and Welfare, 27, 72, 133, 134, 153, 167, 211, 212, 213, 246
professional training, 204
research, 208
U. S. Department of Labor, 123
Bureau of Apprenticeship Training, Appendix B
United States Employment Service, 72
U. S. House of Representatives, 153

V

Variations within mentally retarded

adult, 10, 11
Vennert, Beatrice F., 150
Vineland Social Maturity Scale, 7,
    8, 9, 44
Visiting Nurse Association, 159
VISTA (Volunteers In Service To
    America), 238
Vocational Adjustment Center, 128-130
Vocational counseling, 4, 11, 125-126
Vocational evaluation, 4, 59-71, 116-
    118, 121, 135-136, 141-142
Vocational interests, research on, 47
Vocational needs, 86-88, 112
    least able, 164, 166
    less able, 143-152
    more able, 116-134
Vocational Rehabilitation Administra-
    tion, 12, 55, 117-118, 119,
    123, 124, 219
Vocational Rehabilitation Amendments
    of 1954, 117-118, 150
Vocational Rehabilitation Amendments
    of 1965, 116-117, 130, 239, 241
Vocational rehabilitation services, 12-
    13, 118-120, 128-130, 194-198,
    230-231
    and adult education, 105
    case finding, 194
    in communities, 215
    counseling, 4, 11, 60-62, 125-126
    evaluation, 4, 59-71, 116-118, 121,
        135-136, 141-142
    Federal-state program for vocational
        rehabilitation, 12-13, 59, 117-
        120, *see also* Vocational Re-
        habilitation Administration
    independent living rehabilitation
        services, 149-151, 197-198
    job follow-up, 4, 118, 126, 240
    job placement, 4, 13, 14, 61, 118,
        122-125, 131, 195, 241-242,
        Appendix B
    medical care, 118
    physical rehabilitation services,
        118, 192
    records and reports, 126-127
    see training
    types and amounts in 1964, 119

    work adjustment, 63-71, 118
    see workshops
Vocational training,
    see training
Voelker, Paul H., 15, 27, 35, 42
Volunteers, 23, 106, 111-112, 135,
    146, 151, 163, 164-165
Volunteers In Service To America
    (VISTA), 238

W

War on Poverty, 32
Wayne State University, 35-36
Webster's Dictionary, 27
Wechsler-Bellevue Intelligence Scale,
    6, 43, 44, 46, 60, 63-64, 66,
    98, 131, 150
Wechsler, David, 26, 71
Weingold, Joseph T., 195, 211
Weir, Thomas P., 110
Welfare Federation of Cleveland, 226
Whiteman, Martin, 27, 88, 89, 114
Whitten, E. B., 211
Wide Range Achievement Test
    (WRAT), 66
Windle, Charles D., 36, 37, 42
Wirtz, W. Willard, 123
Wisconsin Division of Vocational
    Rehabilitation, 225
Woloshin, Arthur A., 114
Woody, Robert H., 114, 115
Work adjustment, 63-71, 118
Work Adjustment Evaluation Report,
    63-65
Work as therapy, 100-104
Work evaluation, 4, 59-71, 116-118,
    121, 141-142
Work rate, 64, 102-103, 129, 136,
    137-138, 141
Work sampling, 66-71
Workshop, 118, 195-197
    adult education in, 104-105
    certified in 1965, 128
    chart of organization, 196
    definition, 62

evaluation in, 22, 62-71, 90, 121,
141-142, 220
Independent Living Rehabilitation
Program, 38, 138-143
for less able, 143-152
locations in 1965, 128
long-term, 87, 91, 127, 135-152
in communities, 215
definition, 143
description, 143-149
needs for, 151-152, 240-241
recreation, 144-146
schedule, 144-145, 147
for more able, 118, 127-132
short-term, 118, 127-132

size in 1965, 128
transitional, 118, 127-132
Vocational Rehabilitation Amend-
ments of 1965, 130, 241
Workshop Improvement Grants, 130
Work-Training Center Project, 37-38,
97, 105, 121
WRAT (Wide Range Achievement
Test), 66
WTC Program, 137, 138, 230, 231

Y

YWCA, 146